Indian Women

An Inner Dialogue

Indira J. Parikh
Pulin K. Garg

SAGE PUBLICATIONS
New Delhi/Newbury Park/London

First published in 1989 by

Sage Publications India Pvt Ltd
M 32 Greater Kailash Market I
New Delhi 110 048

Sage Publications Inc
2111 West Hillcrest Drive
Newbury Park, California 91320

Sage Publications Ltd
28 Banner Street
London EC1Y 8QE

Published by Tejeshwar Singh for Sage Publications India Pvt Ltd, phototypeset at Aurelec Data Processing Systems and printed at Chaman Offset Printers.

Library of Congress Cataloging-in-Publication Data

Parikh, Indira.
  Indian women: an inner dialogue / Indira J. Parikh, Pulin K. Garg.
    p.   cm.
  Bibliography: p.
    1. Women—India—Attitudes. 2. Women—India—Social conditions.
1. Garg, Pulin K., 1927–   . II. Title.
HQ1743.P36   1989   305.4′ 0954—dc 19   89–30581

ISBN: 0–8039–9597–0 (U.S.–hbk.)   81–7036–140–0 (India–hbk.)
        0–8039–9598–9 (U.S.–pbk.)   81–7036–141–9 (India–pbk.)

To

Jitendra

*With whom there are shared dreams
and the creation of new paths*

Contents

Acknowledgements

This book has been the gift of many, many women who have shared their experience of living and reflections on their relationship with the world around them. These women shared their inner dialogue with us, often in grief, pain, anguish and pathos. They articulated their experiences with amusement, laughter, bewilderment and blushed at some of the memories. Our first and foremost gratitude and deep appreciation are to them.

These women courageously took the step to open up their inner world, their hearts, wherein they have carried the guilt of the role models prescribed for them by the cultural lore as well as their families. They reflected with us on what it meant to be women in India and spoke a hitherto unknown language to free themselves from the chains and shackles of guilt, shame, victimhood and martyrdom. These women came from homes across India's diversity—daughters and wives, mothers and aunts, mothers-in-law and daughters-in-law, sisters and sisters-in-law. There were young students from schools, colleges and management institutions. There were school teachers and professional women, doctors, lawyers and scientists. We have been witness to their changing roles and the shaping of new values, attitudes and roles.

In order to explore the issues surrounding their role and identity, many of the women participated in summer programmes run by the Indian Society for Individual and Social Development while others came to management education programmes of the Indian Institute of Management, Ahmedabad. By articulating and sharing with us their inner monologue, they created an opportunity for a dialogue. Without their participation and candid expression of their turmoils and discoveries, this book would have been impossible.

We began writing this book in 1983. It has since gone through many modifications and revisions. As we listened, our need to understand and sense the inner world of women became acute. In fact, it became a compulsion. In these moments, friends and colleagues became our captives with whom we articulated and explored the emerging world that the women we met shared with us. These friends and colleagues gave us their whole-hearted support both in terms of time and by sharing with us their own experiences. This has added immensely to the richness of the experience of writing this book. We take this opportunity to express our gratitude to some of these friends and colleagues:

Shashikala Ananthanarayanan
Seetha Ananthashivam
Meenakshi Banerjee
Sushanta Banerjee
Misrak Elias
Pauline Farrell
Claude Faucheux
Nalini Garg
Don Hellreigel
John I. Reynolds
Sarah Reynolds
Barbara Stone
Smita Suri
Dorienne Wilson-Smillie

Our thanks are also due to Jocelyn Foers from Texas A & M University, S. Sridharan and V. Jagannathan of the Indian Institute of

Management, Ahmedabad, and M.K. Madhavan of the Indian Society for Individual and Social Development who typed and retyped the several drafts of this book and the final version with immense patience and understanding.

Since 1983 we have been part of several institutions singly, jointly and simultaneously. Our thanks are due to the following three institutions which provided a context and the time and space for writing this book: the Indian Institute of Management, Ahmedabad; the Indian Society for Individual and Social Development, Ahmedabad; the Department of Management, Texas A & M University, USA.

Besides all the above, there are those from our respective home settings who have supported us in our struggle to express in a meaningful manner the shared and articulated inner realities of women. Often, the dialogue and the overwhelming poignancy of the pathos created despair, futility, exasperation, anger, desperation, and a sense of helplessness. In these moments Jitendra C. Parikh not only witnessed the struggle but continued to encourage us to put down and express in words the deeply held, lived and experienced pathos of women. As an observer and often a partner in the struggle to discover a new ethos, he identified and articulated the ever-replenishing and self-renewing qualities of women.

IJP
PKG

Preface

This book has been inspired by the need to document the inner dialogue as it has emerged in the journey to the self. It has become a compulsion to express the ever-present inner dialogue which women have carried on silently for centuries in their struggle to come to terms with the prescriptive roles, systems, structures and relationships within society. The articulation of this inner dialogue became possible in the generation to which the authors belong. Our journey of personal breakthroughs defined new roles, created new locations, evolved new settings, and redefined structures, systems and relationships.

This book traces the path of growing up in a family, with its idealism and belief in spiritualism and the uniqueness of existence on the one hand, and exposure to newer forms of education and aspirations which beckon towards adventure and the discovery of a world beyond tradition, on the other. Such was the context of growing up, which allowed the self to ask a lot of questions and to discover new meanings in the experience of being and becoming in our society.

What is this struggle that women have engaged in? It is the struggle to grow out of given roles and into new roles; to defy roles and the prescriptive absolutism of tradition but at the same time to carry forward the spirit and wisdom contained in the social structure and in the cultural role of women; and, eventually, to define and crystallise personal identity around meanings which integrate the old and the new and give it a different shape. On this journey we met others who were in search of new directions and paths, and who had crossed similar thresholds of experiencing acute agony in solitude and silence. This book voices the inner dialogue of these individuals as it unfolded to become part of the living process, simultaneously creating new spaces and paths.

Why this compulsion to articulate the inner dialogue of women? Why, in this moment of time, space and history, does this inner world, the sanctified world of the being of women, need to be shared? Will it change anything? Perhaps not. Will it make a difference to the existing nature of the relationship between men and women and women and society? Perhaps not. There is, nevertheless, a deep conviction that it needs to be stated.

Across the centuries, women in India have silently maintained the permanence and stability of society's cultural institutions and the continuities and consistencies of its ethos. In this context, women have been treated as the virtue-holders of society, living a life of roles and doing their duty as daughters, wives and mothers. But the fullness of their persons has never been allowed to break through these bounded roles. Many women have kept it alive by dignifying their roles rather than transcending them. They have sacrificed their personal social aspirations and, for fulfilment, surrendered their beings to religion. They have lived by role-appropriate feelings and by the wisdom of the cultural lore. All this needs to be stated at a time when the contours of the world we live in have changed dramatically. The space for growing up and living now has new coordinates. The land at which women have arrived and live in today did not exist in the past. It is a land where new landmarks have to be created, and in order that women can cross the threshold of a world gone by and enter another world to create new meanings, it is first necessary to banish the bogies of their inner, hidden world.

For centuries, women remained rooted in the social affiliative systems, confined in a network of social relationships as daughters, wives and mothers. It did not make any difference that a large number of them were part of the labour force, that they engaged in varied activities both in the home and outside it. They remained daughters, wives and mothers and society continued to regard them as such. They could not define a new role for themselves as workers independent of the affiliative system. Today, this aspect of women's lives has acquired a new dimension. Educated, armed with knowledge and skills, women enter formal work settings delinking themselves from their social structures and network of relationships. Like their male counterparts, they enter the world of occupation, career, profession, competition and achievements in their own right, and create a space where the need to experience themselves and be accepted as autonomous beings is very dominant. They feel compelled to discover and identify their personal resources as also to discover a vision of life beyond that defined by social structures and the network of relationships. They encounter the possibility of creating a world beyond the horizon which could become their world. And they visualise for themselves a role beyond the micro social one which also contains the dimension of a synthesising human existence.

The fears and anxieties created by this vision affect both the woman and the network of relationships and social structures. It creates guilt at the abandoning of roles, anxiety about being inadequate and about performing the given roles imperfectly and apprehensions about the accusing fingers that will follow. The first response is to hold on to the existing roles and actively disown the process of being and becoming. And, yet, the new cultural milieu not only compels women but makes it inevitable for them to face the emerging reality of rising aspirations.

In this book we attempt to articulate the inner dialogue that women have conducted for centuries at the core of their being. They have heard it within themselves and experienced it as static in their transactions. We believe that an articulation of this dialogue can only bring dignity both to women themselves and to the people with whom they interact. For a long time, women have only been able to express the pathos of their social roles and the prescriptive social structure. And while this has led to reformist movements it has not succeeded in creating a new ethos. We believe that women have a central role in building institutions of culture—that is, institutions of togetherness, regeneration and replenishment. The articulation of their inner dialogue can release their potential for this role. It will also provide a bench-mark for the emerging new realities and contribute to the dissolution of reactive anger, rancour, and other similar emotions which may serve as the source of many movements for achieving equality in social roles but which lack that essential sense of dignity that would make the achievement meaningful. It was this that prompted us to invite women to explore the inner dialogue and give it some sort of shape and coherence.

At our invitation woman after woman came forward to explore and share her inner dialogue with us. The initial opportunity for these explorations was created in 1971 at the Indian Institute of Management (IIM), Ahmedabad, where the authors offered two courses: (a) An identity lab under the title 'Interpersonal Relations' and (b) 'Careers, Roles and Identity'. A second opportunity was provided by the Indian Society for Individual and Social Development where in 1979 the authors, along with their colleagues, offered exploratory programmes like 'Explorations in Role and Identity in Organisations'; 'Explorations in Role and Identity in Home Settings'; 'Explorations in Role and Commitment at Schools'; and a programme of 'Internship in Process Work'. The third opportunity was created in 1981 at the IIM, where a special course on 'Women Managers: Issues of Role and Authority' was specially designed for and offered to women alone. These programmes and courses are still being offered at the respective institutions.

At these meetings, approximately a thousand women, in mixed or exclusive groups, struggled to express their inner beings. It was an act of courage and conviction; for, in order to articulate their innermost feelings, these women had to tear through the shrouds of pain and anguish, the clouds of reactive anger and resentment, the fabrics of hate and bitterness, all coloured and steeped in the guilt of disowning the being and the pathos of human existence. As their inner dialogue unfolded, the participants in the groups often experienced a sense of dignity and the reinforcement of their convictions.

Who were these women who came forth to journey into the unknown, risking the certainty of their roles and the security of social structures; who ventured to accept and assert their beings and face being disowned by society; who were willing to step forward with courage and conviction and confront the possibility of being accused as heretics? They came from all walks of life. They were commoners and the elite, the illiterate and the educated, the housewife and the professional. They came from all over the country—from Srinagar (Kashmir) to Kanyakumari (Tamilnadu) and from Dibrugarh (Assam) to Gandhidham (Kutch). They were of all ages—children between seven and eleven; early adolescents at the threshold of puberty, discovering for the first time their female and male identities; later adolescents and early adults already sensing the indignities of being biologically female and of being classed socially as women. They were housewives, managers and diverse professionals, captives in their social and/or work structures. They had all struggled to create a space for themselves and they shared with the others their aspirations and disillusionments, their relationships and disenchantment with people, their hopes for the future and the nightmare of living. They also shared their need for psychological support; the dehumanising experiences of physical assaults; the occasional gifts of comfort and care; and their feelings of the desperateness of death and the excitement of coming alive.

The exploratory progress was very often triggered off by one of the authors who began by sharing his/her own socio-psychological world. Slowly, the other participants would join in, some tentatively and others more confidently. What rose to the surface at these sessions was the structure of feelings that lay behind the narration of experiences. The participants were soon sharing the poignancy and intensities of living in a joint family, of their relationships with their brothers and sisters, with men and women both within and without the family— some exploitative, ravaging and dehumanising, others kind, supportive and dignifying. The feelings behind socially good and bad events were draped in a confused mass of 'should' feelings and real feelings. Participants frequently discovered that behind a socially good event and its accompanying 'should' feeling, feelings of being used, exploited and undignified, raged like a storm. And sometimes, behind a socially bad event and its accompanying 'should' feeling, there were surging tides of excitement, exhilaration and joy. The initial stages of these explorations were spent in sorting out this jumbled mass of 'should' and real feelings.

Very soon, the participants found themselves talking about people whose imprints they carried in terms of their role adoption. This led them to explore role models, both male and female, over three generations. Thus, personal and family histories, the cultural lore, the myths, beliefs and traditions surfaced for exploration. Again, the participants discovered a juxtaposed mass of sources upon which they had chosen to model their own role identities. This prompted them to pinpoint their own additions, both in terms of meanings and feelings, to the contributions made by family members to the formation of their identity.

Sorting out should feelings from real ones and identifying their own contributions to their identity often meant that the participants had to relive the feelings of harshness and softness, of rejection and affirmation, of shame and guilt, on the one hand, and the joy and excitement, on the other, which attended the discovery of their physical bodies at puberty. At this point, most participants recognised the massive upheaval that early adolescence had created and, in the process, realised how their own existential response to the environment had been distorted, been pushed aside to be held in abeyance, and been associated with doubt, anxiety and perhaps guilt. They discovered that there were many thresholds where they had suppressed their existential response and, instead, given precedence to the desired social response. They also recognised how they had colluded in their own dehumanisation and in the indignities they had suffered in the process of becoming and carving out a role for themselves in the prescriptive role space.

In the final phase, especially in mixed groups, the participants explored the gruesome and fixed contextual processes where every encounter avoids the person and involves instead only transactions with symbols of the male and the female. This exploration involved replaying the kaleidoscope of past encounters between men and women, and reviving memories of the shame and guilt which often accompanied the moment of first awakening and discovering the other person. It allowed for the resurgence of the turbulence and turmoil involved in creating relatedness beyond social relationships, experiencing a person behind the symbol, and making the choice of responding or withholding.

Thus, these explorations went back and forth between idealism, family sagas, martyrdoms and victimhoods, pathos and abundances, tentativeness and assertion, reaching out and withholding, and so on, before reaching a point where the convictions, values, beliefs and responses anchored within one's being could be identified and externalised and where the search for a new path could begin.

While grappling with and struggling to explore the issues of identity and meaningful living, hundreds of women spoke of their inner world. The setting for these explorations created and ensured conditions where the previously unarticulated being could be reflected upon and asserted, unhampered by prescriptions, preaching and pontification from others. It also allowed women to focus upon their struggle in a process of reflection without getting caught up in the reactive mode of accusing, condemning or blaming the family, the socio-cultural heritage and men in general. Here, feelings could be shared without shame or fear or contamination from outside. In fact, the programmes were based on a very clear statement that no human being has the right or the power to accuse, shame or condemn any other human being in the struggle to come to terms with his or her life.

In addition, these women had come to realise that to live as a person and to have the freedom to make meaningful choices in the current era, one has to live and share the inner experience. Without such a process, one would feel suffocated and set in motion forces of fragmentation within the self. Sharing these experiences, which include past actions and choices, is a necessary part of the struggle for those individuals who want to try and transcend old roles and crystallise their identities according to new definitions, roles and life-space. It would also make it possible for them to join in the process of creating a new ethos and of adding new elements to the cultural heritage. It is only by realising this truth that the women could recognise that no action, choice or experience is powerful enough to be held in shame, or guilt, or condemnation, within the self.

Most women realised that in order to discover new horizons of 'becoming' and new unfoldings of 'being' one has to pass over several thresholds and negotiate many crossroads. At each threshold one has to revisit, like the Greek heroes, the hell of past pathos and relive the memories of significant people held in that pathos. At each crossroad one has to encounter the excitement of the awakening of aspirations, and struggle with multiple invitations and evocations in order to touch the depth of one's being and find the freedom to travel towards the new horizons of being and becoming.

They realised that sharing the struggle at each threshold and at each crossroad creates a new relatedness for the self with other individuals and this relatedness is characterised by a profound sense of dignity and sanctity for the identity of the self and others. The ability to sense and experience this dignity and sanctity mobilises human beings, both men and women, to join forces in creating a new ethos. Without this sense of dignity and sanctity, the existential awakening of the self remains vulnerable and the inner space can once again become contaminated. The normative worlds of shoulds and musts can once again surround the existential being.

This book, then, portrays the reflections of women who are homemakers, school teachers, managers, doctors, lawyers and professionals in diverse sectors of life; of young and adolescent girls standing at a psychological threshold and cultural crossroads which will shape their lives and feminine identity; of children born in a tumultous world characterised by flux which confronts them with a complex and contradictory cultural milieu for growing up in; of women who have opted to play out roles and seek spiritual salvation and held in abeyance their personal identity; of women who have opted for a life of career and competition with men and held in abeyance their femininity; of women who have remained frozen in the present; and of women who continue their struggle to remain alive in their identity with courage and conviction and accept the consequences of their choices.

For us, it has been a process of listening and resonating with the unfolding of feelings and meanings and often holding back tears as hundreds of women lived through their pathos and the burden of role idealism. Sometimes the togetherness lasted for a day, or perhaps a week, and sometimes the contacts have continued for years. All this has added to and enriched our articulation of women's inner realities and their space in today's world.

Writing this book has been a journey into a nebulous land and yet being firmly rooted in one's convictions. It has been the witnessing of being uprooted and remaining painfully exposed to the harshness and barrenness of the world around, and of finding dignifying nurturance and sustenance. It has been a journey in the wilderness, and at the same time of discovering the magic of creating a garden and an oasis. It has been a journey of living many, many lives in one lifetime and discovering the wonder of opposites and contradictions simultaneously making a coherent existence. Above all, writing this book has reinforced our faith in the human spirit and its relentless effort to forge a new path, a new ethos and a new heritage.

Ahmedabad
November 1988

Indira J. Parikh
Pulin K. Garg

Personal Statement I

$\mathbf{I}$ have often wondered why it has been important for me to express the inner world and dialogue of Indian women. It has been a personal struggle to articulate my inner world to myself as also to convert the monologue which I have carried on from childhood into a dialogue. To actualise this I have searched for a space and a person with whom I can conduct this dialogue with dignity, grace and maturity so as to help me get in touch with my being. My monologue became a dialogue when many men and women shared their inner struggles with me. Writing about all this became possible only when I discovered that I could share my past and the processes of my growth without regret, shame or guilt. To begin the journey it became very important that I first walk down memory lane to perhaps discover a world which I held within. I have struggled to get in touch with my being; with the role models of both men and women that I carry from the family and the sagas I heard as a child (and which I have in turn shared with my child); the models from the cultural lore that I have cherished; and to discover those processes of my being and becoming which I can add to the heritage that I hold dear within me and then carry it forward.

The family lore which I imbibed from both my paternal and maternal grandparents are of the pride of belonging to the Kutchi community, of being warriors, and of tales woven with the spirit of adventure in new lands. The family held values of honesty, integrity and hard work. Both my paternal grandparents were strong-willed individuals. My grandfather, Gangji Pitambar Varma—a proud man, an idealist and a fanatic Arya Samaji—believed in educating both boys and girls in the gurukul tradition, in widow remarriage and in the concept of equality. He tended to be short-tempered with adults but was affectionate to his grandchildren. My paternal grandmother, Mamma Devi Varma, was vibrant, strong-willed, full of life, an earthy woman—in short, quite a contrast to her husband. She managed a large household comprised of temperamental people of all ages. She chewed tobacco and freely used four-letter words. To the grandchildren, her lap was a place to go to when in need of comfort. As a person she communicated to me—her fourth grandchild and a granddaughter—not only the pathos of being a woman but also the choices and alternatives that were available and the inevitability of the price that went with exercising the choices.

My father's sisters, Shanta Varma and Savitri Chavda, were scholars. In many ways they were pioneers and forerunners of the women to come. My older aunt remained unmarried. She was a Sanskrit scholar, a school principal, was economically self-reliant, strict and very fastidious. She told us innumerable stories from the cultural lore. She inculcated in me the spirit of autonomy and self-reliance through dedication to institutions of learning. The other aunt chose to marry out of caste and out of community. An educated woman, she communicated to me the determination and resilience combined with a gentleness and softness which were anchored in femininity. All these role models have shaped my identity and helped to crystallise my being.

My maternal family has had little direct impact on me. They lived in Africa where my grandfather was a teacher. My maternal grandmother was a frail and subdued woman. I first met her when I was already an adolescent.

My father, Harishchandra Varma, is a quiet, self-effacing man. He is the middle son, dominated by his elder brother and over-shadowed by his effusive younger brother. As a consequence, he ended up being a gentle person. He provided me with stability and security by always being around. He represented a male role model which exhibited the softer and gentler qualities of relationship. My mother, Usha Devi Varma, is a strong woman, a pillar of towering strength. Never one to crumble in the face of odds and hardships, she has an attitude which is anchored firmly in the positive aspects of life. As a child, I had a turbulent relationship with her. I carry from her the strength to persist in the midst of the severest odds with dignity and courage.

I am the eldest of six, four sisters and two brothers. I was born at a time when my father was starting his own business which eventually grew and prospered. My younger sisters and brothers—Sunita Ruparel, Minakshi Varma, Chandraketu Varma, Madhavi Sonpal and Sanjay Varma—were a set of lively siblings. I carry with me fond, nostalgic and bitter-sweet memories of our childhood: swimming in the pond; climbing *imli*, coconut and mango trees; putting up plays and dance performances to earn ice-cream treats; climbing up hills during the holidays; indulging in games and fights to gain attention; and being united against any threat from outside. From my brothers and sisters, I carry the trust which they placed in me as the eldest sister and the demands they made that I invest in their lives out of free choice and not out of a sense of obligation, and all this with love and affection.

I carried the stigma of being the dark child of a very beautiful mother. This stigma—expressed primarily in the form that I was a burden since no one would marry me—was communicated to me loudly and clearly and by all and sundry. The constant comparison with my fair-looking sisters made me feel unwanted, rejected and unacceptable. I lived with this hurt but learnt to keep the hurt within me and put on a brave face that I did not care what people said. I accepted that a fair complexion was important to them. Since I did not have it and could not acquire it, I did not waste much time seeking acceptability. Instead, I learnt to give myself the freedom to speak my mind, to argue with my elders and to counter-question them when they were being inconsistent. I was perceived as being fearless disrespectful to elders and as having an atrocious tongue. Elders did not frighten me and I acquired the courage to be myself, which was partly a defensive reaction and partly so as to protect myself from hurt.

Amidst all this was another aspect. Being the eldest child meant that my younger brothers and sisters gave me all the respect that this role involved. In my father's factory also it gave me a certain status. Added to this was the fact that I did extremely well in the academic sphere as well as in sports. I started a class for the workers' children where I was the uncontested teacher and where my sisters and brothers joined to learn English. I acquired a degree in homeopathy and began to give medical advice, with the help of my father, to many of the workers' families. Psychologically I lived with a sense of discrimination, hurt and anger but socially I had carved out a space and defined a meaningful role for myself in our vast home.

For the first two years of college I went to live with my grandparents, my eldest unmarried aunt and a widowed aunt. These two years meant being away from home and hence from all sources of comparison. This was also a period of relative autonomy for me where I had only broad supervision. It gave me the opportunity to read extensively and provided me with the time to reflect on the traditional roles that my grandmother and aunts performed as also to comprehend their meanings in life. I asked a lot of questions of myself about my life and what I wanted to do with it and found no answers. I dreamt of travel and romance, togetherness and adventure, but doubted if I was acceptable. It was a period of dreaming and reflecting and above all of discovering the emotions and feelings that went with being a woman. These feelings surged forth like a bubbling spring to be contained and restrained by the social norms of good–bad, right–wrong. They generated guilt, anxiety and rebelliousness at the negative meanings that were attached to feelings of being alive, exuberant and young.

These are some of the significant role models from my youth. I grew up in a joint family of two diametrically contradictory tendencies. My grandfather and father believed in the Arya Samaji tradition of *havan* and *sandhya*, daily yoga, vegetarian health food and preventive ayurvedic medicine. My youngest uncle's family, which inhabited the same home, was 'modern'. My uncle drank and smoked, went to clubs, was a non-vegetarian and an atheist. Growing up in such a home provided me with the concept of the co-existence of opposites as also the ability to hold on to my values, philosophy and beliefs despite a conflictual context. It presented alternative modes of living accompanied by pulls and pushes from both as also involved the struggle to differentiate between real choices and wished for choices. This setting demanded a commitment to values and ideals which had deep roots in the positives of our culture and heritage and the pride of belonging to a glorious tradition. One pull was the fun life of my uncle's family and their parties. Yet, the opposite pull of the spiritual heritage of my father's family established more enduring roots in me.

Marriage provided the context for the beginning of a new unfolding. My husband, Jitendra C. Parikh, is a quiet dignified person, absorbed in the pursuit of science. He opened up a whole new world for me. He is a physicist interested in music and books. He introduced me to the world of Indian and Western classical music and English literature. With him began the process of differentiating between being a daughter, a wife and a daughter-in-law. Marriage meant venturing into new countries and lands and meeting new people; locating a space to discover and a world to experience, and the need to grow from being a dreamy bride to a mature adult; encountering a world of freedom, a world of responsibilities, of giving and sharing; and, above all, a process of discovering the inner being. In the new life-space of marriage, I have struggled between the socially desirable roles and the aspired and dreamed of ones, and have learnt to cope with the fears, anxieties and apprehensions of being accused of being socially undesirable. Marriage has been the space where I began the journey to sort out the layers of introjects, internalisations and processes of role-taking. And, finally, after years of wandering, to create a home.

What I brought forward unresolved from my transactions with my mother, I enacted and lived through with my mother-in-law, Kusumben Parikh. My relationship with her has grown from socially desirable conformity, to defiance and rebellion, to gradual mutual understanding, to an exploration of past roles and expectations, and, finally, to a deep trust and respect. She is a strong-willed, domineering woman but has the grace and dignity to respect my struggle to create a path for myself to grow into a professional.

Somehow, when it comes to redefining my role as a mother, all other role definitions seem simple. My relationship with my son, Sushrut, has aroused feelings of ambivalence, guilt, anger, anxiety and apprehension. No role model or behaviour pattern provided me with sufficient courage to make new choices in this relationship. It is through a sustained process and many battles, tears and dialogues, that a concept of a mother who has a career and a profession emerged. The mother's role and its redefinition has been the most tormenting to my being but it has also provided us both with the space to experience a deep and enduring emotional relatedness as mother and son and as two adults.

Those women who have been significant in my life appear in nostalgic retrospect to have been strong, capable, dominant and in control of a large social empire. Yet, with a deeper, critical and realistic appraisal, I realise today that there were areas where these women had no space for themselves. They resided in the homes of their husbands and in-laws and lived for others. Their dominant concern was to be helpful. They managed the internal interface and politics of the family, and were shrewd enough to be able to protect their own and their children's rights in the context of a joint family. They made many a sacrifice and to a large extent believed that their destiny lay in the hands of menfolk. They lived with the routineness of their daily chores and sought to discover innovativeness in their routines.

At the same time, there were women in my family who came through as helpless, were victims of the social system and continued to live lives full of drudgery, deprivation and discrimination. These were the women who surrendered their unique identity, were willing to be moulded for the sake of role-based security and conformed to the traditional role definitions prescribed by society. They rarely discovered their potential as human beings and limited their life-space to the narrow confines of being daughter-in-law, mother and wife.

On one side I carry a heritage of dominant, assertive and capable women who sowed the seeds of aspiration, courage and a set of values and ideals based on self-respect, grace and dignity. Living and growing with them I have learnt to persist against all odds without ever losing hope, to discover sources of support within the system and the strength to fight against injustice. On the other hand, I carry a legacy of the idealised traditional role of being a woman which encourages helplessness, a giving up of aspirations, being bound by role definitions, living for others, glorying in the sacrifice of the self, and learning to live without any legitimate space for the self in the system.

Caught in these dilemmas, I have often oscillated between conformity and rebellion. At every critical crossroad and at every new choice, it has been an effort for me to discover an alternative which perhaps has a bit of the past and yet a little something of my own. Each step in the growth process takes me a little further towards discovering the strength to venture into the unexplored terrains of my being and becoming.

Besides the heritage of the women of my family, the men from my family and from my work world have had a significant and lasting impact on me and have made many direct and indirect contributions to my growth. My encounters with a variety of men have helped me to differentiate my processes of evocation and invocation and provided a clarity of boundaries. They have compelled me to respect myself first. Being able to distinguish between impulse and emotion has helped me to experience the pathos of men and be sensitive to their struggles and dilemmas. Being able to sense the pathos of both men and women has given me the freedom to reach out with compassion to both as also to experience both the woman and the man in me.

At some point of time, a new role—that of work—was added to my life. When I joined a formal organisation, an academic institution, to create a career and a profession, I had no previous role models or landmarks to guide me. It was an entry into an unfamiliar land peopled with strangers. I started my career in 1971 as a research associate with Pulin Garg at the Indian Institute of Management, Ahmedabad. My relationship with him has been the most enduring one at the family, personal and professional levels. In this encounter, besides entering the world of industry, organisation and management, I entered a living world of philosophy, history, culture, traditions, poetry and realms of human existence that I did not even know existed. To me, this was a world which had infinite space to explore new horizons and depths both within myself and with others. This journey has followed a varied path. Sometimes the path has been like a raging river and at times a sky full of thunderous clouds. At times it has been like a meandering river flowing endlessly, while at others it has been like a gusty wind blowing away the cumulative collection of personal contexts to lay bare a raw earthy glow. It has been a space and a relationship which has taught me many things, the most important of which is being human to myself.

The journey through this space has involved walking on uncertain paths to maturity. It has meant a transition and a moving away from being a female and a woman, to being a person and a professional. In this journey I have lived through many an encounter with the self, others and the system. It has meant dealing with social stereotypes, psychological barriers and freedom. I have searched for a definition of sanctity and respect. The social setting combined with the work-setting has involved living through the century old identity of being a victim and a martyr and discovering the resilient spirit of an identity in search of creating a wholesome space. It has meant discarding the baggage of ancient role models and their residues of reaction and negativism and allowing the slow but gradual emergence of personal values and convictions. It has meant releasing the self from the chains and shackles of doubt, ambivalence, guilt and shame to take charge of my own destiny. It has meant building a home where people can walk in and feel welcome.

My encounters with the simultaneous juxtaposition of the social, familial and work setting have been facilitated by the heritage of the Vedic tradition which was provided by my family. This spiritual heritage has provided a resilience of spirit, and a set of convictions and values concerning human existence. These encounters have been tests of fire which have helped cleanse my soul of past residues and helped to forge a tensile being. The laying down of the ghosts of the past has helped me to remain in touch with the magic of life and living.

The encounter with the existential being is an ongoing process. It helps to create an oasis in the desert, security in the wilderness, and generates energy to give birth to that human spirit which can uncover philosophies to live by and create a personal mission to experience a full life. It is a process of witnessing a stranger inside and discovering the unlimited nature of my being and the universe around me.

Shedding the roles which once gave meaning and acceptability to my life has been a painful process. It was even more painful and yet exhilarating to come into contact with the deeply held values, beliefs and convictions uncovered in the process and to act on the basis of those convictions. For, this process meant touching the existential being anchored in the human spirit and creating a new social order in my personal sphere. It meant being alive and in charge of my own destiny. It meant beginning time and again with my self rather than with roles and it meant creating a response by transcending the reactions. Many of my past pains and hurts have acquired a perspective in a much larger context and I continue to discover many moments of positive relatedness and a sense of well-being with myself and others. I carry the feeling that I have the responsibility of continuing to build a new path whose foundations were laid in the recent past. The past which I have access to is comprised of my cultural heritage and the men and women I have encountered, but perhaps the very first landmark of this past was erected with the dawn of humankind. What I can do is to carry the momentum forward. Perhaps with this momentum the men and women of tomorrow may find the strength to begin new adventures to discover their real and unique identity as human beings.

This personal journey needs to be shared if for no other reason than the fact that so many men and women have shared their processes of being and becoming with me. And in this sharing I have discovered many a kindred soul who has arrived at many a threshold and asked the same questions. My personal hope is that this sharing of the inner dialogue of women will provide the awareness of a much larger context; that it will provide the beginnings of new relatedness with the self and the world around; and will help the creation of new foundations to build a better tomorrow, a tomorrow which will be based on understanding between women and men, women and women and men and men. My hope also is that this inner dialogue may provide an impetus for the exploration of inner space, for the beginning of a new journey, and for a discovery of the spiritual identity anchored in human existence which each one of us carries within.

Indira J. Parikh

Personal Statement II

Many of my friends have asked me what I—a male—am doing as a co-author of a book called *Indian Women: An Inner Dialogue*? What do I know of it? And if I do, how come? These questions have been asked as often by men as by women. I do not really feel the need to justify my participation in the inner dialogue of Indian women. Indira Parikh and I have been working together on research and consultancy for seventeen years. Part of our joint work has been with women. In an interdependent mode, we have published various results of our work together over the years. This book is yet another offshoot of this long enduring partnership in the field of documenting data and generating knowledge. Besides this association, I have a familial and cultural background which, when explicated and reflected upon, may suggest some bases for my participation in decoding and articulating this inner dialogue. So, even though I do not feel the need for it, I shall briefly describe my life processes and experiences in what follows.

I am my father's youngest child. My mother died when I was nine months old and my father, an Arya Samaji and a Gandhian, married a widow. She was my mother's younger sister and had a son from her former husband. This marriage was not acceptable to the community and the extended family. As such, my step-mother—whom I experienced as a very genuine, warm and integrated individual—began life in her new family with a great deal of social stigma and displaced aggression which could not be aimed at my father because of his personality and status. As I grew up under her warmth and care, I was witness to many of her silent tears, the painful process she went through of creating acceptance, and finally of her rejoicing when she succeeded in establishing herself as a highly respected person and an anchor of much of our community's life. She became a friend, philosopher and guide to quite a large number of women and helped them to learn to live with dignity. As the youngest son I was present during many of her dialogues with other women.

Furthermore, as the youngest child who was frequently sick and did not relate to the physically active set of four brothers and twenty-three cousins, I was a mere spectator of the dominant male ethos prevalent in my family and society. My contact was more with the females of the system. This created in me an orientation of looking at things and events from a distance and of quietly assessing them. I also frequently found myself responding either in defence of my dignity or by way of reaching out with warmth to people. Actually, I never found it easy to establish deep intimate relationships with males of my own age group. I found it much easier to relate to intellectuals and elderly men.

I grew up in the era of the national struggle and at the time of a sort of renaissance in north Indian literature. The novels of Premchand, Jaynendra and Prasad among Hindi authors, Munshi and Ramanlal Desai from Gujarat, and Sarat, the most avidly read Bengali novelist, all left a deep imprint on me and provided me with insights into the life-space of women. Who can ever forget the Rajalakshmis, Vijayas, Bharatis, Kamals, Sunitas and Manjaris created by these authors? The themes explored by most of these novelists often unfolded the inner dialogue of the woman who is a castaway. These women served as the context for men to discover and integrate their identity. In these novels, most males came through either as impractical idealists or as highly indecisive, ambivalent, unstable and temperamental people. Conversely, other male characters were rigid, manipulative, orthodox and self-centred. None of these male models were acceptable to me. The women characters, however, not only left a deep impression but evoked empathy and very often tears and poignancy in me.

Besides the living literature of the era, I was also very heavily influenced by folklore and folktales. My family and its circle had many a great story-teller. My mother would tell stories of princesses. A gentleman, whom we lovingly called Baba Chhajjumal, belonged to the grand old tradition of story-tellers. Through the balmy nights of March and April and the hot summer nights he would lie on a bed while we young children would keep his *hookah* going and press his feet. He would tell us stories from *Baital Pachchasi, Simhasan-battisi, Panchatantra, Gulebakavali,* the Persian Nights and Arabian Nights, *Kissa-tota-maina* and *Hatimtai.* My grandfather and other seniors, as also visiting friends of my father, many of whom were scholars, would tell us stories culled from the *Puranas* and Indian scriptures. A close friend of our family, who happened to be a Muslim, would tell us stories from the Sufi tradition. All these story-tellers evoked the life-space of the characters and made it come alive. They also reflected on the universe of feelings of the main characters. As such, sagas, folktales and folklore became an integral part of my thought process and influenced my construction of analogue models of social situations and human beings. Essentially, the prototype of the five stories narrated in the second chapter of this book were communicated by my mother and Baba Chhajjumal. Of course, the new format, the evocative language and the settings are products of Indira Parikh's creativity.

Then began my adolescence. At about the age of 16, I left my home and was, in many many ways, on my own. I became the creator of my own destiny. I entered the world as a carrier of shame and guilt, as a person who could not legitimately claim any resources from the system, and who must be utterly self-reliant. What followed has been a life of struggle, lasting forty-four years so far, to retain a sense of well-being, dignity, commitment, persistence and to apply a philosophy of living. It has led me to experiment with new processes of generating knowledge as well as to attempting to define a culture-specific approach in the social sciences. I spent the first eighteen years of this period as a wanderer and a vagabond, roaming all over the country and even abroad. This was also a period of constant investment in the self and experimenting with my convictions and philosophical ideas. All this was very painful and agonising. There were many moments when I felt like, giving up and surrendering myself to a futile existence. It also included three pseudo attempts to commit suicide and three major spells of undiagnosed illness due to this stress.

These eighteen years were rather critical. As I look back upon this period, I truly value the fact that the psychological support for the survival, restoration and replenishment of my being and becoming flowed invariably and exclusively from women. Their support had the quality of grace. Some of them were my seniors in age, others were either peers or juniors. I owe a great deal to eleven women who helped me to become and be a self-respecting individual. One of them was a nineteen-year old tribal girl. Another was the principal of a well known women's college. Eight out of these eleven women had lived through terrible socio-cultural traumas but had succeeded in retaining their sense of dignity and well-being, though often at a price. Three of them were separated from their husbands. Two of them were spinsters and remained so throughout their lives. The other six went through great struggles to find peace in life and adjustment in marriage. All these women shared with me their deep pathos and also their irrevocable commitment to be.

If nothing else, I feel that the experiences of my pre-adolescence period with my mother and her friends, and of my post-adolescence years with these eleven women entitle me to claim a very personalised and reflective understanding of women's inner dialogue with empathy and even a degree of identification.

However, there is more. My first choice of a profession was as a psychotherapist, and the second choice as a process worker in groups set up for developmental purposes. Both these careers exposed me to a large number of women both in India and abroad. In the groups and personal counselling situations I have been involved in, more than 2,000 women have shared their inner dialogue and their pathos of living. This has reinforced my understanding, empathy and even identity with the inner dialogue of women. The culmination of this process has been my struggle to create personal, psychological and professional equations with my wife, Nalini Garg, and my colleague, Indira Parikh. In the course of these two struggles I have had to keep on defining my locations and boundaries and sharing their own processes of doing so. This has given me new insights into my personal identity. It has made me confront my partly disowned and partly manipulative male psyche and identity. I have had to peel off layer after layer, like peeling an onion, of my own male identity. I have lived through periods of my own as well as their anger, resentment and sense of psychic violation of the self. I believe these processes have seasoned me a great deal and I feel more comfortable today with both my identities—the male and the female.

And that brings me to the last statement. Whether I am a male or a female, the fact remains that all human children introject the female identity at their mother's breast at the very outset. This lays the basic foundation of being human. The fact that later socialisation tells a male that to be soft or to cry is feminine and that he is therefore a sissy, often leads males into disowning the introjected female identity and to view it with contempt and even hatred. Perhaps this is what turns women into objects of men's aggression. I believe that my exposure to my mother, her friends and other women during my own period of growth helped me to overcome the stigmas attached to my feminine side by the later processes of socialisation.

Pulin K. Garg

1

The Beginning

Awoman rarely talks of herself. In normal circumstances she talks only of her role, her family and the traditions of society. She may talk of her reactions once in a while, but she keeps her real feelings hidden.

This book attempts to articulate the feelings that women often hold within. It attempts to capture their inner lives and experiences. Some scholars feel that this book represents only a small section of Indian women. Others suggest that much of what we claim to be the inner voice of Indian women is applicable to women universally. Be that as it may, we believe that, at the very least, this book speaks of women from all walks of Indian life.

Why do we believe so? Our experience suggests that the rich heritage of folktales and folklore, myths and epics, and sagas and histories that Indian women share, revolve around a basic symbolic identity and limited role models. This shared universe of Indian women is presented in the first two chapters of this book.

One may well ask, why must inner experiences and feelings be shared? Why should they be expressed? The attempts which have been made over the centuries to articulate and express this inner dialogue do not seem to have made any difference to the status of women. They continue to be recipients of patronage, they continue to be treated as objects to be worshipped, defiled or defied. In short, regardless of their socio-economic class and cultural background, the situation remains unaltered for most women. They continue to live within themselves and the heritage of the past, enslaved by the role models, images and symbols defined by the cultural lore.

Yet, in the outside world, they seem to have become a part of the culture that is evolving today under the impact of new cognitive logic. This duality makes it difficult to forge a viable heritage for a meaningful unfolding. Regardless of the richness of their heritage, women still long to create a new world with a different quality of relatedness. In the moment between dark and dawn, half-awakened women are startled by a partial glimpse of this different world which, however, quickly recedes and disappears into the unfathomable space.

Since women are the source of family continuity, they have to encounter the male identity This encounter is legitimised and sanctified in the institution of marriage. Social custom dictates that marriage for a woman means uprooting and rerooting. It means an entry and acceptance into the space of others. This critical shift in the life of a woman has been romanticised, and its reality of anguish, anxiety, and apprehension has been covered up.

In the reality of marriage, the hope of a romantic encounter remains unfulfilled, creating feelings of meaninglessness in many women. Most women nurse a craving for a space in which they can experience the splendour and glory of a fulfilling human relationship. They also hope to find someone who will receive and share the pathos of their being, held for centuries in their symbolic identity of being women. Somewhere in their pathos, women wish to be free of the captivity of the bio-social and bio-psychological symbols of society so as to be able to touch their existential quality and creativity. This longing continues to survive in women despite all the anguish, pain, and misery that they experience.

However, even longing has become taboo. Women feel that society provides them with no space, no legitimacy. They have often been denied even the basic claim to a spiritual space. Yet they carry themselves through the prescribed boundaries with dignity and grace. Deep down, they continue to seek a pause, a respite, which are essential for survival. These moments allow women to occasionally bury the past, to anticipate the future a little, and weave a fabric of many splendid colours and hues to sustain themselves through the otherwise mundane experiences of life. Without these pauses, all experiences merge into an undifferentiated mass.

Very often, these moments turn into shattered dreams. The woman often awakens from them with feelings of dislocation and disorientation. She loses her anchor, and is thrown into the massive universe of reactive feelings surrounding her limited roles. The sharing of her inner world is one such pause, wherein a woman can not only express and hence relieve her pain and anguish, but also experience the euphoria of being able to touch her essential self.

Indian society demands that a female child grow up quickly. In the process she gets dislocated within herself. She has learnt to accept the burden of socio-psychological uprooting, but the burden of rerooting herself is also entirely hers, and few support systems are available. The onus of fostering, sustaining, and replenishing herself is also very often on her. The only guideline she receives is that she has to live up to a variety of expectations defined by social tradition.

Her search is for a place where she can be without being pushed around or without having demands made on her. In the absence of such a place, she often hides behind the prescribed role-idealism or, when reality becomes too oppressive, in her reactivity. In either case, she postpones action, and holds her being in abeyance. It is really tragic that women are denied their being and are forced to root themselves only within the boundaries of bio-social roles. The demand that they limit themselves is so heavy that even the few moments of respite they might gain lose their real purpose. The woman, instead of getting in touch with herself and using the opportunity to create a new world, tends to fantasise about a touch, a gift of care, a gentle whisper and an invitation to walk along. These fantasies often lead her down the garden path. The let down,when it comes, as it inevitably does, is very painful and disorienting.

The shift from an agrarian culture to the modern urban industrial pattern has reversed the quality of the life-space of both women and men. Agrarian women lived a house-bound life in groups while men walked alone. Today, men work in groups and women live in isolation. Unwittingly or wittingly, this shift has provided them moments of solitude and reactivated their long forgotten search for their inner beings and their desire to begin to live for themselves. However, this has not stopped their search for togetherness with their counter-parts.

Many women begin such a journey. Some get weary and fall back on the prescriptive role models. Others continue along the path to live and discover the changing bio-social, socio-psychological and psycho-existential facets of life. They experience an inner compulsion and an urgency to reach their destination—namely, dignity and freedom.

Regardless of their attempts, the destiny of women still seems to be that of remaining captive to the universe of the cultural lore. They remain within the confines of the role models prescribed by traditional society. They often venture forth in search of a togetherness with dignity but get trapped by romanticism and sentimentality. Their search for a fulfilment, for the restoration of loss and deprivation, only leads them back into captivity. The annihilating grip of the process of socialisation is deep-rooted. Those women who make frequent attempts to redefine their roles invariably return to the traditional choices. And for those who return, their primary focus is on men and relationships with them—they ignore their own proactivity.

At every turn of life they are confronted with this disillusionment. Yet they survive, with the help of their basic resilience and the strength of the ever-battling, ever-inviting spirit they hold within. Destiny may turn them into pillars of salt like Lot's wife, or into stone like Ahalya but, like the Phoenix, they rise from the ashes.

In these moments of disillusionment, women often encounter distorted images of themselves in the mirrors of society. The entire range of imagery contained in the cultural constructs of women being witches and shrews, incarnations of condemned and disowned impulses, of being untouchable, flashes before their eyes, blocking from their view the face which shines and is radiant.

Like the folktale in which the woman is kept in isolation behind seven locks in order to save her from contamination, the inner world of the Indian women is divided into seven chapters in the rest of this book. The first chapter, 'The Magic Space,' presents five folktales which have been current in India over the centuries. These folktales have been reconstructed partly on the basis of oral versions and partly with the help of written versions that have appeared in magazines like *Chandamama*. These tales present five of the dominant symbolic identities which women have assumed in Indian society, and which are still current even among educated, urban and highly sophisticated women.

The next chapter, entitled 'Women in the Tapestry of History,' presents our reconstruction of the historical evolution of the ethos of Indian women. The source on which we have based our reconstruction is the emotive recall of their history by women who shared their inner world with us. History as constructed by scholars may be valuable, but the history that lives within the memory of women and guides their perception of events in their own lives is more relevant to this dialogue.

The fourth chapter, 'Echoes and Shadows,' explores the experiences of the woman in the context of her parental family. It presents the emotive and cognitive maps of significant people in her family, the family as a system, and the system she is supposed to enter into after marriage. Her experience with the parental family is supposed to prepare her with values to live by, and to provide definitions and codes of conduct by which to govern herself in relationships. It also supposedly defines both the quality and boundaries of her aspirations, achievements, dreams and hopes. Today, this experience has become a double-bind as the traditional cultural lore and the emergent modern vistas are simultaneously present in the context of the family.

The fifth chapter, 'Fantasy and Social Reality,' presents the vicissitudes of her marriage and her struggle with the inevitable structure of the woman's life-space. It revolves around the cultural romance of being a wife and a woman, the fantasy of being the beloved and a partner in life's struggles, and her attempts to translate this romance and fantasy into the reality of continuing to be a role-holder with psychological substantiveness in her being.

The next chapter, 'Struggle with Reality,' deals with the arrival of the woman at the threshold where her real struggle begins. By this time she has experienced the social and psychological role-space and contained herself within the legitimacy and purity of its codes. At this threshold, she becomes aware of a lacuna in her life and begins to seek a space where she can redefine and redesign her role, seek new meanings and greater fulfilment, and claim herself to be a person beyond the given role so that she can reach out into the limitless potentials and meanings of being alive.

The seventh chapter, 'Beyond the Horizon: Confrontation with Psychological Reality,' depicts the struggle of women at this threshold in terms of their attempts to redefine their relatedness with the environment. It is at this threshold that most women find themselves emerging on to the paths of their personal lives with the accumulated pathos of centuries where they begin questioning the very fact of being born as women. This pathos has to be not only lived through and articulated, but a woman has to cleanse herself of its influence in order to transcend and rediscover her being for a future journey.

The last chapter, 'Final Encounter with the Self,' describes the confrontation of women with the micro and the macro identities. It is in the course of this encounter that women have to contend with certain inevitabilities of their lives and find the freedom, dignity and grace to be persons as well as women.

Taken as a whole, the book presents an articulation of what Indian women feel and live through. And if it succeeds in this venture, it may provide the readers with a space to reflect upon the world of women. It may also provide them with an experience with which they can empathise: the struggle for attaining wholesomeness. It is through this wholesomeness alone that women can find dignity and respect in themselves and pass on to their progeny a sense of being substantive. It is also through this articulation that perhaps a new ethos can be given shape so that women can begin at last to live like human beings.

This book primarily raises the issues concerning women with women, thus enabling them to reflect upon those issues. We, as authors, are very clear that the book is not intended to be an accusation—of culture, of society, of tradition or of men—nor does it charge anybody with acts of commission and omission. All that we attempt is to point women towards that horizon where, we believe, exists a space in which they can invoke the spirit of their human existence and bring to themselves and to the world the wisdom of the sages, the energy for an evergreen life, and the capability to create harmony between the heart, the soul and the living process.

The stories presented in the next chapter are taken from the oral tradition of the cultural lore. They constitute our attempt to put together those dimensions of the cultural lore which were meaningful to the women we encountered. Many women responded to these stories by sharing their dilemmas, the struggles of their inner world, their dreams and visions, and the pathos of living. These tales also provided them with several alternative responses to their being and the realities of living in the social context. We discovered that the stories provided directions in which women could make choices, and a space beyond the social phenomenon where they could locate themselves and get in touch with their beings, as also with the courage to begin a journey to explore their being. They were a first step in coming to grips with the reality of their roles and in attempting a redefinition of themselves and the space around them.

There were many who at the beginning were apprehensive and fearful. They remained rooted in the traditions of the social lore and their chosen roles. There were others who defied their roles and designed counter-modalities of role-taking for themselves. They had become independent, often single, women, living through broken marriages, were work and career oriented, and were dedicated to the liberation of women from the captivity of men, society and culture. These women were anchored in the ideals of freedom, justice and liberty.

There were yet others who remained caught between their need to conform to the given roles and the urge to seek freedom from them. They could accept neither, nor were they able to define or design for themselves a new location or a fresh choice. These women were caught in the cross-currents of a culture under transition. Although they had made a beginning, they were unable to persist in their struggle. Their personal anxieties and insecurities compelled them to surrender their beings and live with regret.

Then there were a few who could be regarded as pioneers. They chose the uncertain path and encountered in themselves the universal, cultural and social roles. They painfully delved under the many layers and said: 'I am this, and this, and this and more.' But there were also some who went beyond this. They included in their sense of 'moreness' the systems they were a part of. They began yet another journey to discover the 'moreness' of the system and themselves simultaneously so that they could forge a new destiny.

2

The Magic Space

Indian womanhood has yet to be explored, experienced, and understood in all its vicissitudes, multiplicities, contradictions and complexities. As a woman begins her journey at birth and proceeds through different stages, she experiences herself and is, in turn, experienced by others in several forms. Yet she remains an enigma. Much of her life is shrouded in unfathomable dusk or twilight. Endless horizons, defined by various locations, shift and create many forms. Light and dark, beginnings and ends, the concrete and the intangible, feelings, fantasies and actions, all shift and merge like in a kaleidoscope, to form an ever-changing collage.

Her childhood is like a dew-drop on a fragile petal which has a momentary radiance and vanishes; sometimes it is like a shadow to be avoided. Her adolescence is alluring and tantalising, promising the unfolding of many a mystery. Her youth is like the waxing and waning of the moon in tune with the rhythms of the sea: it can also be alluring but, instead, unfolds many ravages. Her middle and old age are like the return of a weary soldier, torn and battered, in search of some

peace and tranquillity; it can also be a moment of suspended anima-
tion, of, her duty done, awaiting the final call. Whichever way her life
meanders, a woman remains a mystery, full of contradictions, where
opposites exist as if on a see-saw.

Sometimes a woman takes the form of the ocean which pays homage
to the earth in an endless rhythm, or breaks itself repeatedly on the
monolithic rock in fury and helplessness; sometimes, she is like the
wind that gathers the dark, thunderous clouds to weep at her oppression, exploitation and dehumanisation, or scatters them to make the
day radiant with a sparkling sun. In her intensity, she turns the world
upside-down and evokes fear. In her gentleness, she touches many a
heart with joy and comfort. Accursed and immobile, she holds on to
hope and strength in the shape of the gushing stream of life which
gurgles and tumbles and touches many a heart.

The woman evokes in man a range of emotions. She evokes lust and
passion as well as devotion; she promises union, physical fulfilment as
well as communion; and at all times she arouses anxiety, apprehensions,
and fears—fears of merger and of dissolution. She goes by several
names. Sometimes she is called a goddess, sometimes Shakti, and often
a witch who is both seductive and fickle. She is the temptress and the
rejuvenator.

How does a women experience herself? Is she a mystery or an
enigma to herself? Who is she? How does she experience her space?
How does she experience her growth in the society in which she lives?
In order to grow, one must cross social and psychological thresholds.
Biological and chronological growth are inevitable. The social roles of
being a son or a daughter are determined by being born a boy or a girl.
The social movement involved in passing from the role of the daughter,
to that of wife, of daughter-in-law, of mother, are all part of society's
institutions. Psychological growth and the crossing of thresholds are,
however, choices that a woman makes by utilising her personal qualities and by investing herself and redefining her roles.

We set ourselves to explore with some women of India the nature
and quality of these social and psychological thresholds and the role-
taking processes that they encountered en route.

We found women sharing with us many of the images mentioned
above. They saw themselves (and were experienced by others) as being
unpredictable, unstable, subject to variable moods, earthy and responsive to the environment. They seemed to live from moment to moment,
and their interface with the environment reflected indecisiveness,

entrenchment, and a tendency to cling to confusion and to disown their own potential resources. When pushed to elaborate, these women talked of their helplessness—both economic and psychological. They talked of dependence, their social vulnerability, the burden of being bearers of virtue, and of compulsively doing the expected thing. Their feelings of being exploited and under bondage surfaced. The woman was the martyr and the sacrificial offering at the altar of a prescriptive society.

However, the psychological threshold is different from the social threshold. Chronological age does not determine the moment of arriving at or crossing the psychological threshold. In the journey of a woman's life, the psychological threshold is determined by the woman accepting her maturity, crystallising her identity, coming to terms with her past, laying down some of the ghosts of childhood and adolescence, taking charge of her own destiny, having a world-view of herself and others around her, investing in the self, in the system and in others, and discovering the spirit of her own being and becoming. It implies a pause, a review and an assessment of her resources and giving herself the autonomy to mould the future. This is the process involved in crossing the psychological threshold and arriving at one's personhood. However, Indian women seem to get stuck at the social threshold and the perspective role models allow them no space to discover new choices. They continue to remain victims and martyrs in the crystallisation of their identity.

The women of India are reflections of the prescriptive society they live in. They continue to experience the society they live in with all its diversity, complexity, glory, poverty, attraction, and repulsion. This society has a tradition and history stretching over 4,000 years of culture, legends, folktales, folklore, myths and epics (which we refer to collectively as the cultural lore in this book) and cultural roles—in short, a rich heritage of social and psychological role models which society makes available to its members.

We set ourselves first to explore the role models available from the cultural lore and then to examine what alternatives are available to Indian women to enable them to reach the psychological threshold with which to create a wholesome world for themselves. We discovered that there are five basic themes in our cultural lore around which Indian women build their roles and crystallise their identity.

The stories which are narrated below and which express these role themes, though Indian in origin, have many similarities with tales from

The Arabian Nights, those of Hans Christian Anderson, *Grimm's Fairy Tales* and other tales from across the world. What we present here are the stories that we used with many women participants in diverse settings to explore and understand the universe of women: their being, their inner realities, their fantasies, hopes and dreams.

The Apple and the Stigma

Once upon a time, just here and just around the corner, there was a kingdom. This kingdom had a king and a queen. The king was just, the queen was gracious; the kingdom was prosperous and the people were happy. After many prayers from the king, the queen and the subjects, a lovely daughter was born to them.

The princess was the apple of her father's eye and was loved and cherished by all the people in the kingdom. She was delicate, soft-spoken, gentle and quiet. She was talented and excelled in the arts of music, poetry, painting and needlework. All mothers in the kingdom asked their daughters to emulate the princess. The days went by and with each day the princess grew more beautiful and as radiant as the dawn. The people in the kingdom adored her and speculated about the lucky man who would eventually marry her They spoke of the talents, the valour, wealth and courage of the man who would befit their princess.

The princess grew to maturity and, lo and behold, one day she was old enough to marry. The queen became anxious about her marriage and kept reminding the king who appeared oblivious of his duty to find a husband for his daughter. One evening, when the queen once again raised the question of the princess' marriage, the king was terribly angry. In his fury, he announced that his daughter would be married to the first man who entered the gates of the kingdom.

There was silence in the kingdom. As evening came, the gates of the kingdom were closed for the night. The people kept an all-night vigil while the princess awaited her fate. The queen and the subjects prayed that the first man to enter would be worthy of the princess. As dawn broke, a lone traveller was seen coming towards the gates of the kingdom.

In the light of day, the king repented his wrath, but being a king he intended to keep his word. He, too, looked out from the window and saw a young man at whose approach the gates were flung open with a flourish. And what a sight met their eyes! Horror, dismay and repulsion filled everybody as they saw that the young man was a cripple. There were sighs, silent tears and wailing. The king, the queen and the subjects were stupefied but saw no way out of the situation. Sad as they felt, the fate of their beloved princess was sealed.

Preparations for the marriage had already begun. The princess, with her gracious charm and the courage of her spirit, remained undaunted by her fate. She was married to the young cripple (stigmatised) and, as tradition demanded, left the kingdom with her husband. She bid farewell to her parents, her beloved people and her childhood home. Years went by and the king turned old and grey. He could find no heir and repented his wrath and hasty act a thousand times a day.

The princess travelled far and wide with her crippled husband. Day and night they travelled and began to discover each other. They went through many trials and tribulations. The princess, with patience, kindness, gentleness, affection and devotion, slowly but gradually restored her husband to normalcy and he, in turn, worked hard to create a home for them. They prospered and had two children. Then, one day, as the princess sat reflecting on her life, she remembered her parents—the king and the queen—and her childhood. She longed to meet her parents. Without revealing her identity, she sent them an invitation to come for a feast. When the king and queen came, they talked of nothing but their sadness and bemoaned the loss of their daughter. The king was repentant. At that moment the princess revealed her identity and introduced them to her two children. There was much rejoicing and tears and the king persuaded them to return to his kingdom. In time, he made his son-in-law the king and retired. And, so goes the tale, everybody lived happily ever after.

Many variations upon this theme are found in fairy tales and folktales across the country. Our experience with women from varied social, cultural and economic backgrounds indicates that their life-space has a similar basic structure and that they identify with the princess of the story. Many young women are married to men far below their social, economic, cultural or educational backgrounds. This happens particularly in homes that revolve around traditional life-styles, values.

and beliefs. The girls, like the princess, are trained in the skills and the art of home-making. Some of them have also enjoyed a certain kind of status by virtue of being the eldest child. Others are educated but do not have a career. Education is regarded as an asset, a factor which could enhance a girl's performance of her role as a wife.

The husbands of these women are chosen according to traditional criteria, often without a proper evaluation of their personal attributes. When personal attributes *are* considered, the man seems to be full of promise, but fails to live up to it. In our context, he is essentially a kind of psychological or social cripple. Women married to such men take on the role of providing support and encouraging the husband towards achievement and success. They devote themselves to creating a context for that quality of life and relationship which fosters success and the well-being of the husband. Many women in India adopt this approach. These are the women who justify the saying: 'There is a good woman behind every successful man.' They tend to accept the ups and downs of life as also their lot without complaining. They shore up their husbands' sense of self-worth. Such women define their role as sustainers of marriage. Their menfolk and the home come first in their lives. These women are often referred to as Sita or Savitri, two glorified Indian role models for women. These women submerge themselves in their role and live only for their husbands and their families. Very few, if any, ever know what is happening inside their beings. They are all love and affection. These and many more are their virtues. However, these virtues can also become compulsions. Without intending to, they often invoke feelings of guilt in people around them. They also use a mild form of emotional blackmail in order to make people conform to their expectations.

The Counterpoint

A reverse phenomenon does take place on occasion. Some women, brought up in traditional families and from a middle class' socio-economic background, end up marrying prince charming—that is, men from the elite social and economic strata. These women are either sought for their beauty or their upbringing, since their families are highly esteemed and respected in the community and looked up to for the ethics and moral values they espouse. However, the women married into economically prosperous and socially elite families walk on a razor's edge. In the parental families, they are pampered after their marriage and often looked upon with awe. However, within the husband's family, they have to struggle to live up to the expectations of the husband and his family. They take on social responsibility for the larger kinship system of the husband's family. Their personal aspirations are set aside. In effect, they become managers of the family's peripheral and marginal social setting with little praise for or acknowledgement of their contribution. The husbands are rarely available emotionally and are usually at the beck and call of the family. These women sustain themselves basically through their children, and experience no replenishment or companionship. They are seen and regarded as poor men's daughters and accordingly treated with condescension. They hardly, if ever, acquire the status of being rich men's wives or experience a sense of belonging, dignity and respect These women remain uprooted and, despite their sacrifices, do not find a location which they can call their own. Psychologically, they live in a barren land.

Such is the life-space, the context of growth and the role model internalised from the cultural lore by a set of women who are often the eldest daughters. They postpone themselves and live for others; that is, for the husband's family. Psychologically, their hopes and aspirations are concentrated on their children. They soon discover that their life is for everybody else but themselves and there is no one for them. In both (i.e., *The Apple and the Stigma* and the counterpoint) the struggle of the woman's identity is to go beyond the threshold of social transition so as to get in touch with her being and personhood at the psychological level. This would mean including her feelings to be and become. However, her personal anchoring and its reinforcement by the social system is so deeply rooted in her role and the family that she continues to disown her own potential.

The Accomplished and the Trickster

Surrounded by majestic mountains and full of beautiful wooded lands, was a kingdom famous for its king's competence. He was a brave warrior, well accomplished in the arts of war. The queen was known for her intelligence, grace, wit and courage. The people of the kingdom were proud of their land and respected their king and queen. They trusted their king and felt safe and secure.

The king and the queen had a lovely daughter. She was indeed a royal princess. She had ridden horses since childhood and was trained in archery, fencing and the other martial arts. She even went to battle with her father. In addition, she was an accomplished scholar. She was beautiful, talented and intelligent. She was also ambitious, competitive, and confident. As she grew up, both her accomplishments and her beauty increased.

The days went by and eventually the princess became eligible for marriage. The people of the kingdom hoped that her suitor would be a brave warrior, worthy of her. The king proclaimed that whosoever wished to marry his daughter must come to his kingdom and match the accomplishments of the princess. If he failed, he would be taken prisoner, cast into the dungeon or beheaded, depending on the wish of the princess. Many princes came from distant lands. They were tall and handsome, talented and accomplished, heirs to the thrones of big and small kingdoms. They came with the hope of winning the princess to be their bride.

The princess devised many tests of bravery, perseverance, and skill in the form of games and competitions. Most princes succeeded in many games and competitions but failed in that one final challenge which could have won them the hand of the princess. Many of them were imprisoned and humiliated, while several princes lost their lives. As their numbers grew, the people of the kingdom became concerned and were angry at the wilful princess. They mourned the loss of the brave and gallant princes. But the fame of the princess brought many more to the kingdom. Then, one day, disguised as a prince, a trickster came to the kingdom and took up the challenge. Through his tricks, he passed every test, including the final challenge the princess set for him. There was much rejoicing in the kingdom. The princess married the trickster and left with him only to discover that she had been cheated. However, she had already left the kingdom and her only companion was her husband—the trickster. She now lived in shame, and regretted her vanity. And, unlike the endings of most fairy tales, she did not live happily ever after.

The lives of many women whom we talked to were essentially analogues of this identity. A search for compatibility and equality is the bane of the accomplished. Before marriage, such women cultivate intelligence, talent and competence. They are ambitious and struggle to be better than others, often turning their vulnerabilities into strengths. In relating to men they are provocative and challenging, evoking in them feelings of anger and aggression. They appear charming but are actually manipulative. Their feminine qualities—softness and graciousness—are used for gaining control over others. Their close relationships are fraught with friction and conflict.

Such women end up marrying men who appear to be accomplished but who in reality are far below their level of competence. Faced with this, these women soon realise that they have to take charge and that, during a crisis, they will have to end up shouldering the responsibility of managing the situation. In their struggle for independence, their relationship with the husband's family is marked by defiance, rebellion and friction. With all their potential, creativity and achievements, many women who exhibit this identity pattern find themselves cheated of life or denied their due.

Our explorations with women in this identity pattern suggest that the structure of the second identity theme follows from the identity structure of the first story, and is experienced as one of the primary identity themes among women. Fear of being married to the 'stigma' and its consequences drives these women to become more and more accomplished and thus avoid the fate of the first princess. It is also a way of preparing against the prerogative of the father to give them away to whomsoever he wishes. Underlying all this is the hope that their competence would ensure them an even more capable husband who is not stigmatised in any way. However, this in itself becomes their stigma. Their psychological struggle is to find confident and dominant males with whom they can feel secure. What they generally end up with are men whom they dominate and eventually hold in contempt. The men react by becoming either primitive or passive, and/or waste themselves. This model provides no space for vulnerability, and the women who adopt it rarely give of themselves to anyone. In work settings, they come across as being aggressive, self-centred and exploitative. Many of them are creative, but often lead a somewhat isolated and lonely existence punctuated by occasional intense intimacies. Generally despised or held in awe, they rarely succeed in having meaningful relationships. They keep hoping that some day they will find a person whom they can look up to, but most of their idols turn out to have feet of clay.

These are the glorified women of India—the Kekaiyis and the Amrapalis, the kept women and the courtesans, the Padminis and the Manjaris, the queens who walk with their husbands as equal partners. These are the women who are either outcasts or who, in asserting themselves, invite destruction. These women, who make history, stand alone in their beauty, valour, courage and sacrifice. They are married to kings and men of valour, but even they, at some point in time, surrender to the wills of these women or to their own vulnerabilities, thus inviting destruction.

The Counterpoint

The counterpoint to this model is the multitude of women who are either handicapped or who do not show any visible talents. These are the average female children. They experience themselves as being insignificant and lacking in self-worth. Often, the only response they receive and experience is one of aggression, abuse, or negative interaction. Many of these women are vulnerable to exploitation through seduction, and are lured by softness, gentleness and a little attention, only to end up being used and cast aside.

In marriage, a large number of these women experience physical, sexual and psychological abuse, at the hands of both the husband and his family. They live a life of drudgery, overload themselves with household duties and stretch their physical and psychological energies to the limit, hoping to earn some small positive response, a few kind words. They are victims of a social system which glorifies beauty, idolises male children, and regards women as burdens.

Women who fall into the identity pattern described in 'The Accomplished and the Trickster' rarely find space for their beings to unfold. They live under their own or the environment's compulsions. They are oppressed by expectations, both their own and of others, with the result that they often experience a sense of futility and anger. Many of them either choose not to marry or do not succeed in finding a man who is worthy of them.

The third identity pattern, described below, is frequently found in The Arabian Nights, Grimm's Fairy Tales, the tales of Hans Christian Anderson and other cultural lore. Here the parents protect the innocence and naivety of the daughter only to find her confronting the biosocial reality through a socially undesirable man—be he a soldier, a commoner or an alien.

The Innocent and the Seducer

Once upon a time there was a kingdom of many waterfalls, brooks, meadows, and gardens full of flowers. The winds blew gently in this land and the breeze carried the fragrance of flowers everywhere. It was a quiet land of gentle folk. This kingdom had a king and a queen who were renowned for being just, kind, and fair. They were gracious and concerned about the welfare of their people and the kingdom. Rich or poor, arrogant or humble, all received just treatment from them. People could go to them without any fear and share with them their woes, miseries, or joys. The people of the kingdom loved their king and queen, who had a dainty daughter. The princess had all the virtues of a young maiden. She was cared for with love, gentleness, and affection. The king and queen and all the subjects were devoted to her. She was innocent, playful, and winsome.

And, as it always happens, amidst all good there is bad, amidst all joy there is pain, and amidst all blessings there is a curse. So it was with the princess. At her birth, the sages and seers of the kingdom had foretold that the princess would marry an alien who would capture the kingdom. Time passed, and with each day the princess grew lovelier. The king and the queen began to think of ways to prevent the prophecy from coming true. They constructed a well guarded palace with seven thick walls, each of which had a door with a huge lock. On the day that the princess reached puberty, she was regally transported to the new palace. She had a maid to keep her company and guards at all the doors. Her room had only one small window. She became invisible to the world and, for all practical purposes, was a prisoner.

The princess began to live in a world of fantasy. She saw the hustle and bustle of life from the window of her room. She saw young maidens, accompanied by young men, laughing and blushing. How she dreamed of being one of them. How she longed to frolic in the sun, have the breeze play with her hair and the raindrops soak her body, to shriek with joy and laughter amidst friends! She pleaded with the king to let her be with them, but to no avail. The king and the queen waited for the right person who could marry her.

The days went by and the princess became restless. Her maid was her only companion and the queen her only visitor. And then, one day, just as the sun was setting and the day was welcoming the night, a young man entered the room. There was magic in the air. The maid was asleep and the princess was overwhelmed by the presence of the man. She saw in him her saviour, her escape from captivity. The man was a travelling magician who had heard of the beauty of the princess. He was charmed by her simplicity and gentleness and decided to marry her.

The princess continued to live in the palace and her lover (husband) visited her every night with the help of his magic. Months went by and one day, to the dismay of the king and queen, they discovered that their innocent child was pregnant. They raved and raged, and demanded to know the identity of her seducer. She stubbornly refused to reveal it. They then set traps and discovered the nightly visits of the magician. The guards then surrounded the room and tried to capture the seducer. A battle ensued and the seducer killed the king and a large part of his army and vanished with the princess. Destiny had its day.

This identity pattern is quite common among a large number of women. The family protects the growing girl from the realities of being a woman. They uphold the girl's innocence, her naivety, and her purity. She is made to deny her impulses and is compelled to live according to an abstract set of ideals far removed from reality. She lives in a world defined by others, especially by her parents. Her life is governed by the ideals of society. She is a captive and is compelled to surrender her being and the process of becoming to her parents who regard her as a possession to be preserved in all its innocence.

Women who exhibit this identity structure are generally unable to make any realistic assessment of men. Their ignorance of the bio-social reality often renders them susceptible to the charms and endearments of the men around, who are often of the undesirable type. The adolescence of many such women is therefore marked by sexual exploitation, disillusionment, and disappointment, which leaves them scarred for the rest of their lives. In most cases, these women feel that they are deserted and rejected as a result of some fault in themselves. Women of this identity pattern often marry men who are of a different caste and religion. Some of them even try and elope. Their search is for a sense of belonging.

The woman of this type often marry men who derive their signifi-cance from the smallness of others. Consequently, any attempt on the part of the woman to acquire a sense of significance for herself results in feelings of anxiety and apprehension in the men. Anxious to be accepted, the woman surrenders her being and willingly plays a secondary role. Their husbands, on the other hand, dream of marrying the 'apple princess,' but end up marrying women of this identity with the view of moulding them into ideal women—i.e., apple princesses of their own choice. In later years, if the woman concerned manages to acquire a sense of her own reality, the marriage becomes the setting for constant friction. She can then choose between rebelling and conforming but, either way, she is doomed.

Alternately, several women who fall within this pattern of identity remain captive. They are married more to the families of their husbands rather than to the husband as an individual. Thus, psychologically, they are never married. They often continue to shuttle back and forth between their husband's and parents' homes. They find no location for themselves. They internalise the denial and deprivation processes generated by the roles considered significant in the social system. They hanker for love and praise, but essentially remain objects of seduction. They disown their assertiveness and creativity, and their being and start playing proxy roles. They dream and fantasise about meeting someone who would value them for themselves and treat them as adults. Outwardly, they remain innocent, naive, shy and hesitant.

The women who internalise this identity pattern surrender their dreams and aspirations, their very lives, first to the parents and later to the husbands. They accept a destiny that is controlled by others, and are guided by a set of values, beliefs, and role processes of a bygone era. They become what can be termed as the echoes and shadows of the social system. In this they feel that they achieve their acceptance and affirmation for they tend to be glorified; in reality, they are merely the victims of situations and people.

The basic structure of this folktale has provided the theme for many Indian films. Films like 'Gaun ki Gori and Shehar ka Chalia' (the innocent village maid and the city-born charmer), depicting the trials and turmoils of this role model, have been box-office hits in India.

Women of this type enter the work-setting more often for economic reasons than by personal choice. The chances that they will be exploited bio-socially are therefore quite high. Most of these women end up doing routine jobs. They are rarely assertive, and are frequently perceived as being reliable and productive. Although they do become indispensable, they are nevertheless taken for granted. They are easily overwhelmed when someone asks for their opinion or advice. And while they are pleased at this indication of being regarded as mature adults, their upbringing prevents them from responding. Since their idea of reality, both at home and in the work-setting, is largely constructed by others, their own impulses and responses are held in abeyance.

Women of this kind often seek solace in God or religion. They feel guilty if their impulses come to the surface and they torment themselves by denying themselves the good things of life. They deny themselves a respite from over-extending themselves in their responses to their husbands, children or their work-settings.

The women who belong to the three identity themes we have described so far, live with feelings of being unfulfilled and of lacking psychological replenishment. They are constantly in search of something to restore their sense of well-being. They experience a sense of acute loneliness, both of existence and of experience. Their search for a sense of psycho-social relatedness often fails since they have very few positive encounters with their counterpart, the male identity. They cannot accept their body and its desires, and end up feeling guilty, resentful, and unfulfilled. Romance eludes them, and their fantasies of a life full of passion and love remain unrealised.

The following folktale etches the fourth identity pattern. This is a natural sequential identity pattern to which Indian women respond quite easily. The search here is for self-fulfilment and psycho-social personhood.

The Lost and the Unfulfilled

Surrounded by the ocean on one side and a vast desert on the other, there was a kingdom isolated from the rest of the world wherein lived a king and a queen. The land was one of plenty, where flowers and fruits grew in abundance. The shops were full of precious stones and the most beautiful fabrics of vivid colours. The land was blessed and so were the people. The king and queen had many sons and seven daughters. The princes and the princesses were trained in the social customs of the land and each had a unique capability. They all contributed to the cherished traditions of their kingdom.

Amidst this plenty, surrounded by many sons and daughters, the king and the queen were very concerned about their youngest child, a beautiful daughter. She had the gentlest of eyes and long, thick hair which reached her toes. When she sang, the woods and the forests, the streams, and all the birds of the kingdom were enraptured. Her melodious voice pierced through the hearts of the people and evoked nostalgia, memories, and elusive fantasies. This youngest princess was absorbed in herself and she would often sit for hours by the sea or at the edge of the desert dreaming of lands beyond the horizon. She was content in her father's kingdom, yet she was restless. She was loved by many, yet she was lonely. She had everything she wanted, yet she felt empty. She had the world at her feet, yet she felt incomplete, and she often brooded.

The princess continued to dream. She wandered through the kingdom. One day, in her wanderings, she came across the body of an unconscious man, a stranger, cast on the shore by the sea. The heart of the princess went out to him, for he was a handsome man. The princess took the stranger to the palace where he was restored to health. They fell in love and he asked for her hand in marriage. The king was troubled, for none in the kingdom had married a man from an alien land. So the king decided to test the stranger by setting him a series of difficult tasks to perform. After undergoing several hardships, the stranger completed all the tasks successfully and so stood the test of his love. The king finally agreed to the marriage and the princess and the stranger lived happily thereafter. Years later, the stranger wished to return to his home. It was then that the travails and turmoils of the princess began.

There are a whole set of women who internalise this identity structure. Their process of growing up has left them unsure of relationships. As a result, they are willing to offer all that they have. These women bring to their relationships all that is considered ideal in society—love, conformity, obedience, unstinting loyalty, and sometimes blind faith. They often ignore the reality of the other person and the situation. In their own way, they have chosen to surrender to one person in life. They therefore become blind to the subsequent manipulation and exploitation and live with the referred status of others. Deep down, many of these women live with feelings of rejection and a lack of self-worth.

Most Indian women marry a stranger with or without their choice. Those in search for an ideal relationship first attempt to create a relationship with their husbands. They devote their lives to their husbands, hoping that his response would fill the void in their lives and help them experience the magic they have dreamed about. However, the men they marry are often self-absorbed and tradition-bound. In their attempts to be ideal sons and responsible members of the parental family, these men become so duty-bound that they often neglect their own primary family of wife and children. The women in such a setting gradually feel disillusioned.

These women are silent sufferers. Their hope is that their husbands will understand their aspirations and potentials, and create for them a context in which to grow. However, the husbands, preoccupied with their own careers and caught up in traditional roles, are often insensitive to the inner needs of their wives. The women continue to sacrifice their lives and are as lonely as they were before. Women with this identity internalise neglect, indifference and loneliness. They come alive once, when they get married, but having displayed their concern and involvement and having tried to establish a link, they retreat once again.

In relationships and in marriage, these are the women behind their men. They become mothers to their husbands. They provide sustenance and manage the infrastructures of the home to provide consistency, continuity, and stability. They make no direct demands for themselves. They provide support to everybody, and are towers of strength in times of crisis. They are often exploited and taken for granted, and are always in demand when others are in stress. Their worth is felt in their absence and most acutely in their death.

Many women of this identity type become desperate when they experience disillusionment. Some see suicide as their only alternative. The slow and gradual disintegration of their dreams is too much for them to bear. Many of them postpone their career opportunities and sacrifice their potential and capabilities for the sake of their marriage. Some of them continue to play the idealised social role which glorifies sacrifice at the altar of their husband's needs. They disown their being and processes of becoming. They are talented and wish to create a niche for themselves in either their home or in the professional world. However, their talents are sacrificed for a home, husband, children and the social tradition.

Many women who fall into the identity pattern and structure of life-space depicted in 'The Lost and Unfulfilled' forever remain unfulfilled. They search for relationships and occasionally even find one, only to lose it. What really sustains them is their devotion, faith, persistence, sacrifice and unstinting hope. The experiences of many women reinforce the themes of separation, unfulfilled dreams, silent endurance and unrequited love. The Indian cultural lore, glorifies and idealises this identity. Sita, Parvati, Meera, Kannagi, Damayanti, Savitri are but a few examples of characters which operate as potent role models, internalised and given social and psychological expression by women.

In essence, these women search for that one person who would fulfil all that which they have been deprived of from childhood, and make them feel worthy and whole in themselves. They search for personal security and unconditional acceptance. They search for their personhood and a context wherein they can flourish and grow.

The women who have experienced and lived through the core identity theme of the four tales outlined above find themselves falling back upon their own resources. They then begin to live through and experience the next core identity pattern—'*The Realist and the Exiled*'.

The Realist and the Exiled

Once upon a time, there was a kingdom at the edge of a desert. The winds blew hot during the day while the night brought a cool breeze from the distant ocean. The king who ruled this kingdom was temperamental. He either blew hot and lost his temper or was cool, calm and serene. The queen, a tall and dignified lady, was generous and wise. People often sought her advice on their day-to-day problems.

The king and the queen had three daughters, each one quite different from the other. All of them had special skills and were trained in the laws of the land, its social customs, and in ways of relating to the people of the kingdom. The king would often talk to his daughters and tell them stories about days gone by. The king and the queen, along with their three daughters, would frequently meet the people of the kingdom who admired the differences, similarities and uniqueness of each member of the royal family. They felt that the kingdom had all the resources they could wish for.

One beautiful, rainy day, the royal family was sitting in their palace watching the rain pour down from the heavens. This hap-

pened very rarely, for they lived very near the desert. The king suddenly turned to the three daughters and asked them: 'Whom do you love most?' The princesses were taken aback for a moment, but the eldest one quickly replied: 'You, father, I love you the best.' The second daughter then replied: 'It is the kingdom that you have created—its palaces, its monuments, the jewels you have brought from distant lands and everything that the kingdom holds— that I love.' The king was pleased and patted the hands of these two daughters and said, 'I like what you say'. Then he turned to the youngest daughter who looked at him for a long time and said: 'Father, it is the salt that I like best.' The king turned red and purple and then, like a volcano, erupted with anger. He roared: 'You are an ungrateful child.' And like the father of the princess in 'The Apple and the Stigma,' *he declared that his youngest daughter would be married to the poorest man in the kingdom. And so it was proclaimed in the kingdom. The people of the kingdom were stunned, for they all knew who the poorest man was.*

The poorest man in the kingdom lived in a hut whose walls were full of holes and which did not have a roof for long stretches of time. It grew hot like an oven during the day and was freezing at night. The people often saw this man searching for shade during the day and huddling in a corner at night to protect himself from the cold. People wondered how the princess—who had lived in the palace, where cool breezes were fanned during the day and where, at night, she slept on a soft bed covered with silken quilts—would survive. They sighed and bemoaned the king's temper and his hasty command. However, the command had been given. Right or wrong, the king's verdict had to be carried out. The poorest man of the kingdom was hauled before the king and the day came when the king married off his youngest daughter to him.

And, like in all stories with a sad beginning, we would like to know what happened to the princess. Did she survive? Did she weep? Did she moan, shriek or faint? Did she curse and live in the heat and shiver in the cold? What happened to both of them? And so the story unfolds. The princess had courage, for she had said what she felt and what she believed in. On the day of her marriage, she dressed as a simple maid, abandoning all the royal fineries, and walked with firm steps to marry the poorest man of the kingdom. The poor man, now the husband of the princess, was dumfounded and at first thought it was all a dream. He looked at the gracious princess and was tongue-tied. The princess took his hand and walked away from the court. They walked past the palace, past the royal gardens, and past his hut. The people followed them up to the edge of the desert and then stood still. Without looking back, the princess and her husband walked on and on and out of the kingdom.

The days went by. The king and the queen married off the other two daughters to the most eligible and desirable men in the kingdom. Once married, the eldest daughter only came to visit her parents occasionally, when it suited her. She was soon absorbed in her married family and grew indifferent to her parents. The second daughter only visited them to demand presents of gold, jewels and money. She was never satisfied. She would rave and rant if her wishes were not granted. The king felt very disappointed. As he grew older and pondered over his life, he thought about his exiled daughter. He wondered where she was and what had happened to her but did not make any efforts to find her.

Many years went by. There came to the capital a rich merchant who sought the king's audience and permission to settle in the capital. He offered precious gifts to the king in the audience hall. The king was pleased and gave his permission. The merchant was honest. His fame soon grew and he was held in deep respect by the people. His wife, too, became the favourite among the wives of the merchants.

One day, the merchant invited the king to visit his home for a banquet. The king was delighted. On the appointed day, the king arrived to find himself in a big mansion where all kinds of delicacies were being served to hundreds of merchants, bankers, and scholars of the city. He was invited to sit on the throne. The merchant's wife, accompanied by a dozen companions, came to serve the king. The king took his first mouthful and, to his dismay, found that the food had no salt. He tasted every dish; each one lacked salt. By this time the king was puzzled and angry. He demanded an explanation. The wife of the merchant looked up and said: 'Once, O king, you considered salt to be dirty and cheap.' The king was perplexed and looked closely at the woman. He recognised her as his exiled daughter. He realised the wisdom of his daughter and rose to embrace her. There was great rejoicing in the kingdom, and in time the king retired after appointing the merchant his successor.

The women who internalise this identity pattern attempt to integrate their emotions, sentiments and feelings with the primary system and, at the same time, to strengthen this structure with their belief in rationality and practicality. Somewhere during their period of growth they have learnt to integrate their head and their heart and have evolved their own code of life and behaviour. These women come across as being secure in themselves and autonomous in their decision-making. Although they are responsive to people and situations, they do not seem to be able to please the people with whom they relate in the primary system. They respect existing societal values but, at the same time, are willing to explore and question them. Their acceptance does not blind them to the shortcomings of these values. If necessary, they experiment and establish new personalised values.

In role-bound relationships, which permit only role-appropriate actions and feelings, these women may run foul of significant roles and are punished for it. They can operate in any life-space, but with a sense of aloofness. Their propensity is to create a life-space which they can call their own. They deploy their resources to create a space where togetherness can flourish. They are neither echoes nor shadows. They are not dependent upon legacies. They can create a new heritage from within themselves without negating the original heritage. They are 'women-persons' and not 'women-roles'.

Many of these women become pillars of the community. They are given respect, and perhaps devotion, but rarely love and affection. They neither negate nor victimise. They live and act according to their convictions. They do not rebel; rather, they create new traditions. However, they are often perceived as rebels by traditionalists. In our experience, these women, once married, stand by their men. They build a strong foundation to create a sense of mutuality and reciprocity. They are able to adjust to the extended social system and often bring families together. There are many examples where, when such a person enters the family, there is a gradual ending of feuds and a growing sense of well-being in the family system.

These women bring functionality, stability and insight to the workplace. They strive to create a caring work culture. They are responsive to the underprivileged and often take on the responsibility of fighting on their behalf. These women tend to be professionally inclined and have a wider perspective of life.

They create a location and a space which is a source of well-being for themselves and for others. They are capable of handling live issues, people and situations without the compulsion to conform. They are accessible to others who are suffering from some inner turmoil. Indeed, many of them end up as 'mother confessors'. Yet, amidst all these purposive transactions, they often live with an acute sense of loneliness. These are the women who cross the social threshold, encounter the bio-social role modalities and discover their own psycho-social person-hood. In this, they find freedom from confining role boundaries and accept the multiplicities of their being. Their maturity lies in their ability to live with ambiguity, uncertainty, similarities and differences. They are able to resolve contradictions to create a meaningful whole and to add their insights to the processes of living. They claim their space, give themselves legitimacy, accept their unique existence, affirm their beings and feel blessed for the life they live.

A Perspective

These five stories, with variations in time and place, are prevalent all over India (and all over the world) in the oral folk tradition. In somewhat more elaborate formats, they are also found in written and enacted traditions. We have put them together in this sequence in order to illustrate the vicissitudes of women's roles and identity patterns. The five core identity patterns form the structure of a woman's life-space where she has to confront different faces before she can claim her real face. Each identity provides a pattern of relationships with their concurrent processes that have to be lived through if women are to lay down the ghosts of victimhood and martyrdom. Each core identity provides space for a confrontation with the compulsions of societal codes of conduct and the deeply embedded stereotypes of women's roles. Each identity also provides the space to explore and discover resources within the self, giving women the choice of either taking their destiny into their own hands or handing it over to other people, to society or to tradition. Hence, the core identities present in any cultural lore can either provide new alternatives, new paths and new directions or reinforce the existing social code of conduct.

In the first story, 'The Apple and the Stigma,' the woman's identity allows people in her life-space to view her as a passive recipient of love and care. She is supposed to withhold her own being and follow the confirmed path. When she completes her allotted span of time as a daughter, she is handed over to the first likely candidate for a husband

and left to drift on her own. To the father, she is a burden and a stigma in which he refuses to invest any further. He gets rid of her at the first appropriate moment. The woman in this role identity introjects the stigma, which is reinforced even further by the 'stigma' of preventing her being from unfolding. The inevitabilities of the structures of her life-space are concerned with dissolving and resolving this stigma and with restoring her own wholesomeness. The stigmatised husband is the symbol of the stigma she carries for postponing the discovery of her being. Developing her resources so as to mobilise the stigmatised husband and thus restore herself through him, is one alternative she can choose, the implication being that her self cannot be directly actualised. The other alternative is to fade into conformity and to live a life of poverty and hard work. The residual feelings accompanying the first alternative are those of regret at having restored others but having achieved nothing new for herself; while, if she adopts the second alternative, she ends up feeling tortured.

'The Accomplished and the Trickster' is the natural sequence of the first story. Having lived through the stigma, the woman's psyche converts the life-space of the daughter role into one where she can not only receive care and nurturance and live a life based on conformity but where she can actively struggle to give shape to the potentials within her. She is admired for doing so, and even respected, but not loved. She is also regarded as a capable woman who is a successful manipulator of the environment. She becomes what she is not supposed to become—the instrumental mode of the male within herself. She carries the instrumental psyche of man in her woman's body. It is this internalised male psyche (in its negative connotation) that the woman encounters in the trickster. The inevitabilities of the structures of her life-space are centred around her becoming, and in this lies her dilemma. If she lets go of the male instrumentality, she will fall back into the life-space of 'The Apple and the Stigma'. In that role she can only serve as the context of someone else's restoration. If she retains the instrumental mode she has to encounter its negative counterpoint and engage in a constant struggle to find an equation. In many Indian stories, like those of Kalidas and, later, Tulsidas and Surdas, these women push the trickster into a positive modality by their contempt and then face desertion and condemnation. In the stories of Tulsidas and Surdas, the women are eventually deserted, while Kalidas glorified them. The message is clear: the being of a woman, when acting in the male modality, invokes desertion. Many career women in India face 'desertion' in the form of divorce or have to live through their life-space as though occupying a battleground. With both alternatives, the residual feeling is that of 'damned if you do and damned if you don't'.

The third story, 'The Innocent and the Seducer,' again flows naturally from the first two. The woman's psyche, having experienced the travails and turmoils of the other two identities, chooses to adopt the role of an innocent. Regarded as a possession, she is protected by her parents and virtually becomes a captive. Her encounter with the seducer is an encounter with the reality that she has never been allowed to experience. The masked reality is that of her own impulses and their gradual rationalisation through the living experiences in her life-space. The parents deny her the opportunity making the transition to the socio-psychological identity of an adult. She is kept a prisoner of her bio-social role within the primary family, and not allowed to enter the secondary system in her own right. Her encounter with the seducer completes this process.

The inevitabilities of her life-space are to confront the reality of the world, learn discrimination and make mature choices. Unfortunately, this identity confronts only shame and reactive violence. The first alternative (i.e., shame) converts the seducer into a protector who takes her away into a new kingdom, never to return. The hope is that she will be relocated in the new universe with respect, dignity and maturity. In encountering the reactive violence of the parents, the seducer has to destroy the parental family and take over. Many women in this identity pattern relive the encounter with seducers over and over again, even after marriage. Their longing for romantic relationships leaves them vulnerable to seduction. If their wishes remain unfulfilled, they find it difficult to live up to their roles as wives successfully, and can only play the role of a mother to their children. They also very often turn to religion. The residual feeling is one of regret at not being in charge of one's own destiny.

The fourth story, 'The Lost and the Unfulfilled,' is another natural sequence. The woman's psyche, having undergone the three earlier identity patterns, chooses to remain uncommitted and uninvolved in the life-space of a daughter. She becomes self-absorbed, and lives in a never-never land which is not anchored in reality. She waits for some sign of recognition, a bestowal of identity. Finally, in her encounter with the wounded and unconscious man, she recognises that she will have to take the first step to reach out and invest herself. The wounded and unconscious traveller is a representation of her own psyche. Thus, she acts, for the first and only time, to nurture and awaken her dormant being—and once again becomes dormant in herself. She takes on the mantle of the traditional, duty-bound role and recreates her earlier indifferent, uninvolved and self-absorbed role.

Many women who exhibit this pattern go through marriage hoping that their husbands will help them to realise their beings. Unfortunately, due to some peculiar process of choice, either their own or their family's, most of these women end up marrying very formidable men who are sons to their mothers—a role that they are unable to outgrow. These women become part of a group whose pathos is so often enacted in India—the good, well-bred bride, tortured and harassed by in-laws. The residual feeling is that of regret at never having begun to create a space around themselves.

The fifth story, 'The Realist and the Exiled,' represents the final choice of the woman's psyche to assert her inner being and bear the consequences of doing so. Her attempt is to create a space for herself in which she can strengthen her being and claim that which is lost with dignity. Her encounter is with the fantasised lack of resources of the other four identities. Her encounter is not with her own symbol, but with the symbol of the woman's psyche introjected from the environment, which considers women to be helpless and dependent and as demanding a continuous generation of resources and their deployment in the environment. It is as if this identity impels her to disprove the belief that woman are not resourceful. In India, these women are the progenitors of a dynamic, new heritage, and in the process are simultaneously glorified and perceived as tyrants. Idealisation and deification is their reward and loneliness their lot.

Men and women, with their unique experiences of the family as a system and with parents and other individuals in significant roles, converge directly or indirectly towards role models, and become part of the cultural lore. For, what the folktales, epics and myths provide, albeit in fantasy, is what individuals yearn for, aspire to, and wish to receive from the system. They also provide a psychological space in which to dream in and fantasise about a different world—a world full of aspirations, assertions, and freedom from role conformity. In essence, the cultural lore is an alternative expression of that which is intensely experienced. It is also an invitation to transcend role models and to create a wholesome life-space for the self and others in the system; in short, an invitation to be a person without being a threat to society.

Social Rituals and Role-taking

While these identities are kept alive in India through an internalisatior of the cultural lore, their enactment is defined by the rituals and messages which express the ethos of the times. An example of such messages prevalent in India is that the daughter is *paraya dhan* (somebody else's property, held in trust). This implies that the daughter has no real psychological space in her father's home, that she is a social transient. The basic import of the definitions prevalent across different regions of India can be summarised as: 'You have some freedom here. Enjoy it with constraints. Once you are married beware of the in-laws;' or 'You will have a hard time;' or 'Your fate is to be subservient to fathers and brothers before marriage and husbands and in-laws after marriage, and to sons if you survive your husband. Your destiny is to live for others. This you can only do by denying yourself.'

Various Indian rituals are also intertwined with stories from the cultural lore and they affirm the inevitable structures of life-space. After marriage, rituals like Karva Chauth are celebrated only by women. The songs and stories associated with these rituals and festivals also reinforce the structural codes of their role models and life-space. Internalisation of these models and their social and psychological expressions continue to dominate Indian women even today.

Perhaps in every culture across the world, women use the models contained in their cultural lore to fashion their life-space and to govern their role in life. It is interesting to note that the cultural lore has become one of the significant sources of introjection at bedtime. Indian culture discourages the telling of stories to children during the day, because in the daytime a child can question 'why' and 'how'. But if told just before they go to sleep, these stories can be imprinted in the child's unconscious mind. Epics read out during the day are meant to be heard in devotion and silence. The occasional interpretation is provided by the narrator who restates and emphasises the moral of the epic which normally reinforces the existing ethos through the role models portrayed in the stories. The taboo on telling stories during the day is supported by the saying that listening to stories during the daytime will make the child's *mama* (maternal uncle) lose his way home.

The Indian epics, with their spiritual and religious context, provide only fragmented insights into the unexplored areas of a woman's being. They praise that kind of assertiveness which helps destroy evil in society. None of the role models, however, encourage assertiveness as an inherent value that a woman can use to act for herself and to live as a whole person. If she suffers indignity she can seek the help of others (for example, Draupadi seeking help from Lord Krishna), but she can never act for herself. The themes of action or assertion on the part of a woman are used only to emphasise a state of anger against the system or against a set of people on behalf of the husband or a son. The epics rarely promote assertiveness as an independent value. The spiritual and religious role models also do not, as a rule, provide women with any hope of integrating the processes of their being and becoming. They do not generate a socio-psychological identity for women, nor do they create a legitimate space for a woman's being in society, other than that of compliance and conformity.

Of course, Indian history and literature do contain a few examples of women seeking the fulfilment of their being. However, it is not surprising that such women are invariably either courtesans or outcasts like Amrapali, or the women depicted in the novels of Sharat Chandra Chattopadhyay and Jainendra Kumar Jain. At one point in Indian history, the courtesan had acquired a high status in society. Her occupation demanded that she be well-versed in the arts, music, literature and politics of her time. It also demanded a strict code of conduct and honour. The courtesan was assertive, articulate, accepted her feminity with grace, made choices rather than compromises, and commanded respect for herself.

Unfortunately, the acceptance of this role in its dignified aspect was short-lived. In accordance with the rigid social code of conduct as it developed, the courtesan came to be viewed with suspicion, was maligned, and held in contempt. All her accomplishments were reduced to being merely the glorification of her sexual skills and expertise. What was once a role that demanded rigorous training, gradually deteriorated into vulgarity. Literature frequently provides role models of assertive women who, by their life stance, restore men, but are eventually left on their own. The man, restored to his wholesomeness and dignity, walks away to create his own space in a new world and leaves the woman—the source of his restoration—behind.

Essentially, then, in her conformity, the self of the woman is disowned and she has no space in the lives of others, not even in the life of the one in whom she has invested. What options, then, does the woman have? And what are the basic action choices embedded in the role models and life-space of Indian women?

The bio-psychological phenomena of sustaining a child in the womb for nine months is a unique emotional experience. Other than that, what a woman lives with is the trauma of the inevitable uprooting from her parental home and rerooting in the husband's home.

Uprooting

Except in some of the few remaining matriarchical societies where they experience continuity, women live in a transient context from the moment they are born up to the time they get married. After marriage, they experience the pathos of being uprooted from the parental family. No marriage, either in real life or as depicted in Indian films, literature, or drama, can avoid this pathos of the woman's uprooting. No woman, even if she has been unhappy living with her family, can disown this reality. It is only in interactions with her *saheli* (her peer and close girl friend), who teases her about her relationship with her future lover/husband, that she can regard this process of uprooting somewhat positively.

It is obvious, then, that the husband's home is the place where the woman has to relocate and root herself, and in doing so can either flourish or wither away. Even today, most families discourage a woman from returning to the parental family, even when the husband or his family are brutal. The message is—that is your place and there you stay. The daughter is showered with advice about the need for adjustment and for giving in. But she is not offered any support. The woman can either become a victim or a martyr. The wife suffers both physical and psychological brutality, accepting it as her destiny, as her lot by virtue of being a female. The parents of such women bemoan the loss of a daughter but remain mute and helpless in the name of their daughter's destiny and their own inability to make new choices in terms of action. If a woman succeeds in separating herself and her husband from the in-laws, she is often condemned and held guilty. Husbands who let this happen are regarded as being *joru ka ghulam* (the slave of the wife) and treated with contempt. Such husbands are tortured by guilt and anguish at having let down their parents. As a result, these marriages often go through a turbulent time as a consequence of the husband's need to cope with this guilt.

While some women manage to persuade their husbands to escape from parental captivity and compulsions, other women are unable to exercise this choice. This may be because of economic considerations, or because of the husband's inability to redefine the son's role. Many such women end up disengaging themselves psychologically from the processes of rerooting in the new context. They remain daughters and make their lives meaningful by being possessive mothers. They rarely become wives.

With the changes that have been taking place in society over the last twenty years or so, other alternatives have become available to women. If the process of rerooting is not facilitated by the husband or the in-laws, if there is physical or psychological brutalisation, or if new definitions of the husband and wife roles do not emerge, divorce is one option that women can take. After the divorce, a few choose to marry again while others prefer to remain on their own. In recent years, an increasing number of women with jobs, careers or professions have chosen to remain single.

Millions of women across countries and cultures uproot themselves from their parental homes to make new homes. Our exploration with a large number of Indian women suggests that the pathos of uprooting and the difficulty of rerooting result in several critical orientations and attitudes. The women find it difficult to use the resources of the husband for the development of their self. Many women, when confronted with the statement that it is legitimate to claim familial resources to develop their own being and to forge a meaningful relationship with the environment, refuse to seek these resources and/or even accept the legitimacy of such a demand from their side. The family normally shows no concern and makes no provision for the deployment of its resources. The women themselves are unwilling to claim these resources. By this time women have learnt to perceive the husband's resources as being 'his' and not 'ours'. They also carry resentments from the past which prevent them from accepting or claiming such resources. Further, women feel that their husbands give them resources either to humour them or because the woman has fought for them, but in neither case are they given out of conviction. The husband's basic attitude is: 'You have everything, what more do you need?'

Many women shared this inner pathos with us. They felt that they were sought in marriage for the resources which are theirs due to the *samskaras* of the family or through personal achievement in the field of education or other areas. As the woman begins the journey of rerooting herself in a new environment, those very resources for which she was sought have to be heavily constrained in terms of the manner in which they will be acceptable. This creates resentment in the woman, as well as a feeling that she lacks value as herself. She often finds herself being reduced to an errand girl or slave, whose resources are used by the husband or his family at will. The woman finds no escape and very little space in the new environment to bring into play the resources of her being.

The inner dialogue which they shared revealed that many women who have had this experience gradually erode their own sense of self-worth and disown their personal resources. They begin to feel helpless and refuse to take any initiative for their well-being or fulfilment. They persist in the hope that the husband will discover them and create a context for their unfolding.

When the early years of marriage have gone by and motherhood has been experienced for a few years, there comes a moment when women want to re-engage with the world and with their beings. They discover that the roles they have so far played have been inadequate and insufficient. They have lived through disillusionment and disenchantment and remain psychologically unrooted. At this point doubts keep surfacing. Women feel that their resources are insufficient and that life has left them behind. Their attempts to rediscover their own resources and to nurture and deploy them lead first to an encounter with another male. As such, most women in effect disown the search and the struggle. Those who continue to seek other avenues of engagement which require the economic as well as the psychological resources of the husband, find the resentment of the earlier disownings surfacing again and now find it difficult to accept the resources of the husband. According to the logic of the inner dialogue,

they have been denied so far. They have remained unappreciated. They have remained performers of service roles. Their duty is done. At the beginning of a new journey they do not wish to be contaminated by the patronage of the husband offered as if to an old retainer. The commitment of the women is to manage through their own efforts and through their own resources. The anguish is held deep inside. The hurts have been many and no gesture is enough to ameliorate the dehumanisation that women have experienced and lived with.

Another set of manifestations are in the form of psychosomatic and other illnesses. Many women are unable to reroot themselves psychologically as members of the husband's family. Nor are they able to find a space in which to mobilise their resources in middle age and, sometimes as early as in their thirties, live through long and debilitating physical illnesses. They will not go to doctors nor take medicines. They prize the capacity of their body to tolerate stress. These women abuse their bodies and hope to create guilt in others. Because of this constant disregard and abuse, many women end up with permanent disabilities and handicaps. These women often keep falling ill but continue to work hard. Their effort is to prove that they are not abdicating their role, but at the same time make sure that the family knows of the sacrifice.

Another dominant anchor of the model of life-role and life-space is the quality and meaning of relationships. In most of the core identity stories, relationships are given more importance, which leads to women losing their identities. The woman is expected to hold her being in abeyance and to define her relationship according to the purposes outlined by the system. The relationship transactions are coded by an ethos of living for others.

As a part of the system, the woman may have many roles. For example, in the primary family she is the daughter but may also be a sister, an aunt, or a niece. However, of them, the daughter's role is the anchor and its transient status permeates the other roles. Similarly, in marriage she is either the daughter-in-law or the mother. Her role as a wife is secondary. Her status of being the daughter of the other house is constantly kept alive in transactions. It is only in motherhood that she finds some integration and rooting for herself. As a result, she sometimes tends to be over-possessive of her children. Even in the nuclear family system, the woman, in a socio-psychological sense, continues to experience her role in the husband's family as that of an outsider.

The dilemma that faces a woman in terms of relatedness is between her status as a transient occupying a position of trust at her parents' place and of being an outsider at her in-laws' place. Her social locations may be rooted in the system, but her psychological location remains nebulous. The dilemma of her psychological location and hence the problem of a stable sense of relatedness and meaning seems to haunt the inner life of many women in India. This dilemma makes it difficult for them to find an emotional anchor in the permitted, legitimised role relationships. There is always the fear that the fact of being an outsider would be thrown in their face. All their efforts to maintain the well-being of the system and its significant roles can crumble into dust and become meaningless by the smallest reference to this fact. Their sense of location is thus very fragile.

The lack of a stable psychological location leaves only two options open to women: they can either turn to religion or find an emotional anchor in another male outside marriage. In the past, society permitted the institution of *dharam bhai* (adopted brother). Such a person can belong to the in-laws' family or be from among the husband's friends. According to stories and legends, the woman's response in the psychological and emotional sense was to seek transient sensuous relationships: the *abhisarika* who against all odds and dangers goes to meet her lover. The extent to which this was a social reality is a matter of opinion. The fact that at one time sex was not really morally taboo in India may have encouraged this alternative in the minds of some women.

The other choice adopted by Indian women is to cultivate an almost pure virtuousness and to adopt a life of duty tempered with faith and the observation of religious rituals. They become highly normative in relation to themselves as well as others. This form of psychological location frees them to create their own boundaries and thus ward off many exploitative encounters. It also creates some space for women, and gives them the role and significance of being the carriers of the cultural heritage and family traditions. They become the moral backbone of the family through the vagaries of social and economic upheavals. Many ravaged families have rehabilitated themselves on the strength of such women. As devoted beings, with a strong belief in religion, many of them also acquire an added sense of meaningfulness by becoming the source of family prosperity and happiness. It is their virtue and faith that keeps the grace of God on the family.

The question today is what processes of role-taking are open to women? The present beckons with newer and wider opportunities of a life outside the home. It provides investments in the self—such as, education—which were once denied to women. Their intelligence, abilities, and capabilities are being realised in areas other than the traditional fields of art, dance and music. Appearing in public as a performer is an act of courage and conviction, but at least it is a choice that is now available to women. The pull of the present is its invitation to become. Many women have accepted this invitation and taken the first steps towards it. How do they feel inside?

Women seem to experience two sets of feelings simultaneously. One set is of joy, pride, respect and affirmation of themselves. They are full of hope and a sense of fulfilment. They feel a sense of being part of the system in which they attempt to carve out a role for themselves, experience equality and are able to influence their own destiny. This brings to them a sense of dignity. However, they are also acutely aware that their success and responsiveness to the present is shrouded in a mantle of societal suspicion, contempt, sexual insinuations and other prejudices. This generates feelings of anger, resentment and sometimes guilt and anxiety. As such, they are often on a see-saw of feelings—on the one hand, joy in the affirmation of being and becoming, and feelings of vulnerability on the other. Presenting a smiling and brave face while being anxious and resentful within seems to be a frequent experience for many women.

The future is a shifting collage. Women have still not found a place, a location—psychological or social—where they can experience themselves without the ever-present ghost of comparison with men and the system.

In the absence of experiencing any space to explore their struggle for a meaning combined with their secondary status as a female, women in India often experience the lack of an anchor within themselves. This, in turn, makes them conform to the social role prescriptions. This conformity denies women the space to come to terms with their body and their psychological being. It hampers the discovery of personhood, and generates in them an unending search for acceptance, instilling in them a desire to please and to render service. Women feel compelled to make themselves desirable, and this reinforces their feelings of being exploited and stigmatised.

Women continue to struggle to get in touch with their substantiveness and to discover for themselves an identity beyond that of a victim and a martyr. In the absence of the system providing any space or role models for such an exploration and being entrenched in the compulsiveness of social roles, they often surrender their search for their personhood and settle down into a reactive mode. Some women have struggled with the system which has often attempted to deploy their potentials both at home and in the work-setting. They have often confronted within themselves the pathos of the traditional past and the aspired ethos of the present times, but in doing so have overloaded themselves with the processes of both. Most of them have sustained themselves by over-engaging in both roles. Others have fallen either into the role of a daughter, or a wife, or a mother. Thus, they have found it difficult to evolve an integrated identity.

Some women continue their struggle to find freedom from dependent, controlling and patronising relationships. Their attempt is to redefine their role to include acting upon the system and to create a legitimate space for themselves. An exclusive emphasis on career and economic autonomy pushes women into a comparative framework and an aggressive mode which, in the long run, becomes dysfunctional for them. Creating a woman–person identity is associated with fears of social stigma, isolation, and loneliness.

Can there be a life without roles? Can a person relate with others purely at the being level? In any social setting or structure, roles are an inevitable phenomenon. Consequently, they have to be defined, not played, they have to be designed, not enacted, and, most important, roles have to be anchored in the being of the woman and not in the norms and prescriptions of social structures and systems. Indian women cut themselves off from the cultural lore with its anchor in the being of the woman and have linked their lives to the determinants of society. However, society itself has lost its moorings from the cultural context and grounded itself in rigidities and uncertainties. As a result, women, having been dislocated from their beings, hold on to the absolutism of social structures and prescribed roles thus divesting themselves of dignity and creating a setting which invites the destruction of their self.

Roles are an inherent phenomenon of social living and relationships. They cannot be wished away, defied or surrendered. Roles added by the being of the woman then have the space to bring to their unfolding the spirit of a human code of conduct and, consequently, a feeling of well-being and wholesomeness to the self, relationships and the system. The current issue is whether there are any alternative role models available to women. Are there processes in the social system that can facilitate the transition from roles of a bygone era to those of the present time and allow women to be integrated persons?

Having explored the core identities and the structures of life-space introjected from the cultural lore through the nostalgic period of childhood, and having glimpsed the inner realities of women's experiences, we now attempt an 'inside-out' look at the path traversed to arrive at the current threshold. We shall take a look at the landmarks of history, at the life-space that women have travelled through in their personal lives, and the thresholds that many did not cross. Hopefully, this book will serve as a brief pause to assess the current reality of the life women live and to identify a set of processes to discover a path to the future.

3

Women in the Tapestry of History

The Ethos of Indian Society

Any understanding of Indian women, of their identity, and especially of their inner dialogue, will be incomplete without a walk down the corridors of Indian history where women have paused, lived and internalised the various role models. The role of Indian women, as it has evolved, been experienced and understood over 4,000 years, has been intertwined with the history of the country which is primarily one of repeated impositions of an alien ethos on its culture necessitating a frequent restructuring of social systems and, consequently, individual identity. Like the country, the role of Indian women is full of diversity and contradictions. Indian history is experienced from its glorious past to its degenerating poverty, from its spiritual ascendancy to its revelling exhibitionism, from freedom to captivity and from violent outbursts to tranquil moments of peace. Similarly, the role of Indian women has ranged from that of a deity to that of a *devdasi*, from the pure to the vulgar, from being supreme to being downtrodden, and as innumerable manifestations of virtue or vice. The role of Indian women has undergone dramatic and drastic changes from era to era, while within the eras themselves there have existed simultaneous contradictions. Furthermore, it has varied from caste to caste and with the various socio-cultural and economic strata of society. It is as panoramic as Indian history. Any composite presentation of this identity, just like any composite presentation of Indian society, can always be challenged. Any attempt to weave diverse strands, different eras, locales and levels of society into a composite whole is open to controversy. This fact has led to multiple interpretations and a plethora of literature on women's role, their lives and identity. This in itself has created problems for contemporary women in experiencing a continuity of their identity with society. What is introjected by a woman growing up in Indian society is perhaps a collage and a flux of attitudes, perceptions, roles and locations of their identity. It seems to be difficult to take a logical look at all this. To every 'yes' there is a 'no', and to every 'no' there is a 'yes'. The introjected collage does not, therefore, make it easy for women to define their role and to enunciate directions and goals for themselves. Perhaps this is the single and most important handicap Indian women face in taking a creative and constructive step to 'be' and 'become' without guilt.

This chapter documents that part of history which Indian women have internalised in a psycho-cultural sense and which affect their processes of being and becoming. It also attempts to link this internalised history with the five symbolic identities depicted in the tales related in the first chapter. Some of the folktales go as far back as the fourth century AD. For example, *The Accomplished and the Trickster* is available in the legend of the marriage of Kalidas to a princess. Some others can be traced to the twelfth century, the period of the Afghan dynasty.

We asked ourselves about the kind of historical context that facilitated the survival of these folktales which have reinforced symbolic identities and role models for women through centuries, and invited our participants to share their perceptions with us. In response, they came up with their own reconstruction of Indian history. They talked of how they have viewed history. They talked of the shift in life-styles related to technology from era to era. They spoke of the significant and critical landmarks, beginning with the Indus Valley civilisation, the arrival of the Aryans and the different stages of the Aryan ethos (they intertwined the Vedic period, Brahmanic influence, and the misinterpreted *Manu Smriti* with all this), the unfolding of the Buddhist and Jain eras, the arrival of Islam and the Muslim era, the rise of the Bhakti movement and its intermixing with the Sufism of Islam, the beginning of Christianity, the impact of British rule and, finally, the era after independence. All these and more depict not only the changing status, but also the continuities and discontinuities of women's identities with their shifting significance in India.

We realised that this reconstruction does not match with the one that scholars provide. A review of the existing literature (see the bibliography) suggested that many scholars have already traced the role and status of women in India from ancient times to the present day. Our effort to record the impressions of history held by our participants and the consequent inner dialogue borrows from the writings of these scholars as well as utilises the historical contexts, processes and role models experienced by the women themselves. We believe that history as viewed by people is more significant in giving direction and meaning to the choices of individuals. The history constructed by scholars reflects the cognitive map; it is not necessarily enlivened by the psychic energy of persons. We also felt that our responsibility lay with our commitment to present the inner dialogue of women rather than with the scholars.

The women whom we met were not scholars of history. To them history was at best a school subject, often dry and boring. It dealt with political events and the doings of kings and queens and with battles. Very little of the cultural and social lives of the common man was made available to them through this history. What they considered to be the history of their cultural milieu and life-space came to them largely through literature which described the life of the common man. Their second source was legends and other forms of oral literature. The third, and the most important, source was the Indian cinema. Finally, many of them mentioned that some of their impressions had been gathered from magazines, journals and Sunday editions of newspapers which, from time to time, carry articles about the way life was and is in the different states of India and among different classes of people. This reinforced our decision to look at history through the eyes of the participants and thus evolve a new framework rather than to fit their impressions into the frameworks established by scholars.

Our participants held that three distinct historical strands have converged to create the context for the evolution of the boundaries and the content of the identity of women in India. The first strand is that of the ever-changing ethos—from the time of the Indus Valley civilisation through the Vedic and the Puranic to the Muslim and Christian eras. In the midst of these dominant ethos, there has been an influx of many other cultures. And although Indian culture experienced many continuities and discontinuities, a primary configuration has always survived within this flux.

The problem, as one participant said, is how do we determine a bench-mark? At one level, the Indian ethos seems to be the product of alien ones. Who were the first aliens? Were they the Aryans? Many participants felt that regardless of the flux and the changes, the primary ethos of Indian society remains anchored in the Puranic period. This is true, at least in terms of the interpersonal and social transactions of men and women.

The second strand is the shift in the technological modalities of society. This, too, is difficult to pinpoint. Did the Indian people go through the normal evolution from a cave culture to nomadic/cattle culture to agriculture and trade and finally to the industrial and technological culture? Epics and myths like the *Mahabharata* and *Ramayana* seem to indicate a shift from the nomadic/tribal culture to the cattle culture of the Aryans and finally to an agrarian and trade society which continued to dominate India till about 1947.

The third strand identified by the participants consisted of the intermixing of religion and the political governance of society referred to as the periods of the Hindu Kingdom; the rise of political states influenced by Jainism and Buddhism; and, finally, the emergence of a national governance influenced by the Islamic and Christian rulers of India. Our impression was that this strand was not considered by our participants as being a distinct and separate one. It was seen as either being parallel to or in the background of the other two. They could only identify some of the changes in customs and practices that resulted from this mix. They could not identify a major shift in the ethos itself. At best, they came up with attempts of the poet saints and later of Swami Dayanand and Raja Rammohan Roy to assimilate the Islamic and Christian ethos into the Hindu context.

In the view of most women, Indian history, like the Indian ethos, is full of contradictions and diversity. Every aspect of Indian life partakes of this character. The role of Indian women also reflects the same contradictions. One participant said Indian history can be experienced in a glorious past or a degenerating present; in India's spiritual ascendancy or the licentiousness of the Maharajas and Nawabs; in the freedom of ideas or rigidity in action; and in periods of violent chaos and enduring periods of peace. Similarly, women in Indian history have been treated as deities or *devdasis*, as being chaste or being *abhisarikas*, as being equals or being downtrodden and, finally, as representing either virtue or vice.

Another problem with a historical reconstruction, either by scholars or in the recall of folklore, is the issue of deciding which part of the historical material represents an overall cultural trend. In the highly stratified life-spaces classified by caste and geographical distribution, there are distinct diversities and contradictions in manifest behaviour. The role of women has varied from caste to caste, from ethnic group to ethnic group and across socio-economic levels. Any attempt to present a composite picture of Indian culture raises the inevitable question: 'Is there such a thing as an Indian culture?' It is interesting to note that those who raise this question also blithely refer to American, British, French or other cultures which they consider to be unified ones. When confronted with the fact that these cultures, especially the American one, are just as diverse and diffused as the Indian, they merely shrug their shoulders. In our view, Indian culture, in spite of its diversity, has a central core which runs across the country. This core is as dominant and significant as the WASP (White Anglo-Saxon Protestant) core of modern American culture. It is this core ethos which the participants identified as being Puranic in its origin.

The various and differing perspectives of Indian history and ethos has led to a plethora of contradictory writings about Indian women, their role, life and identity. This in itself has created problems for contemporary women. Together with multiple interpretations of the past, they are also subjected to a multiplicity of borrowed cultures. Today, women grow up in India with a variety of unrelated and fragmented, almost contradictory, attitudes and perceptions of their role, identity and location. According to one participant, this is the most significant handicap for Indian women in terms of evolving a creative and a constructive stand for themselves. For every choice made there is a resounding 'no,' causing a great deal of confusion, a sense of anxiety and defensiveness. Hence, another reason why we decided to stick with the emotive recall of history of our participants and to identify the underlying pattern was largely determined by this peculiar quality of the Indian ethos.

Indian Women Over Time

What follows is a summary of the three strands identified by the participants. In earlier civilisations across the world and of the Indus Valley in particular, women were seen as being a source of life. They held in themselves the mystery and secret of birth. They represented fertility, and their identity was analogous to Mother Earth. This conception is central to the worship of the Mother Goddess. It is perhaps this aspect of the earliest ethos which continued to evolve through the centuries and in later periods crystallised in the concept of *shakti*. Later, this concept was revived and exploited by the Tantrics. In Tantric practices and philosophies, women became the central means of acquiring power over the forces of nature. They located the woman in the concept of Tripurasundari. The *sadhak* of Tantra sought physical union with Tripurasundari in order to acquire power over the forces of nature. Thus from the Mother Goddess held in reverence and *shakti* held in awe and fear, in the symbol of Tripurasundari, women descended to being the ultimate object of sensuous fulfilment.

The second concept which evolved out of the symbol of Mother Earth and fertility was that of Lakshmi, the Goddess of Wealth. It is common to hear of Griha Lakshmi, even in relatively enlightened homes. An interesting aspect of both these concepts is that they are considered to be unpredictable and of unstable temperament, thereby saddling women with the label of being an enigma or a mystery.

In our cross-referencing, we found that this process appears to have a link with other cultures across the world. In recent times, there has been growing evidence from Europe, the Mediterranean and the South Pacific, that women were paid homage as Mother Goddess and as the Goddess of fertility and plenty. In well-documented myths of Egypt, Greece and Rome, one finds the Goddesses Isis, Athena, and Minerva. At some point in time, the Mother Goddess also acquired the image of a warrior Goddess in the form of Shakti. This suggests that although at the beginning of human history as we know it, women did have a significant location, processes were already emerging which in time would lead to their becoming objects of men's fulfilment. For example, the concept of *bhogya* is linked to the symbol of Tripura-sundari while the concept of *kshtra* relates to the Mother Goddess.

However, apart from their symbolic status, it is difficult to assess the sociological status of women in this era. Depending upon the perspective taken, women in this period seem to have had greater freedom to determine their relationships than they had in later periods of history. According to our participants, the development of women's identity and role in Indian history became diffused and fragmented during the period in which the intermixing of the Aryan culture and the previous culture of the Indian continent took place. Most participants conceived of diverse strands from this period which helped build their definitions and boundaries of the woman's role and identity. These are summarised below.

The Free and Equal Women

Participants referred to Aryan women riding horses with men and joining them in drinking and dancing at public gatherings. The image they held of these women's relationship with men was one of a companion in work and sensuality.

Women: Pursuers of Intellectual and Spiritual Concerns

The names of Lopa Mudra, Gargi and Arundathi as creators of the Vedic *rucha/richa* were mentioned. This freedom to follow intellectual and spiritual concerns and to participate in the creation of an ethos was also substantiated by reference to Leelavati and other women who lived in periods ranging from the Vedic era to the seventh century AD.

As a substratum of these two streams, participants also mentioned the Ghandarvas and Kiratas, the Vanaras, the Nags, Yadavas and other ethnic groups. According to them, their women shared an equal status with men. They walked, drank and enjoyed the pleasures of life with them and even fought alongside them in wars. Chitrangatha, Hidamba, Kekaiyi, Satyavathi, Surpanakha, Shakuntala and other women were mentioned in this context. According to the participants, in both the Aryan and non-Aryan traditions, women were considered to be the equal of men, socially and psychologically. They could, if they wished, woo men, leave their husbands, and even live with another man without going through the sacramental rituals. In the ultimate consolidation of the Aryan and non-Aryan traditions into a more general Indian ethos, this aspect of life was recognised and legitimised. For instance, Manu recognised eight modes of marriage, only one of which was sacramental. Later, Draupadi, Kunti, Tara, Mandodari and Sita, all five of whom had either an open liaison with other men or whose virtue was suspect, were declared eternal virgins. Thus, in this formulation, women seem to have had a wide spectrum of roles, freedom of choice and a comparatively open life-space.

We asked the participants to outline the possible causes of the disappearance of this kind of society and about how women came to be regarded as the sustainers of virtue, home-bound, responsible to males and committed to the eternal loyalty and devotion of a *pativrata*. They had no clear answer, but their contention was that somewhere in the shift from earlier societies, the Brahmin ritualists became dominant and created role boundaries for women. A few of the participants also pointed out that having the freedom of choice, some of the women in earlier societies also chose to be *pativratas* and carved out for themselves the role of a *sahadharmini*. These women followed their husbands in companionship, and were faithful, devoted and role-bound. The ideal wife was exemplified by women like Anasuya, Arundathi, Savitri and Sulochana, and they were used by Brahmin ritualists to promote their ideas.

It was suggested that in the struggle between the Aryan and non-Aryan cultures, women lost out on their social status. They became the victims of kidnapping and violation. Society responded by creating two loci for women: one of the virtue-holder and the other of a free woman. In the process, all the earlier freedom which women shared with men was transferred into the space for free women. The women who belonged to this space were only allowed the role of a courtesan. Courtesans were accomplished and knowledgeable, had a significant function and wielded both social and political power. The classic example is that of Amrapali.

What follows is a summary of the participants' collective visualisation of the shift in women's status.

Women in a Secondary Status

At some point during the Vedic period, it became customary for an Aryan man to have two wives—one who took care of the home and was attributed the role of the *pativrata*, and the other who was his companion in public life and joined him in social and political assemblies. Perhaps women of the defeated ethnic group were allocated the role of the housewife, and the other woman, being Aryan, was retained as the companion. Thus, two traditions grew—one legitimising women's participation in intellectual, social and political processes, and the other binding them to household chores. It is interesting to note that, in many ways, the role of the courtesan still exists in most societies. In certain respects, Madame Pompadour of France is nothing but a throwback to Amrapali, and women like her flourish even today. Similarly, the tradition of separating the housewife from the public setting is still alive in India. If wives are present on public occasions, they have to segregate themselves from men and form their own group. In many cases they are asked to shift to another room so that they are not visible.

The second step in the denigration of women to a secondary status began with rise of the Kshatriyas in India. Buddha and Mahavir, being Kshatriya intellectuals, gave women a secondary status in their religions. In both systems, the *bhikshuni* was given a secondary status and was not allowed to be a ritual-holder. Their status was the same as that of nuns in Christianity. The eventual codification of the social order in the form of 'Smritis' during this period finally confirmed the position of women in the secondary role. This tradition continued and, as no resurgence of Indian culture and society occurred, it became rigid over time. After the sixth century, with the appearance of the Islamic influence and the domination of the Afghans and the Mughals, the same pattern was reinforced. The energy of Indian society was diverted into assimilating and binding these influences on the one hand, and preserving the continuity of its own tradition on the other. This encouraged an enunciation of social traditions in greater detail and increasing rigidity.

However, Indian society being what it is, none of the earlier identity patterns of women ever disappeared completely. Within the isolated boundaries of the Shaivite, Tantric, Shakti and other *sampradaya*, many earlier strands of the women's identity continued to be operative. Similarly, even after the final codification of social ethics in the Smritis, a large number of women, especially those belonging to what were considered the lower castes, continued to be allowed to retain their freedom from the codified ethics.

On the whole, however, the period after the seventh century saw an increasing erosion in the role and status of women. Slowly, education became taboo for women, and child marriages became prevalent. Any accomplishment in the arts other than of decorating the home was prohibited. Widow remarriage was banned and the woman was left at the mercy of the husband's family. Women began to see themselves as beasts of burden, enduring the drudgery of household chores in silence, bearing children and binding themselves in ignorance and superstitions. Their interface with the outside world became severely restricted. According to our participants, this pattern was reinforced by the influence of Islam which, although it allowed women the freedom of remarriage, generally restricted them to the privacy of the household.

Women in the Modern Era

In many ways, the role of women in Indian society remained unaltered for about a thousand years. It was only under the impact of British rule and the second wave of Christianity that Indian society began resisting its decadence. Raja Rammohan Roy and Swami Dayanand were the first to take up the cause of women. They revolted against *sati-pratha*, advocated widow remarriage and initiated education for women. In the late nineteenth century, with the establishment of the Indian National Congress (1885), a more active movement to lead women into the modern era began. Maharshi Karve of Pune and Mahatma Gandhi were its major protagonists. Since then, women have been able to take up careers as teachers, doctors, lawyers, political leaders and social workers. Of late, women have also entered administrative and other public services. Many have become architects, engineers, and managers. However, the economic and other freedoms available to career women, have not been able to change the traditional orientation and attitudes towards them.

Even at the time of rigid orthodoxies, there were women who transcended the narrow boundaries of the prescriptive roles. They had the courage to define and design new roles. In the process, they were maligned, abused and sometimes destroyed, but they suffered this social response with conviction and dignity. Meera, Ahilyabai, Durgavati and Rani Lakshmibai are some well known examples of such women in recorded history. We are sure that there were thousands of other such women in India whose lives have not been recorded. Occasionally, they have been immortalised in folk songs and tales.

Over the centuries, then, like many other phenomena, the existence of women in Indian society continued to experience flux and transition. And with every change, women were pushed further in the direction of becoming objects. Occasionally, there were times when the doors of captivity were opened, the burden of oppression decreased and women could walk towards new horizons. Yet, in their journey across the forbidden territories of society, the ghost of stigma continued to accompany them. These journeys required courage, intense commitment, relentless struggle and a lot of lonely moments of pain, anguish and tears.

Techno-Economic Change

The various technological transitions followed by major changes in the economic processes and structures of the country played a major role in defining the socio-psychological status of both men and women in India. Changes in technology are the product of man's efforts to enhance his physical and psychological well-being and survival. The development and introduction of technology in a society lets loose economic and other forces which compel man to change and adapt his interpersonal behaviour to the new environment. This obviously leads to new definitions of role and status.

Indian society has witnessed many technological changes over the last four centuries, yet many things remain unchanged. In fact, India today retains technologies from the seventh century BC as well as uses technologies belonging to the present. This mix has been possible because the Indian social design has developed ways of sustaining a simultaneity of variety without requiring major changes in the ethos of interpersonal relationships. However, this has been possible only when technologies have evolved in a continuum. Whenever there have been major technological shifts, there have been disruptions. One such example, discussed later, is the confrontation of cattle culture with agrarian culture.

We would like to stress the fact that the value system, which legitimises the social structure and the interpersonal network of relationships, has a tendency to change very slowly. The forces generated by value structures very often create a social inertia for change. Technological breakthroughs, however, unleash forces of dynamism and create new choices in terms of manifest rewards and conveniences of living that are much more attractive.

Confronted with these two forces, an individual struggling to derive some meaning in his social space, is torn between the idealism of values and the pragmatism of technology. Because, ethos apart, dramatic techno-economic shifts tend to influence role parameters, as well as the boundaries and quality of relationships between people. Today, the attitudes, values, beliefs and modes of role-taking by men and women in society are largely determined by the nature of the techno-economic patterns of society. Ethos generally deals with identity, meaning and values. These are held internally, in the form of ideals. Techno-economic aspects are expressed pragmatically.

In trying to find a balance between the two, the individual has to transcend the ethos and create new definitions. He may have to pay a price for his convictions, or push society into institutionalising the new ethos and its processes. In the past, the Indian social structure managed to maintain this balance in its overall social design. However, it seems that the area of transactions between man and woman was more often redefined in favour of the former. The emergence of agrarian society perpetuated a bifurcation into two distinct role spaces for men and women. Women were primarily relegated to the management of the internal interface of social systems. They were also relegated to being the infrastructural backdrop of men and their role in the work-setting. In short, men do the major work, but women prepare the setting and provide all the support which can help men to achieve and get ahead.

A comprehensive view of the evolution of technology in man's life-space and the resulting and continuing changes in social codes and forms of work, suggest that four major transitions have taken place in the last 4,000 years of known history. Each transformation has brought about changes in the definition, concept, nature and meaning of work, and the role of men and women in the social system. With each transition, women have had to contend with diminishing horizons, changing role definitions and societal values, and a reduction in the degree of freedom allowed them within the framework of the social design. Broadly speaking, the four periods are:

1. Foraging and hunting culture;
2. Cattle culture;
3. Agrarian culture; and
4. Industrial culture.

Foraging and Hunting Culture

According to our participants, this culture did not have a society or a community as we know them today. Small extended families or perhaps clans lived in a certain area. Their inability to replenish their environment to ensure a continuous supply of food became the basis of a strong need to protect their own territory and aggress upon others'. Clashes between clans became frequent. Men were often killed and women were taken away as prisoners. According to one set of participants, there was no basic difference between men and women in terms of relating to the environment. Others held the view that the basic roots of differentiation between men and women, which survive even today, were set down in this period. Women were already being pushed into infrastructural and 'objecthood' roles. However, both sets of participants agreed that women were held in some awe as they were supposed to have links with the supernatural. Thus, the prototype models for womens' role and status were available from the very beginnings of human society.

Cattle Culture

With the emergence of the cattle culture, the people's life-style began to be geared to a cyclic movement from one locale to another. This was due to the fact that, like the foragers and hunters, the people of this culture also lacked the ability, technical or otherwise, to replenish the resources of their locale. Their life-style evolved into that of a camp community. They also managed to develop new technologies in fields such as weaving wool, working with leather and wood-carving.

Over time, a sort of community culture developed around their camp life-style. Interpersonal relations started to crystallise and norm-setting began. Some functional differentiation of roles in community tasks between men and women also emerged. According to our participants, besides functional divisions, the nomadic life also encouraged a partnership between men and women. Women were more free to relate to the external environment. They became partners in the governance of the community. Men often concerned themselves with extending the boundaries of their territory in order to discover new sources of food. This process was the first step towards the confinement of women to the home.

Women became the holders of camp life and its interface with outside communities. They sold their goods and bargained in the market-place. They enjoyed a certain degree of equality. Marriage was very often contracted by choice. Since couples could set up their own household, in-laws did not acquire as much power as in the later agrarian era. The pragmatic aspects of life in a cattle culture community, like the Bharvada of Saurashtra, is still managed and dominated by women.

Agrarian Culture

The agrarian culture began as a parallel process to the cattle culture and eventually grew into its counterpoint all over the world. History records the frequent struggle between the protagonists of the two types of life-styles. In America, this struggle persisted till late into the nineteenth and early twentieth centuries. Western novels and films are full of this conflict. In the Indian context, the transition into the agrarian culture is reflected in the Hindu epic, *Mahabharata*. Lord Krishna represents the cattle culture and his brother, Balram, often referred to as Haldhar (holder of the plough), represents the agrarian culture. The struggle between these two cultures has been extensively recorded in other literary forms as well.

The agrarian evolution produced major shifts in the life-space of individuals. For the first time, man realised his ability to regenerate and replenish the earth through farming. This ability also enabled him to exchange the transcience of camp life for more stable habitats. He began building houses and, later, schools and temples. His life became punctuated by the rhythm of the changing seasons and allowed him enough time to develop new skills and technologies.

The stabilisation of the agrarian pattern of life led to the evolution of a more complex social structure. The community was transformed into a society, where issues of stratification, hierarchy, governance, maintenance and interdependence of different occupations, roles and sexes emerged. All over the world and across all societies, the development of agriculture led to a redefinition of the parameters of socio-psychological life.

The impact of the agrarian society was more pronounced on women than on men. The entire scope of their role, the quality of their relationship with others, the very meaning of their existence—everything was redefined. They were pushed into being appendages of men, with no independent status of their own. Men became the be-all and end-all of their existence.

A study of the *Mahabharata* is the best way of understanding the shift in women's role as a consequence of the transition from a cattle to an agrarian culture in India. Kunti, Draupadi and the other Yadava women had much greater freedom and significance in society as compared to the wives of the Kauravas. Gandhari, wife of Dhritarashtra and epitome of the new value of being *pativrata*, lived her life blind-folded because her husband was blind. The Pandava and Yadava women, however, experienced considerable suffering and public humiliation while the Kaurava wives were almost invisible. The Kauravas were supported by Balram, the Haldhar, and represented the emerging new agrarian society which was distinctly male-dominated.

Agrarian Indian society eventually relegated women to the exclusive role of the housewife. To whichever community or caste she belonged, her dominant space was at home. The role of the man was to manage the external interface with the environment, while the women managed the internal interface of the home. Neither could encroach on the other's space or domain. Man's authority lay with the external world while the woman's authority in the home was supreme. Power, authority and decision-making regarding community, caste, and social/political issues rested exclusively with the males.

However, Indian culture displays diversity even in unity. Even today, at the manifest level, one can find differences in the actual enactment of women's roles across ethnic, linguistic and economic segments of the population. A common factor in this diversity is that the women who belong to the middle class across the country have borne the major impact of the restricted and inhibited life.

This process created a complex, closed and, perhaps, rigid social stratification in Indian society, leaving the individual very little scope for mobility—social, psychological or otherwise. Personal inclination and competence were bound by caste occupation. The individual derived his sense of meaningfulness from the dominance of his social relationships and his sense of affiliative belonging. This reduced mobility, circumscribed standards of living and reinforced social and caste identity. This process of Indian society can be described as the structuring of experiential space whereby individuals learn to suspend their experiencing self from the living process of reality. In this way they surrender themselves to the role identity and achieve the ideal of detachment.

Thus, centuries of the agrarian ethos fostered values and attitudes, patterns of interpersonal relationships and meanings of life which became the norm. In fact, they became so absolute that they were assumed to be part of the basic nature of human beings. The concepts of life, predisposition to action, and curtailed aspirations to which individuals adapted themselves came to be treated either as being God-given or as being essentially inherent qualities. Thus, individuals became the victims of their own natural, social and spiritual adaptations, which societies call heritage.

In short, the unfolding of techno-economic transactions tended to narrow down people's roles and status, closed off a large part of the life-space to the expression of the self, created forces of conformity to limited roles, and made men feel more dependent on external rather than on their own resources. The worst victims of these processes seem to have been either women or the destitutes. Both have had to draw solace from being told that they are living out their fate. In living out their fate, women are burdened with the role of being virtue-holders, and the lowest rung of the occupational hierarchy—the very poor—have been made into children of God.

The social design of this phase evolved a new space for men and women. Slowly but steadily, women's role shrank into a limited life-space with rigid boundaries. These boundaries had varied impact on the various strata of women belonging to different socio-economic and caste structures. Women began to acquire a role space which lost its dignity, respect and value. References culled from the writings of social scientists and other literary figures as well as our data from the participants lend themselves to the ensuing descriptions.

Rural Women

For more than 150 years, rural women have lived with a scarcity of resources and the threat of economic deprivation. In many cases, where caste and family taboos are not strong, women joined the secondary stream of the workforce in order to raise supplementary resources. They go out of their homes to work in fields, forests and in other settings. Those who cannot go out engage in economic activities at home. Women are generally allocated menial jobs and often work for others as paid labourers. Research suggests that, across the centuries, the day-to-day life of rural women has been full of hardship, deprivation and the struggle to survive. Apart from supplementing resources through work, these women have also had to bear the exclusive burden of managing all the activities at home. This monotonous and demanding role and the routine of deprivation is quite typical of rural women belonging lower down in the caste hierarchy.

Women closer to the urban areas seek jobs as construction labourers and household servants or engage in small trades like selling vegetables. This is seen to be the only possible life-style. For the women, it has meant that they are born to live life as beasts of burden and to die without having lived one moment for themselves. Their life is meant to be lived for others, to be sacrificed at the altar of society's discrimination and allocation of a lower status to women. It is a life laid waste both physically and psychologically. Surrendering to the lust of men, their withering flesh bears child after child, while they live an insecure life under the constant threat of being cast aside at the whim of men. Robbed of dignity, pride and self-worth, women see themselves as prisoners or slaves doomed to obedience and conformity. A woman finds release and freedom only in death.

Upper Class Women

These women live mostly indoors. Once they enter the homes of their husbands, they rarely go out. They come as brides and leave only for the funeral pyre. The husband's home is their prison, their castle, their palace. They believe, or are made to believe, or have no other choice but to believe, that this is all for their good. It protects them from the lustful eyes of other men or the jealous eyes of evil women. However, within the walls of their home, within the feudal system of a large joint family, run parallel themes of exploitation, intrigue, and counter-intrigue, all revolving around the control of resources through legacy and heritage. This is the only life they know as wives.

Women from the upper classes are trained for this role right from birth. Deprived of childhood and adolescent dreaming, they can only hope that the man they marry and his family will not be too harsh. In such homes, the eldest woman of the family holds the authority, the power and the significant social status. She is the representative of the inner family, and the link between this inner home, which comprises women and children, and the men of the family. She is the managing member who decides when and into which families the girls will be married, and which girls are suitable for marriage to the young men of the household. Occasionally, she is also involved in matters relating to property. The other women of the family, who are younger in age and in the social hierarchy, can only grumble and conform but have no voice of their own. They are duly allocated roles and duties to be carried out on ritual and social occasions.

Except for the locale in which the women move and the level of material resources available, there does not seem to be any significant difference between the role of women belonging to the lower economic groups and those of the upper classes. Women in both categories share the fate of producing children year after year, and encountering sexual exploitation either within or outside the family. The misery of the upper class woman is more poignant as she cannot express her anger in public or make a scene. Poorer women at least have the psychological freedom to occasionally vent their frustrations in public.

Middle Class Women

Women belonging to the middle classes are squarely caught in the shifting sands of culture. They are neither restricted to the home nor permitted to fulfil their aspirations. They live in a half-way house like Trishanku. The legitimacy of their role lies in managing the home, children and husband. Authority over children, a certain amount of economic control on resources, some participation in decision-making, freedom to determine religious observances and, finally, the freedom to meet with friends in her peer group, both in enjoyment as well as in a cooperative effort to furnish a yearly supply of storable food items, are the anchors of her well-being. But behind all this, she carries the same taboos as the women of the other two classes.

However, one must recognise that the women of this class are perhaps the most significant source of family integration and survival and of the transmission of culture. They are the unsung heroines who, while enduring stress, pain, anguish and frustration, continue to inspire and mobilise their men and children towards the achievement and fulfilment of their dreams. They are the anchors of continuity and ensure the persistence of the ethos—in short, they are the source of cohesiveness of Indian society.

There are two other roles in which these women hold sway in society, where their skills are accepted and respected. One is the indispensable role of the midwife in the community, village, caste or neighbourhood. The nature of the social system does not allow a male to play this role. In this role, the woman acquires a position and status which gives her the freedom to say things which no one would otherwise dare. She often plays the role of limiting pregnancies in the name of health, reprimands the male of the household, and often acts as a source of information about the outside world. She occasionally plays the role of advisor and counsellor in critical situations like those involving abortion.

The second category of women who have acquired some status and significance are those in the performing arts. Music, dance and art have been an integral part of the cultural tradition of India. It was only during the Brahmanic era and the decadent phase of agrarian society, that it was relegated to the realm of *devdasis* and courtesans. Thanks to the courage and persistence of a few women, many of these cultural forms have been retained. It was only much later, when art forms like music and dance were encouraged by elite families, that they gained wider social acceptance.

On the whole, barring certain facilities at home—like having some degree of social status and belonging to a significant family in terms of caste, economic status and social authority—the majority of women in traditional agrarian society lived a life which was narrow and bounded by prescriptive roles and traditions. They were relegated to the role of being the upholders of tradition, virtue, stability, continuity and consistency both within the family and in society at large. They were responsible for sustaining the system, and its relatedness with social kith and kin, caste and community. Women maintained the norms, and were often harsh in implementing social traditions which further restricted their emancipation. For many women, the world, life and the living processes, their roles, their meaning and their significance came from that which was familiar and known, even though it was oppressive and largely restrictive. Many women from among the middle classes and the elite were socially powerful and could perhaps have broken away from tradition, but they rarely took this drastic step.

However, in all the traditions of social codes of conduct, both rigid and flexible, there was one role which remained unchanged for a long period of time. This was the woman in the role of a widow. Once the woman became a widow, her entire social status and world crumbled around her. By assigning the widow a non-status or a negative status, the social system reinforced the secondary and marginal status of women and the supremacy of men.

The industrial and technological ethos began when the roles ascribed to men and women had already crystallised into distinctive sets of activities. In terms of the availability and utilisation of system resources, caste and occupational roles were neatly identified, categorised, wrapped up and sealed. There was little space for negotiation or change. Society was governed by the 'shoulds' and 'musts' of a prescriptive era.

Impact of Industrialisation and Education

With the emergence of the industrial era, which coincided with the independence of the country, a whole new process of work ethics, technology and, consequently, a new life-style was introduced. This inevitably had its impact on the social processes of the country. Responding to a call by Gandhi and other leaders, a large number of women came out of their homes to join in the struggle for independence. Their participation in the independence movement provided many women with the opportunity to take their first step beyond the portals of their homes. Once they had taken that step, the world was no longer the same for them. Their roles had taken a quantum leap; their vision had gone beyond four walls. Above all, they had their first inkling of the power of their potential. They became aware of their heritage. It was the first step in discovering who they were, where they were and in which direction they would like to go. Like Sleeping Beauty, Indian women had awakened from years of slumber at the call of an opportunity to shape their destiny.

History has sufficient evidence of their courage, their unstinting devotion to the cause, their unrelenting efforts, their personal sacrifices, and their willingness to walk side by side with men in the quest for independence. There were millions of women who inculcated in their sons and daughters a sense of national pride and the courage to give up their lives for the nation. Many of them unflinchingly watched their sons go to prison or even to the gallows. They walked with their heads held high and with a sense of personal involvement and commitment.

This critical and significant momentum was reinforced by free India which was determined to provide education to its citizens, be they men or women. Girls in large numbers joined schools and colleges.

For the first time, they glimpsed a world which was earlier the exclusive domain of men. A whole new vista opened up before the Indian woman. She discovered she could do well in her studies; that her intelligence was hers to shape and enhance. She discovered the magic of choices, options and alternatives.

Women entered the portals of medicine, engineering, the administrative services, politics, law, teaching, and the mushrooming business organisations and manufacturing industries. Slowly but steadily, they moved into skilled and semi-skilled jobs, and a small number even succeeded in joining what were considered 'elite' professions.

As education became accessible to the vast majority, as industries and organisations required more and more infrastructural support, and as women's economic contribution began to add to the quality of the family's life-style, it became obvious that the working woman was here to stay. There was no force which could stop the gathering momentum of their outward and onward march. Yet the social and psychological barriers were many, obstacles innumerable, and the path was far from straight. There were many twists, turns and hurdles yet to be crossed. Apart from fighting against the existing social attitudes backed by 4,000 years of the agrarian ethos, what women essentially needed to do was to confront the concept of the role they were creating for themselves. They had to resolve their inner conflict caused by guilt and anxiety at being inadequate mothers and perhaps negligent housewives. They had to ask themselves how they were going to design and define their new roles in a new era.

Through education, women from the better off socio-economic strata became aware of the existing social disparities and of the condition of women in general, particularly of those belonging to socially and economically deprived groups. Some of these women joined clubs like the Lions to participate in voluntary social programmes for the socially and economically deprived. It soon became a status symbol to join these organisations, be involved in fund-raising or charitable activities, and be considered part of the emancipated or 'avant-garde' lot.

Another, smaller, set of women started experimental nurseries, kindergartens and play schools for children. A very select few, caught up in family feuds and the distribution of family assets and resources, took charge of these resources and entered the world of corporate business, the world of men. In a sense, these women were pioneers. They were strong and courageous women who chose to take their destiny into their own hands and create a new role for themselves. They went beyond their roles of daughter, wife and mother, and contributed in creating, maintaining and sustaining a new heritage for their families.

With growing urbanisation and an increase in wage-earners, the number of young women who availed themselves of educational opportunities grew. Through education, they experienced the divergent life-styles, attitudes, values and belief systems of a wider set of people, and glimpsed a world far better than their own. Many women excelled in academics and discovered that, if they chose, they could do as well as if not better than the boys. However, in the home-setting, either directly or indirectly, the emphasis on their traditional role persisted.

Parents of educated girls also recognised their high economic potential. To them, their daughter's economic self-reliance was an asset in marriage and could, hopefully, lead to a reduction in the dowry demanded. Economic independence also served as an insurance against future uncertainties, and only education could provide opportunities for this independence. However, caught between the conflicting demands of achievement as both an instrument of autonomy and of insurance, many of these women became highly ambivalent. At one level, they welcomed the opportunities for enhancement and growth but, at another level, found that these opportunities did not provide them with the desired self-worth and respect. It became extremely difficult for these women to value themselves and their existence: the insecurity of their relationships filled them with guilt, anxiety, anger and resentment, and a sense of helplessness at being considered a burden and a commodity.

Thus, young women growing up in traditional homes, who were aware of their potential economic value, were simultaneously pushed in two opposing directions. Often, they deprived themselves of new alternatives only to create another set of conditions that oppressed, denied, and deprived them. What was needed, therefore, was the creation of new processes which would bring respect, dignity and human values to individuals, systems, societies and cultures.

There were also some women who accepted the traditional roles and lived by them. They were content and experienced no conflict. They acquired meaning and significance in their prescribed roles. They provided space to others and in their open, giving, tolerant and understanding stance, created a significant and critical role for themselves. They were aware of the current realities and of socio-political and cultural issues, but had consciously refrained from getting involved and being torn apart in the process. Instead, they had chosen to become the solid foundation and pillars on which the structure of their family rested securely.

There were a few others who had chosen to create a new location and define a new meaning for themselves. They had attempted to redefine their roles, the system and the nature of relationships, and, therefore, to bring something more, both to themselves and to the system they lived in. Essentially, these capable, intelligent, persistent and hard-working women acted with courage and conviction. They carved out a path where none had existed. With each step they took, they had to create space. Each effort demanded involvement and a price. The road they travelled was unknown and lonely and each step was a discovery. These women searched for freedom.

To free their soul, these women experienced spiritual isolation, devotion and homage, but they received no replenishment. They truly became the symbol of Mother Earth, from whom millions receive nourishment but to whom very little is accorded by way of replenishment. Women give birth, nurture life, sustain and nourish it, and, as though by magic, survive without self-fulfilment.

Society thus fragmented the being and becoming of men and women in the name of social order. It left one half of its population carrying the load of over-engagement and achievement in the role of the protector and the provider, while the other half of its population was required to play the role of the giver. The social system thus demanded that each individual experience incompleteness and fragmentation, and become an Atlas or a Hercules of their respective systems. All individuals, both men and women, were caught in the struggle to find a sense of integration—an endless journey on a path of innumerable shoulds, musts and oughts of society. It is therefore imperative that from time to time societies, cultures, systems and individuals realign and redefine themselves in ways that are relevant to contemporary needs. Men and women need to respond to the call of their being to generate new meanings, create new landmarks, pave new paths and envisage new patterns of relationships.

Such were the reflections of the inner dialogue. As woman after woman walked the corridors of history, hope kept pace with them, their resilience never wavered and they identified choices which could be made. This pause to walk down the memory lane of cultural history seemed to give them new insights. However, before they could act on the new choices or feel a sense of integration with which to shape the future, these women had also to explore the processes of their own growing up. They had to voice the personal history of their family and rediscover those dimensions of the heritage which they could call theirs. The next chapter shares our participants' recollections of their personal history.

4

Echoes and Shadows

Childhood

Childhood is remembered through kaleidoscopic images of laughter and gaiety, of running free on sunny days, of sweets and chocolates, of dressing up for festivals, of playing at being grown-up, of the sheer joy of feeling the rain on one's face and body, of shivering in the cold and being huddled in a quilt, of the compulsion to listen to ghost stories and the accompanying feeling of terror, of being inspired by great men and women of the past, and of the desire to grow up soon.

A whole set of conflicting images also come surging forth—of suffering discrimination, denial and rejection; of feeling responsible as the eldest, waiting in line as the youngest; of sensing, as the middle child, that one doesn't belong, that one isn't wanted or loved; of feeling suffocated by the demands and expectations of others. One recalls elders who were to be obeyed or placated; younger ones who had to be indulged or controlled; of being one of many; and, as the only child, of being the focus of love, affection and expectations. All these images are echoes repeating who one should be, who one should become, and what the future ought to be.

In these, the first five or six years of childhood, the female child is exposed to the cultural lore which defines her core identity and the structure of her life-space. She is also exposed to the many rituals, directives and proverbs which reinforce the cultural lore. The child struggles, reacts, resists, defies, but is eventually pushed into accepting the prescribed life-space and core identity. By the time she is ready to go to school her mind has already been imprinted with the cognitive map of the core identity and the structure of life-space.

According to our data, until very recently a girl served as a sort of apprentice in her home so as to help her crystallise her future role. A whole world was shut off from her. Her fate may have been predetermined and may possibly have been tragic, but her conditioning provided convergence and consonance between her introjected identity and the world into which she was initiated. The world she wished for herself was held in abeyance but was presumed to be expressed in the dreams she had about the romantic beginnings of marriage.

Entry into School

Female children who today have the opportunity to go to school confront the forces of being and becoming. Entry into school brings to an end a world which hitherto consisted of defined boundaries, of familiar people, of known expectations, of pushing against the closed doors of being and becoming good, of climbing onto laps, of being carefree, and of being gently pushed and moulded into what is desirable and acceptable for the future.

The first day of school is experienced in several ways. It opens the door into a world of expanded boundaries, where the faces are unfamiliar, some bold, some tearful and fearful, and some coy and shy. The adults evoke fear while they comfort, their faces are at once stern, kind and preoccupied. There is a flurry of movement, a jumble of sounds, whimpers, sniffs, and brave smiles. These are now all but vague memories which evoke sadness and nostalgia, when as adults one struggles to find a place in the world outside the home and beyond the cultural lore.

Schooling offers the opportunity to discover one's intellectual capabilities, widen one's horizons, actualise potentials and build friendships, some of which endure. For some it serves as the beginning of the process of self-discovery; while for those families which had never previously exposed their female children to formal education, it represents the beginning of a new tradition.

To the post-independence generation of Indian women, school offered an opportunity of discovering new dimensions. However, for many people then, and even now, education was not regarded as being the means for achievement and enlightenment or for the unfolding of the self. Rather, it was treated as a prerequisite for a good marriage. It was not really considered to be an avenue towards a profession or a career so much as an investment that could be called upon in the event of a catastrophe and which could ensure economic well-being only if necessary. This view of education still persists in the minds of many people. For many girls, the adventure of going to school ended with the onset of puberty, when they were withdrawn from school. Only a few emancipated families let their daughters continue on to high school; a college education was rarely permitted.

Unfortunately, schools tend to reinforce the feeling of being privileged if born a male and disadvantaged if born a female. Consciously, and often unconsciously, the young girl comes to sense and believe that her role, space, aspirations and future hold a set of coordinates different from that of her counterpart, the male child. Schools, though providing encouragement and opportunity, often generate double messages. If the female child is not too bright in academic terms, there is anxiety about her future, her marriage, her life and sources of support. If she is academically intelligent and performs well, there is concern about finding her an intelligent husband, about the competitiveness and lack of space for her in what is essentially a man's world, and about the course of her life. Will she seek a career? What kind of husband will make her happy? As a way of lessening these anxieties, society legitimises the entry of women into safe professions such as teaching, medicine and nursing. Social work became acceptable only recently. Even today, women find jobs largely in service organisations or in infrastructural roles. The belief that education is the means of acquiring a suitable husband holds sway.

There is ample evidence from hundreds of women to support the fact that the female child receives conflicting messages during the schooling process which undermines her attempts to develop a world-view. Both the school and home-settings initiate a process whereby, for the first time, a fragmentation between the cognitive map of the world and the emotive map of the people in that world, takes place in the mind of the female child. This, in turn, plants the seeds of ambivalence between her roles in the family and the social setting and her roles in the secondary systems of education and work. This leads to a further struggle to resolve her guilt at the failure or inadequate fulfilment of one or the other segment of her life-space. It becomes an uphill task for her to integrate her roles in the social and work space, find freedom from guilt and to feel wholesome within herself.

The Emotive Map of the Family

The birth of a female child evokes many responses from the family—from feeling let down, disappointed and burdened, anxious about the expenses that will be incurred at her marriage, wondering what her in-laws will be like and an overall sense of indifferent acceptance, to a sense of joy and contentment and a feeling of being blessed. Among the educated, urbanised professionals who tend to limit the size of their families, a daughter after a son brings a sense of completion; a first daughter is accepted with the lingering hope that the next child will be a son. The hankering to have a male child, who will be the heir and maintain the continuity of the family, is ultimately a dominant one in Indian culture.

Experience of Being a Female

It is in this context that the female child develops an emotive map of the family. The parents' indifferent acceptance of her makes the female child realise that her status is secondary to that of the male child. She experiences no space for herself and learns to be invisible, obedient, conforming, and careful about creating no stress. She learns to accept herself as unwanted, or as a transient to be cared for, but never to belong. She also acquires doubts about her value as a person. The second aspect of the emotive map of the family is associated with deriving security from being desirable—in appearance, in conduct (both social and personal), and in being useful around the home. Each of these modes of security are then linked to her future. Being desirable in physical appearance ensures a husband. Desirability in personal and social conduct is associated with adjustment and acceptance by the in-laws, and with being successful in her roles as wife and mother. Her potentials have to be converted into qualities and attributes which can make her acceptable to the in-laws. The female child is also prevented from applying her intelligence to the living processes of society. She cultivates for herself a mask, an appearance of being confused by details, by the complexity of situations and by the world of finance. She accepts the image of herself as being helpless and lost in the wider world. All other potentials of herself, like physical appearance, only give her the status of an object. A plain girl is encouraged to become skilful and accomplished in household work in order to compensate for her lack of beauty.

The emotive map of the Indian family is saturated by the ethos of self-denial, sacrifice, of being useful and living for others. The Indian social system reinforces its negative attitude towards females in multiple ways. It emphasises such qualities as being obedient, self-sacrificing, a responsible home-maker and an asset to both her parental and husband's families. It stresses that she be tolerant, patient, nurturing and fostering: a calm, quiet, resilient force which is not visible but always present. If she does not display these qualities, the woman ends up being called a shrew, a witch, a *dayan*, a *chuddail*, and other such derogatory names. Thus, the female child experiences herself as being a liability and a burden. She has no clear-cut anchors for her psychological location either within herself or in the system. Carving out a space and a meaning for herself without threatening her well-defined prescriptive roles is not a risk she can easily take.

The Good Daughter

The experience of feeling rejected and the compulsive need to create acceptance for herself, compels the female child to conform to the norms and expectations laid down by the family: 'You are a guest and must be at your best. Some deviations may be tolerated here but no deviations will be permitted in your other home.' The parents rarely allow a girl to feel that she belongs to them. The dominant refrain is:

'You are always in somebody else's space. There is no space which you can call your own. The only way to gain acceptance is through conformity, sacrifice, and obedience.'

The female child also gradually understands the differential framework which applies to the male child. There are differences in the degree of control and freedom allowed and in the openness or secretiveness of areas of discussion. This realisation reinforces the lack of a sense of self in the female child. It also makes women internalise the role of being either martyrs or victims, to be sacrificed at the altar of the will of parents, husband and his family and/or finally of their children. A very large number of women find it difficult to accept ownership of their own lives.

The importance given to physical appearance also adds to the turmoil within the female child. Having to wear glasses, having pimples, early puberty, early or delayed physical growth—all raise doubts about finding a suitable marriage partner. The female child sees herself as only being an object for the use of others. Most of her transactions are mere exchanges and she hankers to offer her being to somebody.

In the thirties and the forties, educated parents whose work took them from place to place sent their male children to boarding schools or entrusted them to the grandparents for the sake of education, stability and maturity. The female child, however, moved with them often changing schools every two years. She thus repeatedly experienced the trauma of being uprooted. Some women eventually realised that academic brilliance and a profession was the only alternate source of security other than conformity. Many women who experienced this became dedicated teachers, social workers and doctors and remained unmarried.

Growing up within a family which emphasised equality but which, at critical moments, made a differential choice between a son and a daughter, shattered the female child's image of her parents, their values and integrity, and often engendered agonising battles with her parents. Surprisingly, these battles were often centred around inessential and petty things like mixing with peers, especially boys. Contact with males was normally permissible only in the name of education, for instance, with a tutor, at home or in school. The literature of the period between the thirties and the sixties reflects the propensity of the female child to regard these males as heroes and fall in love with them only to end up being exploited. This tendency is found among female children even today although less frequently. A female child who is obsessed with the idea of her own personhood tends to worship the nurturing male. Many young women often felt let down and cheated by their parents who seemed to encourage academic performance and the ensuing promise of a career, but who, at the onset of puberty, turned conservative in matters of dress, social conduct, and the eventual choice of a career.

Some parents, which included both working and non-working mothers, tried to create an atmosphere at home which fostered a sense of belonging and well-being in their children. Although the children were aware of the economic realities, the emphasis in these families was on values to live by. These parents taught their children that academic excellence was necessary for a life of self-respect. Their effort was to cultivate a sense of joint responsibility and an enriched life. Hard work, persistence and effort became an integral aspect of living. Sharing responsibilities and activities in the home became an unquestioned and accepted reality. The parents provided understanding and resources, but the final choices and decisions were left to each child. This enhanced in the child the sense of responsibility for herself and the family. Such families served as firm anchors for their children. Females growing up in these families imbibed a strong sense of self-respect and learnt to value themselves. They experienced their worth in terms of what they were, and not as something arising from their economic or social status. They performed well in schools and colleges and carved out for themselves a set of goals. Instead of joining large social get-togethers with their peers, they were content with a small set of friends. They became the vanguards of the progress of women and models for the forthcoming generation. However, the number of these women was small.

The Cognitive Map of the Family

While the emotive map of the family has remained more or less continuous as a sub-stratum and is often reinforced by society, the cognitive map of the Indian family changed after the country attained independence. In large, urban centres and in the families of professionals, a new and different approach to life evolved. Instead of being a privilege, education became the right of women. The earlier views of education as a means for acquiring a good husband, and as a means of security and self-reliance in times of crises, were replaced by the conviction that education was necessary for development, autonomy and socio-psychological independence. Consequently, parents operating with this cognitive map, encourage the female child to perform well academically. The emphasis on house-work has decreased and participation in the living processes of the family has become a matter of routine. Like her male counterpart, the female child is also pushed to work hard, to show good results and to apply herself towards academic success. As much money is invested in her education as in that of the male child. These parents are proud of their daughter's academic record, treat their male and female children as equals and approve of their daughter's participation in debates, sports and other extra-curricular activities.

For many women, performing well at school is not a difficult task. It awakens their hankering for finding a meaning and sense of personhood for themselves. Given the opportunity, they pursue education with a certain degree of absorption, and hope to escape the roles and the structures of life-space prescribed by society. This opportunity also gives them a new sense of significance.

The development of a new cognitive map has not fully masked the simultaneous continuity of the emotive map. It is therefore more poignant when many educated mothers try to realise their own frustrated ambitions by insisting that their daughters choose specific careers or seek professionally qualified partners. This process has often turned these women against the female identity and sometimes made them adopt the syntax of women's liberation with vehemence. The contradictions between the emotive and cognitive maps generates emotional conflicts, arguments and an increasing gulf between parents and female children. Many young women decide that the only way they can escape a fate similar to their mothers is by doing well academically and by achieving professional and economic independence.

Although the cognitive map of the sort described above also emerged in district and smaller towns, it created quite a strong cleavage in the goals and life-style of the female child. She became a victim of double standards on many fronts of her life. Many of the women who shared their experiences with us were like Tantalus. They were caught between a heritage which denied them their selves and the new ethos which held out promises but at the same time left them open to the accusation of having destroyed their heritage. They struggled with compromises and developed a set of platitudes that would help them hold on to their role and its meaning. At one level, they admired those women who could polarise and take to careers; at another level, they were their worst critics. They experienced pride and shame, virtue and martyrdom, and contentment and emptiness simultaneously. They possessed, indulged and confused their children.

In the ultimate analysis, there is not much difference between these two modalities. The female child is left in both settings with a growing feeling of not having been able to really choose a psychological location for herself.

Adolescence

For the female child adolescence is a period in which the multiple dualities of her being and becoming emerge simultaneously. It is a period when every answer can be countered by another question; every affirmation be clouded by doubt; every certainty be eroded by unpredictability; every direction lead to a dead end; every response be met with censure; every bit of encouragement be qualified by an underlying condition; and every action be a judgement. Each step is a discovery and a confrontation, with joy on the one hand and repulsion on the other.

In early adolescence, the emergent maturity of the body locates the girl in an experimental space which is very confusing. Within her is the experience of unfolding, with its accompanying sense of thrill, shame and embarrassment. Outside her, she finds that she is suddenly visible to both males and females, especially to males. Some of the experiences narrated by young women (summarised below) reflect this confusion:

Men who previously never looked at me now smile and put their arms around me. They pat my cheeks and make me sit close to them. They are suddenly eager but my flesh cringes. Many males stare at me. I stand erect in glory but also feel as though an insect is crawling over my body. I feel as though I am being stripped naked and want to run. There are a lot of compliments and welcoming smiles but there is also something sneaky behind them. I learn not to trust myself with any male. Even the most trusted men in kinship display this pattern. It becomes a question of how to fend for myself.

Many women also recalled that mothers or elder sisters were of some or very little help in their dilemma. They neither shared their experiences nor advised them about how to tackle the situation. They only made vague references to the ways of the world. All that came through was the fact that each woman had to cope with it as best as she could. It is during these experiences that the female child becomes aware of herself as the object of lust, and at the same time senses within herself the sexual cravings of her own body.

While she undergoes this psychological experience, society starts feeding her with different messages: 'You are the holder of virtue. The burden of chastity is yours. If anything happens to you, you are the temptress.' From her family, messages about her forthcoming marriage became loud and frequent. In a period of dreaming and searching, reality is thrust upon her more blatantly than it is on a male child.

The Indian female child grows into adulthood and wisdom more quickly than the male child. Her experience of attaining physical maturity and the messages received from the social world around tend to converge in the girl's mind and create in her the hope of achieving an ideal relationship in marriage.

Entry into College

The second stream of experiences narrated by our participants relates to their entry into college and their choice of a career. The female child is aware that hopes of continuing the family and being its economic resource rest with the son. She knows that she is looked upon as a responsibility. She has already witnessed her mother's life in which creativity was suppressed, potentials denied and her economic dependency emphasised. In the social scheme of things, she is destined to become a school teacher or secure a post in the infrastructural services, as perhaps a lab assistant or a pathologist. If we look back at enrolment trends in college education around the time of independence, women in India preferred to take up courses in the arts, languages, literature, history, philosophy, home science, social work and, later, psychology, sociology and anthropology. Even in the fifties, only a handful took up science and medicine. The sixties showed a large number of women pursuing courses in design, architecture and commerce. Entry into science, engineering and management courses is a relatively recent phenomenon. The social phenomenon of education still confronts women with their secondary and dependent status. Even after they complete their education and embark on a career, women continue to be regarded as being incapable of taking decisions or of exercising authority and as being unstable in jobs.

Many women who have lived through this process have ended up feeling alone and desperate. They fought, argued and pleaded to gain the freedom to pursue a course of study and a career of their choice. But very few have succeeded in doing so and, as a result, have lived with the wrath, disagreement and disapproval of the family. However, those women who succeeded in gaining acceptance for their choices found that the family's emphasis shifted to her academic performance. Her achievements became a source of joy particularly to the mother who took an active interest in her daughter's education and monitored the time spent on studying. The daughter was also treated as a source of pride and status among her family members and neighbours. The father, too, joined the mother in encouraging the daughter—a good academic performance would bring satisfaction and a sense of achievement; there was time enough to play and engage in other activities. She was even excused from household chores and responsibilities.

All said and done, education for women continues to be seen as an investment in a future which excludes their personal aspirations. Education is meant primarily to help a woman to marry well, be socially useful to her husband, be adept at bringing up her children, equip her to render social service, and is considered to be an insurance policy against a broken marriage. It is true that women in urban India have acquired some degree of autonomy in their choice of a marriage partner, in determining the area of education they wish to pursue, in their choice of occupation before marriage and in their insistence to remain employed after marriage. But most women have had to fight their own battles to obtain the freedom to make such choices. No social ethos yet exists to support it.

Tradition and Modernity

Contemporary Indian women experience their life-space as a battleground between the prescriptive roles based on idealised models of a bygone era and the emerging cognitive map of modern society which pulls them towards wider horizons. Caught between the traditional past and a future inspired by their own dreams and aspirations, Indian women walk a tight-rope. They carry the burden of both traditional and modern role expectations, yet are denied the privileges of both. Unable to resolve the duality of their existence, many women tend to become indecisive and confused, angry and reactive, entrenched or polarised. Their husbands may want a traditional wife at home and a modern companion in public; their children may seek nurturance but resent discipline; they may need to go out to work for economic reasons, yet still have to shoulder all the domestic responsibilities without support from husband or children; or they may be forced to assume the responsibility of being the daughter-in-law, but be denied the accompanying privileges. Whichever way she chooses to face these situations, feelings of guilt, anxiety and stress pervade her being. The experience of many women remind us of Hercules who laboured endlessly in the hope of getting his heritage back. But his efforts were futile. He never recovered his heritage and went mad. That most women manage to keep their sanity is a credit to them.

Childhood, schooling, puberty, adolescence, and higher education are the landmarks of a female child's life-space. Her life-space during this period is largely occupied by significant family members. How were these significant figures experienced? What is the heritage she derived from them?

The Experienced Mother

Some mothers, who are educated, intelligent, and sensitive to the changing environment and their daughter's qualities, emphasise the necessity of regular hours of work. They personally supervise the daughter's homework and, while ensuring that the daughter has some freedom, do not allow her to wander from the beaten track. This mother monitors the daughter's relationships with the opposite sex. She is experienced by the daughter as being a rigorous, strong but supportive woman. Another set of educated women are absorbed in and preoccupied with their own struggle. They are left with neither the time nor the energy for any involvement with their child. As a result, the daughter grows up with no sense of belonging.

Another set of mothers, who grew up in socially significant and economically secure homes but without emotional security, define their role through marriage. They are happy to leave behind the daughter's role and the domination and control of the parental family.

They are willing to offer their best to their husband and children. Such mothers are determined to ensure that their daughters perform brilliantly and create all the space in the home for their daughters to imbibe the values of self-reliance, both economic and social.

A similar pattern is in evidence among less educated mothers. There are mothers who do the right things because they are involved with their children and others who do so out of a sense of duty. The maternal side of the family makes a significant impact on the lives of most Indian women. Some women identify with the maternal family, while others merely disown the location of their identity in the paternal side of the family. On the maternal side, female children experience some nurturance, some indulgence, some pampering and a freedom to express and experience themselves as children. That side of the family is experienced as closely knit and providing emotional support. The growing child perceives her mother as having a different status within the maternal family, where she is accorded respect, love and affection. In contrast, in the paternal family the mother is seen as an alien and an object of either criticism or praise in the performance of her role. These contrasting experiences of the mother's status in the two settings leaves the child wondering about her own identity as a woman.

Women who are the only children experience their mothers as loving and encouraging on the one hand and controlling and seeking their fulfilment through them on the other. Their mothers seem to be saying: 'Be like us but become different from us.' This means they have to find their location and identity in self-reliance and autonomy. These daughters mature rapidly and learn to depend upon themselves at an early age.

Heritage of Women's Identity

To begin with, then, the life-space of a female child is directly filled by the mother and her circumstances. As she grows up, she introjects the core identities from the cultural lore. As she enters school, she is exposed to the identities of women in Indian history. She is, however, also a witness to living models. Among these models, the ones that stand out clearly are those of women who accept the traditional role of being the shadows of their menfolk yet retain their substantiveness, who are echoes of the prescriptive social system yet retain their voice in times of crisis. They are a source of silent but dependable strength to their families, weathering the storms of family feuds and struggles. They protect their sons and daughters, sometimes their husbands and even whole families from annihilating transactions. In fact, although these women accept the denial of their selves and their social imprisonment with grace, they sow the seeds of new aspirations in their female children.

These women are experienced by the family as being strong and capable of engaging in multiple roles simultaneously. They become the resources of the family. They manage their homes, sometimes with the minimum of resources and with many constraints. They swallow their bitterness and rise above the discriminations and denials imposed upon them by the social system. These women transform their roles into anchors of stability, continuity, security, and consistency. In effect, they become the context wherein others derive the autonomy to be themselves.

In experiencing the living role models of such women, the female child is either aware of or ignores the processes of deprivation and denial of aspirations, meaning and well-being that these women go through. The female child experiences not only personal pathos but the pathos of being a woman. She witnesses ravagement but receives no replenishment. Yet, amidst this, the female child also experiences infinite patience and persistence. She discovers the capacity to regenerate herself from within. She derives strength from her commitment to live, to give birth to life and from her capacity to nurture and foster. She discovers in herself the capacity to cultivate the quality of mother earth in order to be a woman. Surprisingly, in India, this is the only stable role model that women have for their living transactions. It is also, to a large degree, a positive model for survival. It provides immense capacity to come alive and fructify.

For women currently struggling to transcend the inevitable structures of their life-space and create a new space for themselves, this role model of traditional Indian women evokes admiration and awe, but it does not mobilise them to act for themselves because it also evokes pathos and a sense of inadequacy. The entire dialogue centres around the question, if not this (the model of traditional women) then what? The struggle to transcend the traditional role is too painful and risky. The universe of the past is familiar. It is easier and safer to navigate in calm and chartered waters.

The Experienced Father

Female children perceive their fathers in many and varied images. There are some fathers who appear to be comforting and full of fun to their young children, teasing and pampering them. They even favour the daughter in situations where the mother appears to be harsh. These very fathers who appear to be liberal, encouraging and supportive during the childhood years, later become traditional, conservative, restrictive and determiners of educational and career choices. Thus, between the years of ten and fifteen this liberal father becomes a symbol of the restrictive society. During this period, it is the mother who becomes the daughter's new ally.

There are other fathers who appear to be silent and aloof. They evoke fear, sometimes anxiety, and are apparently harsh in their outward behaviour. They are hard workers and also appear to be taskmasters. When such fathers are at home, the mother tends to push the children into corners, into talking in whispers and generally into keeping quiet. These fathers rarely make direct demands. Occasionally, they display their fondness, affection, and love, and affirm the success and achievements of their children. However, although they remain a mystery, their children look upon them with hope and affection.

In both these images, the father is idealised, somewhat romanticised, and looked upon as an object of hope. Because of this cathexis with the father, the role that women introject in relation to men is characterised by dependency, a need for their approval and security of location in a contained environment. Some of their temperamental behaviour in marriage arises out of this cathexis.

Other images of the father lead to a negative cathexis. Here, the father is experienced as ruthless, discriminating, depriving and hostile, and as the direct source of the demand to postpone the realisation of the self and its expression. Physical battering is frequently associated with these fathers. He becomes the symbol of the shame of being women instead of men and reinforces their introjected role as helpless victims. The experience with such fathers reaffirms the message that women are *paraya dhan* and therefore secondary and outsiders.

Some fathers are experienced as being inadequate and helpless, and appear to have a status lower than that of other members of the family. Daughters witness the discrimination, deprivation, and other processes of denial and rejection which their fathers are subjected to by other members of the family and even by neighbours. As a result, they are often perceived as failures, and sometimes as men who have been denied their due. Many of them become the objects of pity. The daughters helplessly watch them fail in their attempt to maintain dignity and self-respect. These fathers trigger off feelings of empathy and sometimes a deep sense of identification. The cathexis from this experience often invokes in the core of female identity a need to offer her own resources to men without making demands on them. Some of the women who experience this cathexis display a tendency to mother or reform the male.

Infrequently, but persistently, we come across women who experience their fathers as the eternal lustful youth: sensuous, zestful, flirtatious, and generally witty. The experience of such fathers, who tend to have a great need for physical contact, is never openly stated, only shared in private. In their own way, these fathers are responsible for their daughters' initiation into the world of adolescence and adulthood. They also provide some intellectual and developmental inputs, but only incidentally. Most women with this type of father seem to internalise the shame of being women and treat their body as an asset for transactions. Alternatively, they continue to foster in themselves the identity of the 'innocent girl,' whose every encounter with the male invokes the image of the seducer. The image of this type of father is often fused with the woman's experiences of her uncles—her father's younger brother or his friends. Underlying this image of the father is the physical battering they receive from him. For some women, this physical battering is the most poignant recall of their childhood and adolescence. Their cathexis with the father is largely negative.

As with the mother, the female child's experiences with her father also reinforces elements of the cultural lore. Men remain the inevitable counter-identity and the quality of relatedness between the mother and father and the male and the female continues to revolve around the inevitabilities of the structures of the life-space.

Father's Heritage

While the mother's heritage is linked with her status and location in the two families—her parental and that of her in-laws—the father's heritage is grounded in his location in the parental family and his place of origin. With regard to origin there are two clear trends. The first one is of the grandfather or the father who, as a migrant from the rural area, created a space in urban places ranging from semi-urban settings to metropolitan cities. They became entrepreneurs in trade and business, civil servants or worked in mercantile houses and became 'sahibs'. Others became doctors, lawyers or professors. Their heritage is hard work, a commitment to succeed, the ethos of being self-made and a strange culture in which traditionalism and modernism operate simultaneously but in isolation—traditional at home and modern outside. At home they retain the life-style and rituals of traditional modes of behaviour. The women are compelled to dress in traditional attire. Outside the home, however, they can ignore these practices.

The second trend is related to grandfathers and fathers who have lived in urban settings for generations but have persisted in following traditional modes of living, values and attitudes. Members of these families enter the civil services and/or become professionals. Thus, from the urban centres, there are two distinct locale-based heritages. One is constituted by the business class, the other by wage-earners and professionals. The heritage of the business class remains very conservative in ethos but also promotes the value of acquiring possessions. In the heritage of wage-earners and professionals, it is acceptable for a woman to pursue a career, if not on a regular basis, at least in times of crisis.

The heritage emanating from the status of the father in his own family has many dimensions but the three most significant are: the nature of the transactions between the father and the mother; the nature of the transactions between the father and his mother; and the quality of relatedness of the father with the rest of the family members.

Other Transactions

Father and Mother

The father's transaction with the mother is the source of both the pathos and the context in which the daughter learns to regard men in her encounters. Sometimes, when the father is idealised and the daughter develops a positive cathexis towards him, he becomes the symbol of the kind of man she seeks in later life. The positive cathexis forms the basis of her dreams and hopes. After her marriage, attempts to realise the pattern of this positive cathexis persist. However, the negative cathexis also surfaces during her marriage and becomes a source of confrontation and a matter for resolution.

It is not very surprising that there is a great deal of symbolic transference from this universe into her marriage. The father's transactions with the mother are often compared by the daughter with his transactions with herself. This comparison creates the dynamics of the struggle between the centrality and marginality of a woman's identity. It creates the harrowing dilemma of choosing between being and becoming, of being an object or a person. There is a strong feeling in the female child that she has very little choice but to be an object.

Father and Grandmother

The status of the father in the family is often caught up in the father's ability to resolve his son's role. His efforts to preserve his own status while remaining silent at the treatment meted out to his wife by the mother and his family at large, seem to be the most significant aspects for the daughter. It also reinforces the inevitability that her life-space will not have any psychological location except in herself. Very few fathers seem to provide a model which can counteract the residual feelings resulting from this aspect of their status in the family.

Father and Kinship

The father's status outside the family, if it is positive, becomes very precious. In moments of psychological dislocation, it is this heritage which the daughter holds on to in her life. This reinforces the proxy role of being 'the daughter of the house' and many women try to reproduce it in their own lives. The values they enunciate for them-selves emerge from this heritage. But in case the father's outside status is negative, it leaves the woman lonelier in terms of resources. The feeling that she is her only resource gets reinforced. Some of them commit themselves to create their own heritage.

In the Indian setting, the transactions of the mother with the grandmother become significant introjects for the woman. These trans-actions constitute a cultural lore where the mother-in-law or the grandmother acts as a persecutor of the bride. In combination with the experience of various kinds of mothers as described earlier, the experience of the grandmother adds ambivalence to the status of being a woman in society. The inability of the father to resolve his son's role adds to the intensity of the pathos of being a woman.

The emotive map of life-role and life-space as internalised by the female child from her experiences with the mother, father, and both their heritages, has many common points with the emotive map introjected by women from the cultural lore. The most common theme is of psychological location. It is always transient. It appears stable and firm but always collapses when needed. A woman's life appears to be like a rudderless boat, drifting, occasionally in serene waters but frequently in turbulent ones. Escape from this drift is possible only by grounding the boat in the swamps of traditional ethos and pathos. Attempts by women to take charge and navigate, or to establish anchors, to stop the drift, requires a very strong commitment to deploy their resources on their own and to make adjustments with socially defined situations. Attempts to take charge and navigate beyond the traditional waters invokes a wide range of feelings—of anxiety, terror, shame, guilt, joy, hope, and dreams. Managing this struggle requires not only conviction but tolerance to withstand many accusations.

Many of the women who shared their experiences of their life-space, appear to have emotionally blackmailed themselves to stop the struggle. Some of them reminded us of the folktale where if one looks back while embarking on a journey one turns into a stone or a pillar of salt. These women had become entrenched in a perspective of the world and in a pattern of transactions with men with which they had begun initially. Their success in having crossed many a threshold did not give them enough courage to go beyond the initial pathos which mobilised them for action.

The second common theme was that of the 'fate' of women. The universe of this theme is often accompanied with the feeling of 'damned if you do and damned if you don't'. So why struggle and why not surrender to the inevitabilities of the structure, the life-role, and the life-space? To suffer while acting out the given role is desirable. This permits women to hold on to the helpless (that is, both dependent and innocent) aspects of their being. It allows them to be immobile while reinforcing their feelings of being victims.

Emergence of Role-Identity

We now review the three primary locations of women's role-identity, i.e.; the adjuster, the asserter, and the drifter, as also some of the variations of these roles.

The Adjuster

Some women, having introjected the cultural lore and having internalised their experiences with their father, their mother, and their heritage, develop a context for their role. They accept the role of recipient and performer. They accept the construct of duty and role-appropriate feelings and behaviour. They commit themselves to render their best to the family, children and husband with a smiling face. They respond to a houseful of people, to the sudden arrival of guests, or the unannounced descent of in-laws and other emergencies without losing their poise. They tend to create a feeling of sufficiency and plenty in the midst of a low or inadequate flow of resources. They build up reserves in their personal resources as well as in those of the family. Their home is well-run, neat, orderly and clean. It is quite homely if not decorative.

Eventually, these women are seen as being reliable and dependable. To a large extent, their status as an outsider gets dissolved. By middle age they start acquiring social status and power. They can then influence the choices facing the family and are held in regard. The same people who would have fought them earlier and created situations, now avoid open confrontation. They never completely give up but become more amicable. Such women begin to be heard in their system. They also become visible. Essentially, these women become echoes and shadows of ideals promoted by the cultural lore. Once they are in 'power' they reinstitutionalise the cultural lore through their transactions with their husband, son, daughter-in-law and grandchildren.

This is their adaptation and they are justly proud of having successfully managed their social and phenomenological transactions. In many ways they become upholders of the system. Some of them even become creators of heritage by dropping some of the traditional compulsions. For example, they may support the daughter-in-law's modernity. As long as the daughter-in-law is duly respectful she may not have to cover her head. Daughters may be encouraged to go in for education and be freed from participation in rituals. This heritage is largely of the type which fosters some autonomy and transactional ease in day-to-day living. In this role, these women make themselves available to everybody. But their personal feelings are never stated. They are gracious and earn their dignity. They do not voice any regrets. What is happening within them is rarely known. Most of them take to religion in their later years in a more concerted way.

The Asserter

Some women, though exposed to the cultural lore, seem to react to their experiences of their mother, their father, and their heritage by internalising assertiveness. They do not like the restrictive life-role and the inevitable nature of their life-space. They try to establish for themselves the role of a navigator and to take charge of their lives. They actively attempt to carve out a space for themselves where they can find expression of their being.

The response of the environment to such efforts pushes them into a fighting mode. They are seen as assertive, aggressive, sometimes impulsive, stubborn and get labelled as fighters or as being unmanageable. This often settles them in the role of a rebel. These women are pushed by the response of the environment into such intensities of feelings that they crystallise either the ethos of being restorers of women or make it a personal issue to be themselves.

Their assets are their academic excellence, ability to mobilise themselves, and of being good at doing things. They see no justification in being denied a psychological or social location as partners in life. They are not satisfied with being echoes and shadows. They seek out relationships in situations where their own limitations, weaknesses, and vulnerabilities can be attributed to society and male domination. The syntax of their behaviour is: only opportunity can be had or created. They would like to show what women can do, achieve and contribute to life.

Within themselves, however, they are aware of their limitations, weaknesses, and vulnerabilities. These they postulate in a search for a relationship where a mutuality of resources and vulnerabilities can both be accepted. This search gets partly romanticised in the concept of an ideal relationship where there is no censure, criticism, accusation or punishment. A whole generation of potentially assertive women got caught up in the myth of experiencing 'communication'. Their inability to find a relationship where they can communicate finally turn them into rebels and proponents of women's lib in India. Others, who have some core of traditionalism still intact in their identity, turn to the ethos of reformation and they attempt to start programmes for the development of women.

In our experience with most women, their search for and effort to create a space leads to interactions with people who are hostile, sarcastic, and reactive. In turn, the women affect a style that portrays them as callous and as rebels against social norms. Every issue becomes a major one where they can prove themselves as right and as seeking justice. Very often a fight rages around non-essentials. They present a stance of defiance and intransigence. They learn to appoint themselves as spokespersons for all women.

The pathos these women are trying to circumvent or get rid of is still that of being accorded a secondary status, of a lack of psychological location, of being treated as objects and of being restricted to the recipient role. The pathos of the 'crippled,' the denied, the deprived, provides them with the energy to hold on to this stance in a dedicated manner. It is interesting to note that most of these women exhibit a tendency to take on the role of patron with a large number of women, specially those with the 'drifter' identity. Their own relationships, however, are directed toward people who are intellectually and other-wise their equals if not superior. Even while adopting this role, they continue their own struggle for inclusion and for finding a viable psychological location. Many of them are not even aware that they are behaving like patrons.

For some of these women, the fight revolves around a struggle against centrality versus marginality. Though they tend to couch their arguments in terms of seeking equality they are seen as seeking to displace men. They also enunciate the credo, 'women for women and no man can empathise with women'. They become representatives of disillusionment, disenchantment, and scepticism, of having trusted men in the system and of having been repeatedly let down.

On the whole, women who awake to the pathos of women and who sense some hope and a way out in the context of the new ethos of the West, tend to adopt this stance. It is unfortunate that a meaningful awakening and an assertive stance leads to the creation of a fighting arena with battle lines drawn. Very few of these women succeed in retreating and thus creating a personalised world of a wholesome nature. A handful of those whom we met during our explorations were sagacious women who had discarded both the diffused traditional ethos and the reactive stance and had been able to synthesise the pathos, the goals of a new ethos and the affirmation of the old ethos to create a pattern of fulfilment for themselves and the outline of a new path for others.

The Drifter

Beginning in the thirties, as the culture of transience gathered momentum, a socio-cultural setting was created in India where the introjects from the cultural lore and the internalisations from the experience of living moved increasingly away from each other. This led to a great dissonance. Sometimes even the experiences of familial life were in disarray—they were suffused with double-binds. Besides the introjected cultural lore, the female child was exposed to the constructed lore of a child's life through the writings of popular psychologists and authors from the West like Enid Blyton. Thus, both the introjects and the internalisations created a fog in which counter-points, contradictions, and analogues and identicalities evolved and dissolved from time to time. This process (and its product, the fog) made the problem of psychological and social location all the more difficult and acute. Those with the drifter identity felt deeply disowned and alone. They were restless, desperate to clutch on to something, to experience stability and direction.

The post-independence era intensified the culture of transience. This was a period of hope and turmoil, of an awakening of aspirations, of perceived opportunities, of plans of transformation, and of a feeling of having arrived in the promised land. It also triggered off a greater mix in the introjects and internalisations. The female child had to decide what kinds of social location to search for and cherish. The models of social location began to get polarised into either/or, the traditional and the modern. Models of psychological location were, as usual, lacking. This converted the choosing of social location into an illusory exercise. For most women it was difficult to let go of either. Consequently, they adopted variations of the drifter identity.

Our experience with most women with the drifter identity revealed that each of them had developed a set of tenets to operate from in multiple life situations. They had no cogent perspective of life as a whole. They were concerned with consequences and the kind of things they wanted. They were more logical in their syntax as compared to those who exhibited the other two identities. For example, compatibility and commonality of interests with the marriage partner was one of the tenets. They would have great debates about it. They refused many offers of marriage. Yet, to our surprise, many of them had eventually married men with whom they had little in common. They often ended up with a 'tall, dark, handsome, stranger who held out the promise of success' and ended up living out the theme of the 'trickster' of the folktale mentioned earlier.

One aspect of the universe of women with the drifter identity was anchored in the female child desperately seeking to be affirmed, to belong. The deeper influence of the cultural lore has maintained that this affirmation can be provided by somebody else—God, the father, a guru, the husband and, in modern times, a cause. Caught in the fog of the culture of transience, the models of affirmation became unstable and diffused. The women struggled as a result. From their narration we found four sub-sets of the drifter identity which converged around this theme of need for being appreciated or affirmed.

The Unappreciated

The 'unappreciated' are women of great commitment who are always ready to give their resources to the system. They render support in all family interactions. They can be relied upon to do all the right things. Surprisingly, however, they also attract criticism, sarcastic remarks, occasional disdain and even condemnation. Their families and the people around them will use their services but will not necessarily include them in their affective relatedness. In time, these women feel unappreciated, occasionally exploited, but persist with their approach. In discussions we found them using the syntax of comparison, evaluation, and logical justification of their feelings of disenchantment. There was a sub-stratum of mild disdain and contempt and a search for significance and exclusivity. These women can always be relied upon in a crisis. In fact, they are often treated like errand girls and are used to manage uncomfortable and time-consuming interfaces. But, in general, they are accused or criticised for having airs.

In our experience these women are unsure of their self-worth but very sure of their competence. As a result, they became great do-ers and tend to be efficient. These women also have great potential. They continually invest in their own self-development and in that of their children, and eventually become perfectionists. Most people consider them to be critical, self-righteous, and finally unmanageable, yet indispensable. In the context of the traditional cultural lore, this is the syndrome of *badi bahu*, *jethani* or a 'drudge'.

THE MISUNDERSTOOD

A variation of the drifter identity, anchored in the same dynamics as the 'unappreciated,' is a comparatively passive person who does not seek visibility. She employs her resources in silence and in the service of a chosen few of the system, which invariably includes all those younger than her. Her intentions are always right but she is not considered to be a perfectionist. She does not initiate things on her own but waits for a command or to be given an assignment. She is always around but never in the centre of things.

The drifter identity, caught in the need of being affirmed, develops the pathos of being misunderstood. Such women are reflective and perceptive but, unlike the unappreciated, cannot mobilise themselves into action. In final desperation they are reactive, become negative and claim that they do not need to be appreciated by anyone and that they will make it on their own. However, whenever they attempt to do so, they often find themselves out of their depth. They have a sense of self-worth but they have no trust in their own competence and abilities.

They act as counsellors for many. While they are capable of playing the empathetic proxy role, they cannot act for themselves even in desperation. They make good alter egos, the *sahelis* of the bargains in Indian classical drama and folklore. As they go through this process of holding out promise but achieving far less, they generate the feeling of 'oh well' or exasperation in people who empathise with them.

The pathos of being misunderstood is constantly reinforced in their lives. They also experience desertion. In the cultural lore they are the 'becharis' who are seen as whiners and as being the source of their own miseries. After a time, people learn to leave them to their lot.

THE UNAPPRECIATED MISUNDERSTOOD

The two other variations of the drifter identity are the converse of the above two. The 'unappreciated' becomes both the misunderstood and the unaffirmed.

Like the unappreciated, women in this pattern are action oriented. They too wish to render service in action, but somewhere a conditional

clause of equitable reciprocity makes its presence felt in their transactions. When things do not go according to their expectations they
feel misunderstood or cheated. 'I am misunderstood' is their response
when the other person states that he or she expected more from them
as a reciprocal part of their transactions. They get angry and resentful.
They also experience a feeling of being 'cheated' when the other
person does not fulfil the expectations aroused in the course of the
transaction.

This variation of the drifter identity likes to keep all her doors open
and has problems in making commitments to any relationship. In her
syntax she appears doubtful, sceptical, paranoid, but definitely preoccupied with apprehensions as to whether the other party will come
through or not. Such women spend hours airing and discussing these
apprehensions but arrive at no conclusion. Their ultimate response is,
'all right, let us see'. Their basic syntax is to establish clarity so that
there is no misunderstanding later on. However, misunderstandings
are inevitable in their lives. Eventually, they are seen as manipulative,
selfish, and as castrating. Being really talented in certain respects, they
are also seen as arrogant and as possible threats. There is a certain
degree of righteousness in their pronouncements concerning other
people and the world in general. They eventually develop such clearly
defined maps of people's behaviour towards them that they are always
ready with their responses. As a result, other people see them as
carrying a chip on their shoulder. In the cultural lore, they are the
pampered *nanad* (daughter of the house) or the archetypal females.

The Unaffirmed

A parallel identity, characterised by passivity and an overt sense of
innocence, the unaffirmed is another manifestation of the drifter
identity. Such women tend to come from 'lower' economic, social and
cultural strata but have had the opportunity of going to good schools
thanks to their parents' efforts. Some are the youngest daughters or,
perhaps due to a stigma concerning height or colour or because of
some other phenomenon, did not experience a sense of belonging. In
the case of these women, the search for being affirmed takes the form
of a search for belonging at any cost.

Their fear of commitment comes in the way of any search for
relatedness. As such, the acuteness of the need to belong makes them
seek temporary warmth and approving relationships. They get into

these relationships with a sense of innocence and often find themselves exploited. As against the misunderstood—who become defensive, doubtful and sceptical—these women adopt a hopeful and trusting stance. This creates situations where they face many kinds of exploitation, including sexual.

Some of them appear erratic and quite unpredictable. During our discussions, some of these women admitted to having experimented with drugs and other phenomena associated in their minds with freedom. They carried deep scars from their childhood and displayed a strong resentment against their parents (especially the father) whom they considered to be dogmatic and pushy. Their behaviour in adolescence and after seemed to be one of wasting their potential. Their need to punish themselves and, by proxy, their parents is very strong. Their sense of worth both in terms of the self and their competence is shaky. Their strategy is always to attach themselves to somebody in order to go through life. In the cultural lore they are the innocent or the dumb.

There are a few other versions of the drifter identity. Some are merely mixtures of the four patterns delineated above. Others appear to be different but no clear-cut underlying theme—like the search for being affirmed—seems to emerge. The one distinct pattern attached to a drifter through school and college is that she is generally admired and is considered to be accomplished and an achiever. Her modalities are close to the cultural lore of the 'accomplished'. We conceive of this type as a drifter as many such women fail to consolidate the early gains or mark out a direction for themselves. They are good at whatever they do, they always make their presence felt, but they also avoid making self-oriented commitments.

The adapter, the asserter and the drifter are the three nuclear core identities. They seem, in part, to have continuity with tradition and, in part, are products of the current social and cultural scenario. What is the nature of this scenario?

Socio-Cultural Scenario

Increase in Nuclear Families

With the growth of the wage-earning society, the number of families which, in physical terms, can be described as nuclear has increased.

The nuclear family provides a setting where the configuration of role models is strikingly different from that of a large joint family. Born and brought up in a nuclear and small family, the female child's competitive traits, struggle for attention, and need to establish a centrality in the emotional space of the family get reduced. However, confrontation between the male and female identities becomes either more severe or is masked. On the whole, living in a nuclear family leads to the development of an attitude of being special and of some awareness of being different from the women of cultural lore. The family provides a setting where a sense of inclusion, well-being and positive support from concerned people is experienced. There is a sense of personal involvement. The child sees herself as a member of the family, in spite of references to her transient state. Essentially, this consolidates the daughter identity.

The nuclear family also exposes most children to the turmoils and travails of their parents' marriage. Parental conflicts range from tense and irrational transactions, through suppressed hostility, to open confrontations. The issues include money, children, friends, parental families, grandparents. Very often, parents either shut the children out (leaving them in a state of anxiety) or try to win them over to their respective sides. This creates a sense of guilt. Thus, in the midst of security, a daughter faces insecurity and doubts about the quality of relatedness. The social location, which is secure, gets contaminated with the insecurity of psychological location.

When such a child goes to school and later college, she moves from a personalised world of stable social locations to being one of the masses. The female child who is talented takes the path of achievement and competition. Given her articulateness and intellectual abilities, school becomes a stage where she can shine. The need to stand out and outshine others makes her overlook her similarities with other people. She often learns to develop strong likes and dislikes. This moulds her into a woman who is the life of the party but lacks meaningful relationships. These women frequently experience stress in building closeness and intimacy. They are either put on a pedestal or left alone. They often become prone to encounter the trickster.

The nuclear family also directly exposes female children to the life-space of the father and the mother. They see their parents struggle and sacrifice, compromise and persist, and yet retain the sanctity of their life. They experience the helplessness and determination of their parents. All this has an influence in fashioning their identity. The female child from such a family tends to be committed to autonomy and adopts a stance wherein she will not be subdued, controlled or made economically helpless and dependent. She learns to concentrate on the search for psychological location and not the social location. Despite various vicissitudes, some nuclear homes retain the quality of emotional security. Such homes are full of space to talk, discuss, explore and share. Women who grow up in these homes acquire an ability to deal with reality. They can handle the negatives of the larger situation while still charting a path for themselves. Some of them grow into adjusters while others, though called rebellious in the initial stages, create their own heritage.

System of Secondary Socialisation

The nature of secondary socialisation has also changed from the traditional pattern. Earlier, the secondary socialisation of the female child took place in the home, neighbourhood and community. She was initiated into rituals, forms of social behaviour, household activities and other desirable accomplishments which would ensure a good location in the husband's house. The new socio-cultural scenario created schools and colleges for secondary socialisation. Initially, women's colleges were cloistered settings. They were well-protected and guarded. The teachers and the principal acted as surrogate mothers. There was heterogeneity among students in terms of culture, origin and religion, etc., but there was homogeneity in the school or college culture. This became a setting and a period to discover the inner world, to sense the unfolding of the woman—the laughter and chattering of friends in the midst of participation in dramas, debates and sports; the awakening of aspirations and dreams; the discovering of the forbidden through books or, by proxy, from some adventurous classmates. Yet, throughout this, the female child retained her doubts and apprehensions about her future.

Encounters with the male were largely transient. They happened in the public settings of debates, dramas, picnics, and college trips, or on train journeys when male and female children travelled back home in groups. Deeper personal contacts were rare. Most of these 'relationships' led to periods of mooning around. Most women could not break the modality of bestowal; they still felt that freedom was to be bestowed and not taken. The women of this period ended up living the life-role and life-space of the cultural lore but did better for their children.

Over the last thirty years the nature of secondary socialisation has changed further. For a large number of women, co-education has become the preferred mode. What did it bring to the female child?

Legitimacy of Profession and Career

More women can now aspire, plan and struggle to establish a professional status or career to end economic isolation. Previously, the main occupations open to women were as teachers, doctors and social workers. Now, a whole panorama of careers has opened up for them. They can enter the fields of business, drama, dance, engineering, space science, etc. Job opportunities, except in business, are more easily available to women in India than almost anywhere else in the world.

Along with career prospects, the new secondary socialisation also exposes women more directly to the Western ethos and social forms. This creates the rationale for freedom, autonomy, equality, and companionship. While, on the one hand, it opens women's eyes, it also shatters the roots of cultural continuity which Indian women had always carried within them. It is not that women have to carry this burden but that their role in the past provided for an evolutionary process. Their exposure to the Western ethos, modes of living and social conduct perhaps come in the way of their developing integrated identities. However, the most critical contribution of the secondary socialisation provided by the school and college setting is to expose both the female and male identities to a direct encounter with the inhabited world of heterosexual intimacy and closeness.

These heterosexual encounters lead to mixed responses—some disillusionments, some disenchantments and some tragedies. The experience of falling in love is like any storybook romance. The person *per se* is not important, but the discovery and experience of an awakening generates a mixture of fear and excitement. Many women have described this feeling as a 'mid-summer night's dream,' where the young woman awakened to her womanhood and fell in love with a man with a donkey's head. The first flush of this awakening transforms the world into a magical one—where one walks a few feet above the ground, where the air, the sun, the colours and the flowers all acquire a unique and intense fragrance and luminosity. Feelings of both pleasure and pain acquire an intensity, and every moment is experienced like life and death.

These are also critical moments where a path to the future and life-roles get crystallised and acquire a shape and a form. Here, the centuries-old and universal themes of Sleeping Beauty, Cinderella, the mermaid, the folktales, folklore, legends, myths, epics and psycho-dramas get enacted and re-enacted.

Young women from all over the country, with their unique configuration of experiences of the family and the social system, respond differently to this awakening. Some accept the role of a Sleeping Beauty who lived in her parents', family's and society's reality and now wakes up in the world to the reality of her prince charming. She makes no demands and creates no reality of her own. As a result, her hopes of living happily ever after are dashed. She finds herself once again in the realm of echoes and shadows, where she has to live by duty, and by rendering her best to her husband and children. It is like a life of captivity interrupted by a brief moment of freedom.

Some women become Cinderellas where a life full of rejection, deprivation, and discrimination seems to end in a moment of acceptance. They are ready to give everything for that one acceptance. They overload the relationship with expectations only to be disillusioned and let down and so end up repeating and recreating the past in the present. Insecure, anxious, and apprehensive, they keep repeating history. They keep on waiting for a human touch from outside. Their being is like a bottomless well where the deprivations and denials are so intense and deep that a lifetime of gifts from others is not enough. They live in a world of fantasy and dreams and hence often get exploited and used in the encounter with males. But, thanks to their strength and resilience, they survive to search again and again for that one unattainable relationship.

Women who adopt either of these two modalities in their encounter with the male, essentially become victims of the structures of the life-space prescribed by the cultural lore. Their introjects are deep enough to inhibit them from using this opportunity to discover their ability to heal their own deprivations as also to realise the strength they carry within them to create, first, their own reality and, then, one together with a male.

There are some women who, in the moment of falling in love, take upon themselves the entire responsibility of sustaining and fostering the love. They commit themselves to a life of sacrifice and become possessed. The male counterpart in such relationships discharges all the negative residues of his mother's identity on them. They constantly seek solace and comfort. They prick and deflate and then turn gracious. They are hostile, throw temper tantrums, and walk off but always expect to be begged and pleaded with to return. And some of them do return, like bad pennies. It becomes difficult for the woman to let go and break the neurotic pattern. In such a process, the woman lets herself become the beast of burden. She is willing to sacrifice her own needs and desires, lives for others, carries the emotional burden, and, with devotion and faith, finds a space in other people's lives. The pathos of her lack of space, however, remains. These women end up believing that they have no ability to create their own space nor can they ask others to give them space. They are forever bouncing on the see-saw of too little or too much. These women find it difficult to create a world of people or relationships for themselves and they forever experience emotional poverty. Their efforts to become involves trying to fill a void or a felt lacuna from the past. In this attempt they mortgage themselves to other's needs. They have a great deal to give of themselves but cannot discover the will to give it to themselves.

In summary, women who experience this socio-cultural scenario have a strong need to retain their individuality and find it difficult to create a complementary role. The need to possess, claim and own their accomplishments and achievements is obvious but it is difficult for them to make it their anchor for security and location. Although presenting an external image of being outgoing and confident, their inner insecurities create anxiety, uncertainty and doubts about the self. These rarely get resolved. The need for validation, affirmation and assurance from outside is never overcome. Loneliness is frightening and a large amount of their energy is spent in creating relationships. While they consider social relationships to be shallow and meaningless, yet these women have a fear of creating meaningful and close relationships. The apprehension of losing oneself, of merging one's identity, of remaining marginal, of losing centrality, of being possessed and controlled and being turned into insignificance, continue to keep them on the see-saw of life. With their chosen role and identity having lost content and meaning, the psychological location remains elusive.

Reflections

At the threshold of a new world, a world of work and marriage, the young female blossoming into a woman wonders whether the battles of achievement, the drive for excellence, the striving for economic independence, and the struggle to create a space and personal meaning—whether all these have any meaning at all. Why does economic insecurity make her anxious, why does the thought of emotional dependence create apprehensions, why does affirmation/belonging evoke rebellion, why does conformity evoke a reaction? And, at the end, she is left wondering whether her struggle to achieve a space has made her lose an acceptance of herself.

Work has become an anchor without which a woman's life would drift like ,a boat whose navigator has abandoned the helm. A life without work evokes fears of being rootless, forever being a shadow and an echo, and of following in the footsteps of all those that have walked the beaten path. The conflict between the demands of a traditional role imposed by the family and society and a modern role based upon self-aspirations is intense. The traditional role, as experienced by the female child, involves obedience, conformity, and following the path charted out first by her parents and then by her husband's family. To the woman this implies disowning of initiative, self-motivation, aspirations, dreams and goals. Having continued to persist in what she believes in, argued for what she aspires and dreams for, and having acted on her convictions, being faced with a life based on a traditional role reduces her to helpless fury, tears and guilt. Their dreams and aspirations persuade some women to step into the avenues and opportunities of the blocked option in order to discover some meaning in their lives.

Caught between the emotive and cognitive map comprised of experiences of the family, school, college and society, the woman survives with many scars. Her future: the social role of being an obedient Indian wife who puts family before personal meanings. That part of her being and becoming which propelled her to create both a meaning in life for herself and to create a home, leaves her stranded on an eternal see-saw. Thus, being on the threshold of entering the adult world evokes terrors—that the ghosts of the past and the beckoning of the future will create pulls and pushes forcing her to make a commitment. If she chooses self-goals, it will evoke and lead to accusations of neglecting the family. And if she chooses others and family, it will not only mean repeating the history of sacrifice and futility but will also involve the guilt of wasted potential and creativity. A painful choice thus awaits the woman at this threshold—a threshold where the door to a nostalgic world has to be closed as she steps into the unknown; a world to discover and a world to create; a reality to experience and to add to; a reality to aspire for and dream in; a reality to mould and shape; a reality to live in with its numbing pain and exhilarating joy; a reality which carries centuries of pathos and the seeds to create a new ethos; and at all times to experience the pulsating life that is to unfold just beyond the threshold.

Many women have woven romantic dreams about love and marriage, about a prince charming or a knight in shining armour. Most women standing at the threshold of the adult world, however, hold the experience of growing up, which has tempered the dreams and fantasy with social and cultural realities. Many women—educated and intelligent, capable and confident, eager and aspiring—have eventually come to terms with the fact that while love may spring from looking deep into each other's eyes, it requires a deeper attempt at understanding and a commitment to each other if it is to survive. Consequently, many women at the threshold of a professional role and a career have accepted the social reality of an arranged marriage in the hope that it will work out. These women hope that the man they marry will be mature enough to accept a sharing of inner realities without social norms and evaluations; that they will be able to laugh together at the follies of adolescence and be able to integrate in effort and meaning. That, together, they will create a space where they can combine.

Mature women have come to terms with themselves and accept that they are not competing with men but need to create an equation. They anticipate a sharing of responsibilities at home, at work and in living a life of togetherness. There is a need to arrive at a meaningful convergence of their various roles—that of being a traditional *bahu*, of being a social asset to the husband, and of carving a career for herself.

Having a profession means a sense of autonomy, self-respect, being mentally alert, and experiencing a sense of worth and meaning in life. A life without this meaning is one of a slow and gradual decay, deterioration and wastage of one's 'being'. Work today has a deep meaning in the woman's life. It is the only way to break through the cultural lore, the limited choices in identities, and the inevitabilities of the structure of the life-space.

5

Fantasy and Social Reality

On the threshold of marriage, juggling with both anxieties and the anticipations encoded in the cultural lore, the woman envelops herself with the cloudy and misty theme of 'living happily ever after'. To her, this juncture is bewitching and enchanting. It contains messages of hope, of future dreams, and of new aspirations. New relationships and a strange family await her. The parental home had primarily been one of adults, where she had been a child, a daughter, and a transient. Her network of relationships were given, her role well-defined and her expectations limited. Within these boundaries, her passage through adolescence had been full of kaleidoscopic emotions with joys and thrills, pains and pleasures. Her encounter with the self and the male identity at home as also her educational aspirations made her struggle to fashion an identity for herself. This period is not always clear and cogent. It is often marked by many doubts and the woman lives through contradictory cognit' and emotive experiences.

The threshold to marriage has been romanticised. Some women arrive at it with thumping hearts, with plans for the future, and with the feeling that they have a heritage to create and to continue. To others, it is a dream—of romance, of love and of a bewitching relationship where rainbows abound, eyes speak and silence communes; in short, a world surrounded by magic and fragrance. And yet for others, it is an awakening, a beginning of an unfolding to discover a touch, to dream of togetherness, a moment to merge and unite and to weave a world where there is no pain and sadness, no hurt and no anguish but where there is love and affection.

To some, it is at this moment that the search for the right one, the ideal one, for the self and for a new life really begins. The new family is at the periphery, not in the centre. To still others it is an entry into a world of new faces, new people, and new relations. There is an anxiety to create a space—the magic space where they can experience and give free rein to their potentials of being a person. And to all women, it is a moment to bid farewell to the role of being a daughter and a child, to wave good-bye to the past both pleasant and painful, passive and turbulent, a past of a childhood denied or of being treated as a child for too long.

The act of marriage transports the woman into a world of many new social relationships. She becomes *bhabhi, kaki, chachi, mami, bahu, jethani, devrani*—and all at once. These relationships have varying degrees of freedom which allow her to relate to a whole new set of expectations. This network of relationships is either supportive or a source of stress. The ease with which she adjusts or fails to depends upon the quality and nature of the interaction between her and this new network of relationships. She has no experience of them though she may have witnessed models which may not always have been satisfactory. She had probably observed the poignant struggles of her own *bhabhi, chachi* and *mami* to adjust to their new family and had wondered whether these models would work in the new context.

A sense of uprooting and concern with rerooting is the core dilemma of women in a male dominant society. Most women confront questions concerning what to carry with them from the past and whether what they select will be assets or liabilities. It is a drastic uprooting where the doors of return are shut fairly tightly behind. Henceforth, she can return to her parental home with a sense of respect and dignity only as a visitor or a guest. This is perhaps the most significant inevitability of the structure of the life-space of women. Men may go away for long periods for educational reasons or on business and may experience enforced or perhaps self-chosen exile, but the psychological uprooting that women go through at marriage is not part of men's experience. This trauma is faced by women alone, each woman facing it in her own way.

In the past, customs, rituals, and the individual traditions of each family provided some infrastructures and processes which enabled women to face this trauma. For example, traditional societies, with their structure of social living by women in groups, created a space which helped women to share and hence contain this pathos. Such social structures acted as channels of catharsis, togetherness and replenishment. Various rituals and festivals were also rooted in and associated with this tradition and ensured the fulfilment of this role. Another example centred around the belief that women's beings were anchored in spiritual salvation and this was one area where women were left to themselves. These two processes periodically gave women some space to express and share the cumulative pathos of being women. They drew strength and sustenance from each other and hence were able to protect their beings from facing destruction.

The emergence of a secular ethos has eroded most of these supportive social structures. Even where they still operate they have lost their meaning nor have they been redesigned to suit the present. Urbanisation and modernisation have engendered the phenomenon of living in isolation. Modern society has not yet generated new processes whereby women can have the space to contain their pathos. At the same time, uprooting and rerooting continue to be an integral part of the institution of marriage and women are left to sustain themselves and survive as best they can in the harsh environment of the new context.

At the threshold of this uprooting, confrontation with both a stranger and a strange world await the woman. She is inextricably bound and bonded to them. The stranger is the male—an identity which until now was only a source of uneasy anxiety for her. This identity excites yet frightens her; it is held in suspicion yet is desirous. The woman also has to confront a stranger in herself. For years, her feelings have been held in check awaiting a person, a new setting and a new direction to enable her to create a space for herself. She has nurtured expectations of romance, of being accepted for herself, and of experiencing a sense of mutual meaning. The parental home, a transient location, is a mix of security but uncertainty, legitimacy, and permanent space. Her sense of belonging is similarly fragmented between the primary family and the family to be. Her fate lies beyond the threshold of uprooting.

Standing at this threshold, the young woman visualises herself in many roles which are largely juxtapositions of the traditional and the modern: the home-maker; the wage-earner, who will be protected, cherished and loved by her partner; the strong one who will join hands to form a team. She sees herself as a loving and devoted wife, a doting mother, a competent woman, efficient, capable, outgoing, and with a career. These are among the many images with which she struggles and which hold her in their sway. Apprehensive yet excited, she awaits to behold and experience the man, who will be the context in which her future will unfold.

In reality, however, for many women the quality of life after marriage turns out to be a replica of the old world in many ways. It, too, is the location for a role, not for her person. Only here, the convergence of demands and expectations is different. Very often this life becomes a process of discovering what she can do and what she cannot. She discovers that here, too, she is her own resource. In this new space she has to prove and win for herself trust, credibility, acceptance and finally even her role status. The journey towards earning social membership, social status and social belonging starts at this point.

The Assimilator

These women come from families who cherish their heritage and values but are free from its orthodoxies and rigidities. They allow themselves the flexibility to adopt enlightened ways and newer forms. They retain the beliefs, attitudes, and respect for the traditions and rituals of their context as anchors of their identity, but adapt modern modes to enrich the quality of their lives. Women from such homes do not feel overwhelmed, and can gracefully move into any role with assurance and confidence.

Such women have the sense of security in themselves which enables them to evolve a role. They feel equally at ease with the traditional roles of being a wife, daughter-in-law and mother, and with being modern (i.e., the ability to relate in social settings with ease and grace). They are outgoing and manage the external environment with confidence and poise. They win trust and an acceptance of their role easily. Without nagging or being too eager, these women encourage their husbands to achieve beyond what they had themselves planned. They create a space where the husband can share his aspirations, achievements and options. Their ability to assure the husband that they are willing to stand by him and bear any consequences of the risks involved in actualising his options provide him with the strength to forge ahead and be confident of returning to a secure and stable home.

Many of them start working or develop a career after they see their children through the dependency of childhood and early schooling. They are the backbone and anchor of the family and allow its members to experiment and grow. These women create homes which are comforting and where people sense harmony and affection. Differences and disagreements rarely become major conflicts. Rationality and affection tempered by commitment and concern make such differences a part of reality and do not evoke panic, threat or anxiety. It is in this setting that marriage as a social and cultural institution has the best chance to survive.

The mother-in-law issue, like in virtually all families in the Indian cultural context, is a source of stress. However, the cultural introjects of the assimilator and the deployment of these introjects in their role behaviour keep the stress within tolerable boundaries. These women are able to persist and modify without defying. Similarly, these women are firm and flexible enough to retain their autonomy in many essential and critical matters concerning their home, husband and children. They encourage traits of self-sufficiency, self-reliance, and discipline. They face crises without whining and whimpering, anger or futility. They have the resilience to continue to build and create a family with a sense of togetherness, loyalty, affection, concern and direction. In many ways, these women anologously belong to the cultural lore of *The Apple and the Stigma*.

The Twice Uprooted

These tend to be young, intelligent and competent women who come from families with Westernised life-styles and beliefs. These families have consciously abandoned the religio-philosophic traditions of their heritage. They are the 'enlightened' ones who espouse a strong rational scienticism as a perspective for life and its problems. There is an undercurrent of a certain degree of contempt for superstitious knowledge and the traditional life-style. These families converse in English and rarely use their mother tongue. Western festivals like Christmas and New Year are celebrated with greater enthusiasm than some of the Indian ones. Their reference group is British or American and they have a penchant for foreign goods. To them, the West represents quality, opportunity and progress.

Hence, in these families the first uprooting is from the cultural moorings. In adopting an alien life-style they only internalise its superficials; the basic assumptions and the ethos and pathos of that alien land are not introjected. At marriage, women from such families confront another uprooting. However, it seems that they either ignore this uprooting or continue to be rooted in the life-style which prevailed in their parental home. In such families, both boys and girls are pushed towards academic excellence and achievement. Participation in sports and extra-curricular activities are encouraged. Adoption of modern social mores and sophisticated personal appearance are emphasised. The children are sent to anglophile schools. Family life centres around social entertainment, clubs and parties. The friends of the family include significant social, cultural and political figures. Visibility and social appearance are the hallmarks of their lives.

Many girls coming from these families are prepared for a life of companionship in marriage but not the life of a housewife and daughter-in-law. They are well-groomed but lack roots. They have learnt to live efficiently but not effectively. They do not know how to deploy their resources to build infrastructures of living. Their work goals are aimed at social visibility and they covet glamorous jobs. To them, marriage is a continual series of parties, outings, shopping sprees and chats with friends.

Most of these women rarely stay very long with the in-laws. They create a separate base in the same town. Acquisition of a decorative, modern home, a place to entertain and to set out from, is very important to them. And if the marital home lacks the wherewithal to sustain such a life-style, it results in stress and conflicts. A modern life is central to their concept of marriage. Economic well-being tied to social status and a decent life-style are essential for having children. Life is a planned sequence according to a list of acquisitions. If the sequence does not unfold as envisaged, life becomes one long string of dissatisfactions. These women feel even more unsettled if they do not work. Their urge to socialise and compete with women in the elite social set is very great. They gradually get involved in a pattern of life which revolves around being a hostess for their husband's business interactions. Eventually, their marriages are held together by reflected social status, lavish homes, a retinue of servants, and a large budget provided by the husband. They live in horror at the thought of social ridicule and of being shunned. They are constantly anxious about losing economic resources and social standing. Part of the universe of these women is analogous to the cultural lore of *The Accomplished and the Trickster*.

The Working Woman

The women who exhibit this personality type come from homes where the father is a self-made man and has risen above his ascribed socio-economic status. Such families maintain links with their traditions without embarrassment. The father's success probably stems from his academic achievements and/or work skills. The family is loosely linked with all the traditional kinships and the extended family. They get together for ritual events and on occasions such as marriage and death.

These families emphasise education aimed at a job or a career. The importance of work for economic autonomy and security is central to their cognitive map of future life. The home and the skill of home-building and maintaining family links are equally emphasised and cherished as inherent values of being a woman. These women prepare themselves for roles as teachers, researchers, bank employees and similar other middle range service professions. The belief is that such professions provide a setting where women can manage both home and work with ease. If married early, these women continue their education and soon take up jobs, while those who are already working do not give up their jobs after marriage.

Such women often set themselves the Herculean task of being socially traditional daughters-in-law but end up being ambivalent about this role and thus adding to the stress in their lives. While the in-laws like the income and the consequent increased buying power that the daughters-in-law provide, they also resent their autonomy and freedom. They make familial life difficult for such women and also capitalise on the daughter-in-law's guilt at being away from children and home. Caught between social and familial relationships and the expectations centred around their roles on the one hand and the reinforcement and encouragement of their role in economic partnership on the other, the marriages of such women often involve a swing from the husband's participation in domestic chores to periods of strife, tension, and suspicion concerning the wife's relationship with her male colleagues. These women maintain simple and functional homes where a visitor feels comfortable. There is no pretence at social glamour or acquisitive competition. The neighbourhood is a living reality where there is both camaraderie and squabbles. The home is filled with friends, children, neighbours and relatives. They appreciate what they have and treat their trusted friends, relations and neighbours as a source of security. They are never alone socially. Their sense of belonging is strong.

Life, however, is not a bed of roses for them. It is a continual struggle of something gained, something lost; some deep satisfactions and some regrets; a squabble and some love; arguments and togetherness. Such women arrive at middle age with a sense of pride, of having pushed back the walls of captivity a little farther and of having created a space for themselves. Some turn critical and temperamental for, in retrospect, their struggle appears to them to have been a hard and perhaps lonely one, but they have a sense of substantiveness about them nevertheless. As persons they are experienced by others as harsh and demanding on the one hand and supportive and tender on the other. At one level, success leaves them alone psychologically. In middle age, task orientedness and a commitment to persist in it tends to be viewed as strength. Occasionally, some of them are seen as inflexible, uncompromising and overbearing about how and when things should be done. The children of such women feel that their mother's love is masked by the need to control their children's lives.

The universe of these women reflects diverse strands from the cultural lores of *The Apple and the Stigma* and *The Accomplished and the Trickster*.

The New Middle Class

These women often come from families which started as small entrepreneurs but became successful and joined the ranks of the well-to-do. As such, these families experience a substantive rise in their socioeconomic status. However, their cultural and social status lags behind. Many of these families adopt a pattern of conspicuous consumption with a conscious display of their economic power. They enjoy possessing foreign goods though not necessarily those of quality.

The fathers in such families display an attachment to their daughters but are harsh to sons. They educate their daughters but do not expect them to excel. Instead, the daughters are encouraged to become accomplished in the arts or in a craft. In adolescence, these women tend to get addicted to the Mills and Boon type of romantic literature. They are contemptuous of men of lesser economic status but somewhat apprehensive of intelligent and educated men who hold degrees in subjects like mathematics, physics and chemistry.

The mothers in such families are normally dominant women who, from being silent sufferers accustomed to economic scarcity, acquire the magic wand of purchasing power almost overnight. They control their daughters critically and plan lavish marriage celebrations. They search for sons-in-law from families of some standing and with urban backgrounds but within socio-cultural and caste boundaries. These mothers also insist that their daughters acquire domestic accomplishments.

Young women from such families are trapped in the role of being a daughter. Even when they enter adulthood they continue to live in the world of adolescence, romance and marriage. To them, the in-laws are ogres and they decide that they can never get along with them even before they meet them. They often dream of absorbing the husband into their parents' home. If they marry an educated, professional man, they resent his limited economic resources and gradually become contemptuous of the husband. They visit their parental family frequently to bring back material resources for themselves.

Many of these women feel uncomfortable in the marital home. They compare the husband and his family with their own and find them wanting in many respects. Their syntax is one of constant comparison. They rarely, if ever, develop a basis of psychological relationship with the husband. In the first few years of marriage, they treat the marital home as a transient place and their emotional loyalty and sense of belonging continue to lie with their primary family. They start putting down roots in the husband's home only through their children. Having failed to integrate their husbands in the parental family, they foster in their children a feeling of belonging to the maternal family. The *mamas* and *mamis* often become their models.

By middle age most of these women begin to feel empty and meaningless. Many of them put on excessive weight by this time. They also start to limit their life-space and narrow their social boundaries to a select few within the neighbourhood. Their main stance is one of criticism and disapproval. They, too, fail to manage the process of uprooting. Fatalism and the traditional dictates of society became their platitudes. Some of them turn to religion. The universe of these women is analogous to the cultural lore of *The Lost and the Unfulfilled*.

The Self-Reliant

These women come from families where the father is absent either psychologically or physically. It is the mother who holds such families together through work and self-reliance. These mothers neither impose rigid controls nor allow too much autonomy. The children are expected to be mature and responsible. These mothers naturally encourage the ethos of self-sufficiency, of standing on one's own feet and making choices with self-respect. The children, daughters particularly, of such families grow up with a certain clarity of direction.

The daughters of such families tend to marry men who are also largely self-made, and are intelligent, hard-working and committed to create something for themselves. The wills and values of both partners are strong and clear. Such marriages often become a setting for intellectual stimulation and a sense of commitment and purposive living. Yet, given the sharpness of the male and female identities involved and the fraught nature of the attempt to create a life-space together, such marriages also contain a threat to harmony. Some couples end up parting while those marriages which endure are treated in the neighbourhood as models to be emulated. Their own children grow up with a sense of confidence and poise. The universe of these women is analogous to the cultural lore of *The Realist and the Exiled*.

Such were the realities of the roles enunciated by the women that we talked to. These women grew up in an era where the macro culture was in transition from a traditional agrarian society to an emerging modern one. Confronted with their experiences and aspirations, being rooted and uprooted, having a glimpse of an alive and inviting world and given the cumulative feelings of being a woman in Indian society, these women responded with an overwhelming desire not to quietly follow in the footsteps of past models.

However, as we review our dialogues with these women, we find a striking commonality in the experience of standing at the threshold of marriage. Regardless of which families they came from and regardless of the cultural lore and their personal introjects, most women arrived at this threshold with mixed feelings. To a certain extent, the women were incomplete, unfinished and open in their identities—open to new introjects, and new internalisations. Very few arrived at this threshold closed and with entrenched role identities.

Psychological State at the Threshold

The threshold to marriage is beset by dreams and hopes, anxieties and threats. Women hope for husbands who are mature and educated and on whom they can rely; who will be tender, affectionate, loving; who will be responsive to their desires and will spring pleasant surprises; and who will also demand from them an involvement in their lives. Awareness of the need for self-sacrifice and of holding themselves in abeyance to create a stress-free space for both to grow together, compete with the need to fulfill the residual feelings of deprivation, discrimination and of being transient in the parental home. All these pulls and pushes evoke contradictory and mixed feelings in women.

Most women are basically searching in their marriage for a space where they can be a person and be treated as such. Most women want affection without control and love without guidance. They want a specific space which will be their very own but they do not wish to intrude in another's space. These wishes are tinged with doubts arising from their exposure to various models of marriage during their formative years. As children they had witnessed conflicts, arguments, fights, stress, tension and violence; some had also witnessed love and affection and experienced security. Their own expectations and hopes are sometimes defined in reaction to what they have witnessed but they are also aware of possible realities. So, at this threshold, women tend to have already overloaded the institution of marriage with contradictions—with superhuman expectations of a life full of love, tenderness and concern over-arched by the theme of 'living happily ever after' on the one hand, and the pain, poignancy and tragedy tucked away in some corner of their minds on the other.

Women who are confronted with the pressures of day-to-day living and the socio-economic realities of their situation, with the need to generate economic resources, and having to manage the complexities of both the home and the workplace, find themselves torn. All this is compounded by the expectations surrounding the role of a daughter-in-law. Having crossed the threshold, some women experience patterns of dominance—they are confronted with a demand for total surrender, conformity, obedience and devotion. Their role is to give unstintingly and to receive what is given without complaining. In a way, these women find a continuity from the parental home in the form of expectations concerning what to do, how to do it and when to do it. The only discontinuity is that what was a state of transience now becomes a state of captivity.

Confronted with these realities, women try and generate new responses. Our discussions with various women suggest that they have the feeling that they are constantly under the microscopic scrutiny of their husband and his parents. Most women feel damned. Whatever they do is critically appraised. The only guidance they get is in the form of sermons or preachings, the main message of which is that they are insensitive to something or the other in the in-law's family. Eventually, feeling cornered and harrassed, many women regress to utilising the same coping processes and patterns that they had developed when they were daughters.

Other women, however, respond with maturity and gradually help the husband become sensitive to the existence of their person and their dreams. These women quietly help their husbands to gradually grow out of the traditional role of the son and acquire an adult, mature role. Yet other women wait patiently, but with commitment and support, while the husband fulfils his family obligations and achieves economic autonomy. Many young men have sisters to marry or younger siblings to educate. Some of them have loans to pay back or have to provide for their retired parents. Whether the marriage is by choice or is arranged by parents, these are the realities of their existence which many women confront when they cross the threshold.

In cases of marriage by choice, many women have to confront the possibility that the marriage may not take place, as their mothers, and/or would be mothers-in-law, nearly always have different aspirations for their children. Any partner selected solely by the son or daughter is, almost by definition, not the ideal match visualised by the mothers. In this situation, many young men and women patiently wait till they obtain their parents' acceptance. A large number of them just drift apart. Those who finally win through and receive their parents blessings, still have to work towards affirmation and approval from their respective parents during the first few years of the marriage. Some women turn angry and bitter in this process, and this sets the stage for an unhappy and a fractious start to the marriage. These women do not modify or reappraise the situation but, instead, constantly demand proof of love, affection and security and often drive their husbands up the wall. Others sacrifice their earnings, assets and jewellery to the unending economic demands of the in-laws who turn into parasites feeding on the struggling young couple trying to set up a home and start a family.

Marriage: The Cultural Setting

Marriage may mean many different things to different individuals but to society it is a social institution providing legitimate entry into the adult life of sexual and psychological togetherness. It is marked by a shift to a new location, a legitimised uprooting from one context to another. The woman leaves her home, changes her name, accepts a new context, attempts to call it her own, accepts the past and present of the new family, and then tries to weave a future which includes her.

The Indian ethos conceptualises the institution of marriage in many ways. At the psychological and philosophical levels, the woman is told that the marriage is her space where she is *ardhangini*. This concept evokes the image of physical togetherness and completion and also implies co-ownership of resources. She is also told to be *sahadharmini*. In its essence, *dharma* stands for a value-anchored mode of living and conduct. *Sahadharmini* as such implies the status of co-chooser of values and co-designer of conduct in life. She is also told that she is *priya, rambha* and *shakti*. This implies that sensuousness and fullness of sexuality is her right as is the responsibility of being the sustaining force of man's struggle in life. These concepts, rooted in the institution of marriage, provide her not only with freedom of space, but also with the dignity of being a person.

Not too long ago, the marriage ceremony in India used to last for a week. A host of other rituals were centred around the main ceremony. These rituals were meant to evoke in the young couple the realisation that they were ending their social role of son and daughter and now had to evolve the new role of being adult members of society in their own right. However, during the declining years of the agrarian social set-up, the concept of joint family demanded that the young couple remain within the social system of the husband's family. They were not allowed to set up a home of their own as was done in tribes and in many other cultures. This institution (i.e., joint family) created much of the earlier confusion surrounding the unfolding of married life. Perhaps it would have been easier on the young couple if they were permitted a separate location and were allowed to explore their own processes of integrating with the social system. Traditionally, like all other aspects of life, the institution of marriage in India had been designed as a setting where individuals could make choices to define and redefine meanings. It was meant to reflect the Indian community at large, which is a fusion and flux of socio-psychological, socio-temporal, socio-economic and psycho-cultural communities. The spirit behind it had been to create a setting where multiple universes could converge to let each person struggle to achieve his/her own unique integration.

With the changing complexities of Indian society, this organic quality was lost and the individual got caught up in the conflicting demands and choices generated by the changed social setting. In the sphere of marriage, the termination of the psychological roles of daughter and son was marked by different processes in the face of retaining the social role. The social role, in fact, became a continuity and could no longer be refashioned. Today, young men and women find that the only solution for them is to create their own nuclear families. This choice, however, leaves them with a whole set of residual feelings of guilt; while those who cannot exercise this option find that the family setting becomes a source of continuous struggle, in which the seeds of mistrust, stress and doubt are sown. The unfolding of married life creates loneliness, restlessness and a gradual erosion of the stable processes of rooting.

Struggle to Create Role-Space

The first few years of marriage are filled with turmoil, anxiety and contradictory expectations. The bride is chosen by the husband and his family on the basis of her being educated, intelligent and capable of being an asset to the husband and his family. Yet, when she displays or employs these very qualities, she often faces criticism and accusations from them. In fact, what is really required of the wife is conformity, submissiveness and acquiescence. Thus, entering a new home and faced with the need to perform multiple roles simultaneously, leads to the creation of anxieties and apprehensions in the new bride. The roles are given to her as part of marrying the man. Social membership is also given but its unfolding is dependent upon several factors. The most critical and significant role transactions are between the bride and her mother-in-law and between the bride and her husband. The demands from the husband and his mother are often inconsistent and contradictory.

For example, some husbands espouse a modern model and demand from their wives open expressions of affection, social skills to relate to his friends, and participation in social life. The mother-in-law, on the other hand, wants a coy bride who is invisible but always at her beck and call. She needs essentially a traditional, ideal *bahu* who would be obedient to her. Caught between the two, a woman lives in a state of anxiety and often in fear. She is torn between two conflicting sets of values and her own expectations. The introjects from her childhood and her education, both emotive and cognitive, are also challenged by the experience of being married. Faced with all these, often contradictory, pressures, the woman attempts to redefine what she as an individual would like her role and space to be. But she has very few options. When she comes, with her own expectations, and joins her husband who is, in turn, moving away from his role of being a son, she incurs the wrath of her mother-in-law. Conversely, when she attempts to please and accommodate the mother-in-law, she faces her husband's resentment of being let down. Torn between the two, the woman ends up in a 'no-role' situation and has to keep her own expectations in abeyance.

Role-taking Processes

Upon entering this new home, those women who had grown up in traditional homes learn to dress in Westernised ways, cook Western food and participate in activities which were taboo in their parental homes. They learn to cook meat, go to clubs, dance with male friends of the husband, and go to the races. But the husband, who on the one hand demands all these changes, is also uncertain at each step. Thus, married life turns into one which is full of doubts and suspicions and is a source of many conflicts and arguments. The woman lives with guilt and conflicting demands and suffers the torments brought about by changing values. She finds it difficult to be both completely modern and traditional at the same time and, in the pendulum swing between the two, she gradually loses touch with her person as well as with the concept of her own role. At some point in time, she begins to hope for a child as a way of earning respite from the demands of the multiple roles.

Other women experience a different pattern of role demands. If there is no day-to-day interaction with the in-laws, it is the husband who takes on the role of teacher and critic. Given the traditional social design, the husband wants to be the decision-maker since he is the breadwinner. He believes and demands that his authority be absolute and unquestioned and that he be given the central space and significance in the family. The woman feels compelled towards surrendering her autonomy and expectations of partnership. She has to pay homage to her husband and provide him total affection and even adulation. The wife feels that she is slowly but gradually being pushed into the role of a mother to her husband rather than being the *ardhangini* or *sahadharmini*.

Most women we talked to said that being born in the modern era left them stranded at the crossroads. The mothers-in-law's demand that they play the traditional role was something they could tolerate but the tragedy was that they were denied the privileges that go with the traditional role. Similarly, they said, they could respond to their husband's demands that they be modern and a companion, but the husbands were even less tolerant of the privileges that ought to go with being a modern woman. These women faced the demands of two different kinds of behaviour in two different settings and could claim no locus for themselves. Some women went so far as to state that the denial of the privileges of either role had reduced their psychological status to that of being 'kept' and it left them with no dignity. The economic helplessness emanating from their own introjects served to keep them in this undignified position. They would have preferred to break out, fight and demand but passive withdrawal, sullenness, and learning to suffer their indignities seemed to be the only options they visualised for themselves. In sum, they experienced an erosion in the sense of well-being not only for themselves but for their families also.

Consciously or unconsciously, slowly but gradually, the woman finds herself being edged into all the role modalities suited to the new family. She realises that she has to be understanding, undemanding, devoted, and an ideal housewife on the one hand, and a modern, social, capable woman, managing the environment and contributing to the husband's growth on the other hand. Amidst all this, she also has to find the time and space to create an acceptable social role in the neighbourhood, be a worthy mother and occasionally even join the workforce.

Pushed into this kind of dreary life, many women revive the fantasy of the romantic encounter with that one person where they will experience their own personhood. Our explorations with many a woman suggest that this pre-marital fantasy reappears and acquires great potency for a large number of them. Most of them fulfil this fantasy vicariously by becoming addicted to Gothic literature or novels in the Mills and Boon tradition. Some even search actively for the fulfilment of this fantasy but such encounters nearly always leave them empty and with the realisation that this fantasy can probably never be fulfilled in real life and that it could, at best, only be an episode. To many of them, encounters of this type serve to reinforce the belief that women can have no personal space. Such experiences also tend to reinforce their mistrust of all men. Further, it encourages them to identify with the macro-identity of women, i.e., women as a class of martyrs and victims who are deprived and discriminated against. Some of them end up being active in women's forums. Others develop a general philosophy of withdrawal and settle helplessly into the confines of the given role. Still others become bitter and turn into shrews.

Management of New Roles: The In-Laws

Many women find it difficult to give up the daughter's role and cross the threshold to enter new roles. In such situations, the home becomes a battleground centred around whose attitudes, values and ways of living are appropriate and valid. The woman, loyal to her upbringing, becomes adamant. In the initial encounter with the new role and as she begins to explore the expectations of the new family, she encounters criticism, some snide remarks and constant evaluation. This process evokes all the internalised apprehensions rooted in the cultural lore of the in-laws. The woman hardly gets any time to sit back and manage the ensuing transactions. The fact that the feared transactions are actually taking place serves to block the woman's mind and, instead, leads her to reassert the daughter's role which is rooted in the belief that her parents' ways are right. Many confrontations begin with insignificant issues but often acquire the form of battles of will power centering around subjugation, domination and surrender. The home becomes a setting for hostility, sarcasm and barbed comments. Alternatively, the new bride or the mother-in-law (or both) inflate the issues, often out of proportion, and the husband ends up caught between the two.

The mother-in-law, anxious that she may lose her son and uncertain about the continuance of her central role, tries to continue to hold on to the ownership of her son and his surrounding space. The young woman finds it difficult to fashion a new response. She finds herself being pushed into the role of a 'maid-cum-errand girl' in the family. The concept of creating togetherness and a richness of emotional experience becomes a mirage. The young couple snatch a few moments together only to be confronted with the harshness and emptiness of dehydrated living processes. These processes further reinforce the woman's response of holding on to the security of the role of being a daughter. She creates as many opportunities as possible to visit her parental family, while in her in-laws' home she experiences feelings of anxiety and insecurity. This makes her very defensive and, as a result, tentative in her responses. Her behaviour only elicits further critical remarks and the net result is that a vicious cycle is created. In this situation, the lack of active support from the husband leaves many a young bride desperate for a respite and for a corner where she can breathe. This type of transaction often encourages the young bride to increase her efforts to integrate her husband with the parental family and thus deprive the mother-in-law of a son.

Not all marriages involve the severity, intensity and trauma of adjustment. There are many relationships where the transition from one family to another and to a new role is easy and meaningful. Such marriages have the space and people with whom to feel free and comfortable. The new bride is pampered, loved, teased and helped to feel a member of the new home. The mother-in-law—aware of the hopes, dreams and aspirations of the younger generation—provides as much space as possible to the son and the daughter-in-law to grow together. A sort of camaraderie develops between the young bride and her peers in the husband's family. Many young women are encouraged to go in for higher education and to take up activities which are beyond those prescribed by tradition. The infrastructure for this kind of transaction is provided by the husband's family as a whole and the woman is integrated with the new family easily and with grace.

We also encountered a set of young women who did not experience conflict with their in-laws. They defined their role, goals and priorities, their career aspirations, their desire to be a professional, right from the beginning. Such women accept the husband's family, whether nuclear or extended, as a reality. They have a clear vision of their role which they know will require tremendous investment, hard work and effort to actualise. They tolerate many of the dysfunctional processes arising from the social setting. Self-contained and self-reliant, they cope as best they can and continue to work towards realising their own vision of their roles. Their convictions about themselves and their lives are the sustaining force. They display the courage to accept the consequences of their choices, and have faith and trust in their ability to get up and walk away from most setbacks.

After marriage, many husbands find themselves caught between their role as a husband and as a son and end up mediating between two women. Unable to confront either of these roles, husbands often escape to the workplace to find peace and sanity. The passive stance adopted by such husbands adds to the burden of the young bride. Our conversations with many a woman suggest that as compared to women (who are often eager to discard the daughter role), men are deeply and perhaps forever attached to the son role. The cultural lore at least prepares the woman to uproot herself and relocate her anchor. But in the case of men, the cultural lore very often reinforces the commitments of the son role. As such, the Indian male as husband is often confronted with the need to resolve the psychological as well as social role of being a son. At best he ends up establishing the bio-social role of a husband, but rarely fulfils the psychological one.

The man is often unable to take any initiative to create psychological togetherness. Love, affection and all the other softer feelings often tend to be expressed only in the form of the sexual act. This obviously cannot create the fundamental security and trust needed between young men and women. The man discovers that the only socially approved alternative available to him is to get over-involved in work or in other settings of the masculine world.

In such relationships, women have to confront the pathos of living a dependent life. Their role is to provide security, stability and a sense of continuity and consistency at home. They are relegated to the symbolic state of being nothing but a context for the husband and his mode of life. Women thus become captives with no sense of their own location. Over time, this results in women being accorded a secondary status and gives rise to patterns of subjugation. Such a relationship also promotes myths about women being fragile, helpless, and needing constant protection.

Brought up in the social design of Indian agrarian society, Indian women have over the centuries internalised various processes which they actually detest. They, too, have come to believe that women are like chattels to be owned and protected by a successive set of males: father, brother, husband, son. At no point in time are women encouraged to believe that they are human beings who can be autonomous, can make choices for themselves, and can create a life of their own. At best, the only role allowed to them is to adjust, adapt and accommodate to the setting they find themselves in. They are not supposed to define or redefine any of these situations through their active participation. They are expected to sacrifice, suffer and, through patience, create a context for the well-being of the family.

Caught in such a situation, today's woman often sees her only escape in physically moving away from the husband's family. In the name of work and the travelling it involves, many young couples opt for geographically distant locations. Information obtained from Indian families settled abroad also reflects a similar pattern. Migration abroad is often justified in the name of better opportunities and economic security, but many of these young men and women admit that at a deeper level their inability to deal with the monolithic social processes of the family in Indian society influenced their decision to leave. Men and women who have migrated abroad carve out roles which appear appropriate and meaningful to them today. These women have adopted roles and taken up activities which even their mothers could not have dreamt of actualising. In our experience it is the migrant woman (and not the man) who does not want to return to live in India.

However, physical distance and the acceptance of new roles and activities do not in themselves free the young couple from the deeply ingrained social attitudes, orientations and ways of relating to the world and people. In many direct and indirect ways, their role expectations continue to be embedded in traditional role models. These deeper internalisations still continue to affect the couple, and the woman, and even the man, remains psychologically unfulfilled.

Marriage is an institution as well as social living and both aspects are loaded with expectations emanating from traditional roles. Marriage is no longer a transaction between two families where the respective expectations of the woman and the man were secondary to the expectations of the context. Today, marriage has become a way of overcoming the loneliness of existence, of experiencing deeper intimacy, and of gaining the freedom both to redesign relatedness with the wider world and to engage in meaningful activities. The deeper introjects of traditional roles, expectations and attitudes run counter to this conceptualisation. As such, marriage has become an institution where, besides fulfilling current expectations, men and women seek to be free from various emotions—of deprivation, discrimination, and 'dominance–subjugation'. Each partner therefore loads the other with expectations of support in the effort to seek psychological fulfilment, though the fulfilment that is being sought may not be clear to either. As a result, marriages today have become rather fragile.

Despite genuine efforts made by both, men and women keep regressing to older models. Men regress to the role of provider and the controller of relatedness outside the home. They do not sustain the new role of sharing the turmoils of the outside world. Similarly, woman tend to regress into the roles of home-maker and mother. They expect the husband to bestow love and care on them as also to sustain the initiative to maintain their marriage as a partnership.

Essentially, men and women remain preoccupied with their residual feelings as well as with the framework of role expectations, both emotive and cognitive. They fail to make the most of the autonomous state they have already created by virtue of having got married. They often display the prisoner's dilemma in their behaviour. Thus, both men and women end up visualising marriage as a process for replenishing the barrenness and dehydrating experiences of the past and as the location of an ever-flowing spring or an oasis. These expectations leave very little space for men and women to explore and discover each other as human beings and as themselves or to design and create a new life-space.

Caught between the emergent aspirations of a new world-view and new role definitions, and the persistence of beliefs emanating from centuries-old Indian traditions, women end up as martyrs and objects of persecution. Their life-space is dominated by the struggle to create a sense of psychological equality, respect and autonomy. The forces of tradition and modernity turn both their internal and external lives into a battleground. Instead of any constructive outcome, this struggle has acquired an either/or polarisation. Women's lib and male chauvinism, along with their accompanying stereotypes and arguments, rage through their life-space. While the slow fire of discrimination, deprivation and denial burns inside women, their external lives are characterised by helplessness and resentment.

This attempt of women to focus the issues on the social and inter-actional level has often led to a dysfunctional confrontation with society which, in turn, generates fear. What women begin in a heroic mould ends up with them denying themselves their legitimate space. They ignore their real resources and potential and get entrenched in demanding equality and an affirmation of their competence, indispensability and functional abilities. The males respond by getting entrenched in their own need to bestow patronage, marginal support, and the inadequate and insufficient resources at their command. This leaves women feeling marginal and secondary, and of being included only in a half-hearted manner.

The current social and economic realities in the urban setting have further compounded the struggle of Indian women. In the traditional agrarian society, women lived and worked in groups. They had well-designed infrastructures where they could experience some kind of personhood with their own kind. These infrastructures prevented the accumulation of 'frustration and aggression'. Thus, life, though it still lacked both autonomy and a fundamental location, had sufficient support to ensure their psychological well-being.

Today, however, women live alone and work in mixed, heterogenous groups. All the infrastructures for role sustenance have been eroded or destroyed while no new institutions and infrastructures have been created. The persistent social stereotypes of women deny them any setting or space to experience their own personhood. In our experience, those few women who tried to create such infrastructures or who tried to experience their personhood found themselves facing sexually exploitive or degrading relationships. For these women, therefore, the psycho-drama of the male-female entanglement becomes a broken record. Besides, the universe of identities based on the cultural lore is also replayed by the Indian female child. Perhaps the role models of the cultural lore are internalised as deeply as the universe of identities is introjected. The three significant and persistent models running through mythology and history are the virtuous woman who suffers, the virtuous and assertive woman who fights, and the one who escapes into religion.

Sita, the mythical heroine, is the archetype of the first model. A series of such role figures, culminating in Rani Padmini of Chittor, symbolises loyalty to the role of being an ideal, chaste woman. These women spent their lives following in the footsteps of their husbands. In times of crisis, when they had to act for themselves, they had the choice of sacrificing their dignity or accepting death. These women are glorified not for the choices they made as persons but for the chastity with which they fulfilled the role ideal. Evidence that this role model has been internalised by many women today is provided by numerous incidents of an almost diurnal nature. Self-immolation, being burnt by aggressors, and other kinds of aggression within the bounds of the family are not uncommon. Caught in inflexible role expectations, the will of the husband and his family, denied the opportunity of being themselves, badgered into conformity, women either suffer indignity, oppression and exploitation or choose the path of self-destruction. The only alternative they are offered is to give in and turn into an ideal mother and wife.

Kali in the myths, Kannagi in literature and Rani of Jhansi in history depict the model of virtuous but, in the final analysis, assertive and aggressive women. These women overthrow the belief that women are fragile and helpless. They take up arms against an unjust system bent on victimising the weak and the helpless: They either fight and succeed or die fighting. There are plentiful instances of women taking this stance and functioning constructively in their own life-space. Such women are often the nucleus of voluntary work and they succeed in establishing an ethos of dignity, justice and well-being for women. They sustain their role consistently so that society eventually comes around and not only accepts them but provides them with resources. Soon, however, these organisations are taken over by elite groups, thus defeating the purpose for which they were set up. The role-holders become patrons and the victims continue to remain victims; in short, the existing social processes are perpetuated. These organisations end up getting lost in the wilderness of mammoth and monolithic traditions. An alternative form that this role model takes is one in which women create a viable space in their community and become sort of resident counsellors for women undergoing stress. They are trouble-shooters and often intervene supportively in the struggles of women in the neighbourhood.

The third model of virtuous women is those who escape into religion. This is by far the most common role though there are no examples of it in mythology. However, history and the present times are replete with such women—Sant Sukhobai, Meera, Anandmai Ma, and the 'Mother'. Trapped in the social and familial milieu, disenchanted and disillusioned with people, desperate to hold on to their sanity, these women turn to religion and God. Religion becomes their anchor which enables them to counter the stress of being women. In their lives, they have experienced a barrenness of emotions and lack of support for their pursuits. The shackles of traditional ideals clasp them in their mighty grip. Society allows women to suspend their role and drop out of the system in the name of religion and spiritual salvation. Being the repositories of virtue in the mind of society, Indian women find it easy to turn to this path as the best source of solace. In our experience, many women from urban as well as rural settings resort to this option. Gathering around gurus, *kathas, pravachans* and joining religious cults is something many of them do.

Within the framework of these three role models, women either react to or side-step the system without directly confronting it or modifying it. All models suggest death—either physical or psychological—as a final alternative. Those women who become martyrs, though with all good intentions, actually perpetuate the processes which dehumanise women in the system. Women try and transcend the social milieu using various role models but are unable to create any real space for themselves. They attempt to define new roles but fail to trigger off new processes within the system. In the ultimate analysis, they are captives of social traditions and role prescriptions.

Neither the identity of the various princesses nor the role models described above seem to fulfil the basic need that a woman has to find and sustain that one relationship where she can be herself and give free expression to all her potentials without being subjected to aggression, exploitation, criticism, condemnation, and so on. In living out their identities, women have to take on the burden of proving themselves. Yet, in the final analysis, they also have to belong and have to earn social acceptance, and in this process they are once again squarely put back into the role.

Indian cultural lore provides many other social, historical and religious role models. Models like Durga, Kali and Chandi are but a few examples. These models attack unjust individuals in a social cause and are forever deified and glorified. However, their acts of positive assertion have not been institutionalised as a living reality for women. History has many examples of women performing heroic deeds in times of crisis. For instance, there is Kekaiyi from the *Ramayana* who in a war put her finger in the crack in King Dashratha's chariot and thus contributed to the winning of the war. But these and similar acts are transient ones enacted only in times of crisis. Once performed, the woman returns to her socially prescribed role.

In the face of these models, women find it difficult to actualise their potentials and achieve an integration. In the process of experimenting they are confronted with the inevitabilities of these models. Their struggles assist them to gain many insights into areas of the self, though they are virtually prohibited from actualising or even exploring that self. The framework of these models and identities are themselves so compulsive that women rarely achieve the ideals in which these identities and models are anchored. The 'fall' is inevitable; there is always room for the accusing finger. Sita, who is held up as the most ideal of them all, falls short in the eyes of a single washerman and the king, her husband, exiles her from the kingdom. The cultural lore provides no role model or mechanisms whereby a woman can integrate her processes of 'being' and 'becoming' to generate a socio-psychological identity for herself in the system.

Independent of these models but within the framework of identity, there are women like Gargi and Lopa Mudra in the myths and, in recent times, characters from fiction who have taken recourse to an intellectual life. Lopa Mudra became an outcast from her group while Gargi and the others stayed within the boundaries of the role. These figures serve as models of role integration while being able to acquire their own meaning. However, even they cannot modify the processes of the system.

Today's Indian woman is caught in fragmented and narrow roles. Opportunities of education and of discovering her own intelligence and abilities, and encouragement to learn the arts and to actively participate in the world of work alongside her male counterparts have opened a whole new vista for the woman. However, the social and psychological stigma attached to playing such an active role leaves the woman vulnerable as a person.

Our experience is that most of the women who finally succeed are accused of having one or other of the popularly conceived attributes attached to courtesans. For example, their success is often considered to be the result of their having linked up with a male. They are rarely given credit for achieving what they have through personal integrity and dignity. The social system does not seem to have any conception of or willingness to help women acquire womanhood and personhood. A majority of women get stuck in the dilemmas of woman–person encounters. Each attempt they make to get out only serves to suck them deeper into confronting the interpersonal relationships surrounding their social and work roles and into the vicious grasp of the double-binds of the role processes connected to social systems and work organisations.

Women are thus permanently stranded at a crossroad. The question is whether they have any alternatives which can help them to define a new locus for themselves. Are there any models available in society to facilitate such a new location? The answer to the first question is 'yes' but 'no' to the second one. To take the latter first, in today's times a single charismatic woman cannot generate an ideal model which other women can follow. This kind of a leader–follower model would only repeat the historical process of turning women into echoes and pale replicas of a giant model. The only alternative, to take up the first question, seems to be for women to become 'heroines' in themselves and that they initiate an individual search to discover their own identity.

Those women who have attempted to integrate their woman–person role in both social and work-settings have had the courage to choose a path which has not been travelled before. At each critical moment they have made choices, not compromises. They have accepted the intended and unintended consequences of their choices without bitterness. They have had the courage to travel beyond the crossroad. Like heroes of the past in search of their existential identity, these women have time and again asked the old witch spinning a wheel at the crossroad: 'Which road do I take?' The witch answers:

One road goes to the right. This road will take six months and a day. It is a widely travelled road. It has familiar landmarks. It has many travellers who can be companions. There are shelters for rest and food along the way. It is an easy road and a road of little effort; a known and familiar road which has existed for ages. The other road is the road to the left. It is a road with many dangers. It is filled with unknown paths, barriers, turbulent rivers, deserts and high mountains. Very few people dare go that way. In fact, there is no road. You will have to create your own path. There are no land-marks and no shelter. The road takes a year or more and is a lonely one. And you may not come out alive. CHOOSE.

Indian women at this juncture get caught up in the dilemma of whether or not to choose the familiar road with its landmarks of Sati, Sita and Savitri. They get caught in the iron shape of the social system which demands a price—that they surrender their existential beings so as to acquire a role-based security. However, some women have opted for the road to the left and blazed their own trail. They have had the courage and the conviction to choose the road of adventure, to discover the vicissitudes of their existence and to grapple with the arduous process of discovering an integrated identity which includes the multiple facets of social and work roles. They have claimed their existential and psychological identity beyond the social roles. Only then have they been able to achieve fulfilment and been able to actualise and experience wider horizons. We now identify these pro-cesses in the remaining three chapters.

6

Struggle with Reality

Standing at yet another threshold the woman once again asks herself the question: 'Is this my life forever?' In times of solitude and loneliness, this threshold represents moments lost and doors firmly closed. At this threshold, she confronts the reality that youth and womanhood have started to recede into the realm of what once was, what could have been, and she is left with nostalgia, with a past which is largely fantasy and a present which is harsh reality. In retrospect, her life appears to have been one of engaging in multiple activities without feeling productive; of being many roles without being herself; of putting on many masks; and of being at the beck and call of all and of performing given roles. There has been no respite from demands and no time for confronting one's real self. In being many things to many people, she has not been sure of being true to herself. At this threshold, the woman wonders whether she is made out of clay or wax; whether her life is her own or belongs to others; and whether she has lived a life as she had wished to or has been made to change shape according to the wishes of others. It seems to her that she has become a stranger to herself.

Standing at this threshold, the woman experiences a whole host of feelings and images. Everything around her is familiar—the forms, the shapes, the sounds, the smells, the people, the house, the neighbourhood; and yet there is a strange sense of being lost. It seems that she has been involved in a charade in which she is a late entrant, having waited in the wings for too long. In the midst of all this, both reality and unreality prevail. She feels that she has been in a strange land peopled with strange faces and that she herself is the strangest of them all.

She stands at this new threshold and recalls the one where she had once stood—young and breathless, with spirits soaring, with the dream of building a heaven on earth and a world of meaningful existence. The space beyond that threshold had beckoned with promises of companionship, of the joy of adventure and of a glorious future waiting to unfold itself. She had hoped that once she had crossed the magic threshold she would be able to claim a space for herself and fashion a life of her own. She had waited a long time to come alive and to live her life as her own. But once she had crossed that threshold, she waited each day for the magic to unfold and the enchantment to appear. However, the living process turned her dreams into a nightmare. The living reality brought with it the anxieties of insecurity and the search for security. She found that the realities of that land only contained, even more poignantly, the experiences outlined in the cultural lore. She lived with people who were her own yet she could not call them hers. She experienced her existence in private and in isolation but the compulsions of belonging to a network of relationships were very strong. She had to seek acceptance and prove her worth. Her efforts to work through and create a new identity pulled her deeper into a sense of pathos, sometimes futility, and, occasionally, led to an outburst of reaction.

Confronted with the reality of the land across the magic threshold she reflects on her life. The most poignant feeling that she had experienced was related to her struggle to locate the anchors of her existence in her own being and to create a space to be together with her loved ones. She often recalls how her attempts to achieve this were invariably shattered by the prescriptive modes of social relationships. In her search for anchors in her own being, she had perhaps even idealised her dreams. Attempts to actualise these dreams in new settings accentuated the poignancy and intensity of helplessness. All her attempts to create space and some degree of freedom for her being, only resulted in her being judged. She had to face too many rights and wrongs, dos and don'ts, and this frequently evoked guilt, shame and often despair.

Constantly faced with emotions of guilt, shame and despair made her desperate to take hold of her destiny and give herself direction. However, there was no point of departure, no clear choice of action and not even a direction. Whichever direction she wanted to take or whatever action she contemplated, she knew she would have to encounter the same responses. She clutched at many a straw and was tossed around in the sea of exploitation and humiliation. She had floated too long and too far away from the shores of her being and hence floundered frequently.

The woman felt helpless and fragile. She not only felt vulnerable but lived through the agony of being violated. In her desperation, she was often lulled into a false sense of security by expressions of concern and sympathy and promises of support from individuals. But if she accepted such offers, she only ended up encountering new demands and fresh exploitation. She often had to surrender out of a feeling of obligation or guilt and then experienced an erosion of her sanctity and values while pursuing these tantalising chimeras of security.

And, thus, the magic turned into evil, hope into despair, dreams into nightmares and the spark of her life gradually faded into a dark emptiness. It was only at such moments—when she came to confront the inner loneliness, the feelings of being stifled and strangulated, and a wish to die—that some women finally heard that voice, that inner voice, which had been drowned in the noise. The world had failed her but in reality she had failed herself.

Chains and Shackles

The woman now stands at a new threshold—that of middle age. She is a grown up woman, experienced and worldly, but when she looks into a mirror she confronts a stranger's face. She is not the woman she had anticipated in her dreams. What she sees is a worldly woman, bound by chains and shackles. These chains and shackles are the traditions which had made her accept the compulsions of the given roles—roles which she had never integrated into her personhood. She had been a daughter-in-law, wife and mother but not herself. Those women who made their home their primary domain had anchored themselves in the social roles of the family. These social roles divided the life of the woman into the public one of being a *bahu* and, within the confines of the bedroom, the private one of being a wife. For most women, these two worlds remained separate and fragmented. And while the expectations surrounding the daughter-in-law role were all-pervasive, the wife role occupied a miniscule portion. Their experience was that their whole existence was subsumed into being a *bahu*. This meant that the private world of the bedroom and of being a wife was also largely barren, as it failed to compensate for the traumas of being a daughter-in-law.

In the process of being pulled and pushed between these two roles, the woman had little space left to allow herself to unfold. She was also left to manage these roles on her own. The husband normally gave her very little support as he was, first and foremost, his mother's son and thus an ineffective mediator and, in fact, became an object of significance or a possession to be fought over. The Indian male can be effective neither in his role of being a son nor a husband. His dilemma is how to respond to the mother's anxiety about losing him and her consequent possessiveness on the one hand and, on the other, how to handle the anxieties, insecurities and meaninglessness of his wife's existence in the new family. Invariably, he is unable to provide the love and tender care that his wife needs.

Confronted with the traumatic reality of marriage, most women initially find that they have no other alternative but to surrender and cope, to give and not demand, to withhold and disown themselves and not compromise the family's status. If the woman contemplates any action in her search for new alternatives, she ends up facing the possibility of being deserted, physically brutalised and/or living in the family as an outcast or as a kept woman. In fact, the central theme of many women's lives is that of violation. Violation takes many forms— from the physical to the psychological.

As a consequence, many women slowly but steadily let their sense of confidence, respect and self-worth as individuals be eroded. They find security in a mechanical and restricted role performance. They harbour feelings of denial, discrimination, deprivation, anger and frustration. Even in the midst of material plenty, many women live with harrowing feelings of psychological insecurity, lack of personal status and a sense of not belonging. If the woman attempts to create a space for togetherness with her husband, he feels oppressed, confined by two dominant sources of affection and love—namely, his mother and his wife. He complains of a loss of space and experiences stress, tension, anxiety and conflict. A stifling atmosphere pervades the home. The husband becomes a guest, a visitor in his home, using it only as a place to sleep. The only recourse women have in this situation is to accentuate the mother role, and thus attempt to possess the husband in emotional bondage.

Realisation of Realities

After about fifteen years of marriage have passed, most women come to understand the realities of their social existence. They know only too well that married life is a strong prison from which there may be escapades but no escape. They also come to realise that men are as helpless and perhaps less capable of releasing themselves from the hold of traditional roles. This recognition that men, too, are victims does not, however, help women much.

Our data suggest that both men and women are keen to create an atmosphere where they can experience personalised togetherness, but neither is willing to take the initiative. At critical moments the old pleas—that 'the time is not yet ripe', or 'may be the parents will now be reconciled and let go'—always crop up. Procrastination and postponement become a way of life. It is a strange fact that while both egg the other on to make a break, to take a stand and to initiate, neither of them ever do it.

Having encountered and shared the living realities of the many roles acted out by women, we have come to recognise that Indian society leaves no scope for an individual to transcend the role boundaries. In our experience, hundreds of young men and women enter the world of work with hopes of carving out a space for themselves and of redefining their roles but they are confronted with time-honoured models of the subordinate type. Even the workplace generates processes which demand a good son's role. Very soon, the young men and women lose their dynamic impulses and creativity and fall back on modes of adaptation and/or manipulation. They either do not give of themselves completely either at home or in the workplace, or they end up being owned by their parents and/or the organisation they work for.

Men and women trapped in these kinds of roles fail to create reciprocity, mutuality and interdependence with each other either at home or in work-settings. The entire network of relationships gets categorised in terms of superior and subordinate. At home, wives are treated as subordinates and hence to be acted upon. Gradually, there is little time, space or even predisposition to relate to each other in a meaningful manner. The social setting becomes a series of islands where each player performs his or her role without any feeling.

While the woman lives out the pathos of the chains, the shackles and the prison, she often wonders if there is a door through which she can pass and thus experience a different world. This different world is often vaguely conceptualised as having freedom, no responsibilities and no demands or expectations. To most women such a door opens occasionally by way of an unexpected encounter with another man who appears to be entirely different from the models they have so far come across. Inevitably such an encounter leads to an opening of all the floodgates. The woman experiences a resurgence of anticipation, hope, joyousness, a desire to offer her whole being. Life and its surroundings acquire a new meaning, like the arrival of spring.

However, such encounters take place within the living world. The old setting is alive and so are many residual feelings from the past. Commitment and guilt, joyousness and shame, momentary fulfilment and persistent emptiness, toss and turn the woman. She becomes restless, impatient. Such encounters only serve to accentuate the painful realities of her married life. The need to throw it all away and walk off becomes very intense. It also triggers off a process of reappraisal. All the internalised values from the past not only raise questions but also point accusing fingers. This appraisal of reality also sets in motion fresh anxieties. The fear of social disapproval can be faced but most women find it difficult to accept the role of having deserted their children. The woman ends up remaining immobile and thus actually reinforcing the very same processes she resents in the social system.

In the moment of this encounter and in responding to it, the woman often forgets that one anchor of relatedness lies in the nature and quality of transactions. All transactions are intrinsically circumscribed and operate within certain constraints. These constraints not only arise from the circumstances but also emanate from the psyches of the two people concerned. She continues to blame the world and sees herself as the victim. Eventually, the universe of transactions crystallises and it is in this crystallisation that she seeks freedom. The wholesomeness of being oneself is over-shadowed. The emergent reality of the encounter is perhaps further distorted by the internal struggle and the environmental constraints. Thus, the reality of the encounter seems to offer far less than it promised. Finally, the nature of the transaction confronts the woman with the question: 'Is this real, or am I once again stepping into a world of somebody else's making and being used as an object? Do I really mean something as a person either to myself or to the other?'

So, for many a woman such encounters end up being an idyllic interlude, to be forgotten; or a sordid affair, the shame and guilt of which she has live with. Some women find the strength to go through with such an encounter and do come up with a critcal personal appraisal of their values and reality. They encounter in themselves and in their living processes a role which has dignity and set themselves the task of discovering ways to derive meaning beyond the roles. These women discover the quality of persistence and endurance in themselves as well as the ability to define the world around them.

At this stage, some women give new meanings to their role and make new choices in terms of action. They either go in for further education or join their husbands' enterprises or carve out new activities for themselves. Making such a choice also involves reappraising all their existing roles. The quality of being daughter, wife, daughter-in-law, mother needs to be redefined. Women not only confront these issues within themselves but often encounter protests, doubts, ridicule and occasional support from without. Exercising a choice of this nature means that the woman has to extend herself beyond the home and to interface with the wider environment and the world of men. It means accepting her legitimacy in the wider world and stepping beyond the stereotypes.

For many women this threshold is a short-lived experience. Fear, terror, anxiety about being isolated, loneliness, and accusations, all encourage a woman to return to the prison rather than to experience autonomy and freedom.

A Glimpse into the Mirror

By this time a large number of women are desperate to find some meaning for themselves. Until now they had been caught up in the processes of the cultural lore. They had searched for meaningful relationships, had followed the path of conformity and surrender, and had ended up feeling futile. Some had followed the path of faith and thus gained some respite for themselves. Others had grown out of the daughter role and acquired new roles with grace and dignity. Yet in all cases the search was for something more fundamental and more existential. Women arriving at this threshold can either anchor themselves there or can cross the threshold; they can either live with regrets or walk into the unknown and create a new world.

The encounter with the other person and the consequent enchantment normally elicits one of three responses from women. One set of women turn bitter and allow this bitterness to pervade their own life-space. They become shrewd, critical, negative and always bemoan their fate. They communicate a streak of vindictiveness, wrapped up in concern, to all female children. In a way, they become the conscience-keepers of the younger generation. Others locate their bitterness in the concept of being a woman in a world which is unjust, unfair and harsh. They carry the baggage of historical and social stereotypes and use them to bestow the same meaning on every experience.

The second response also involves bitterness. Instead of focusing on the younger generation, however, these women become the conscience-keepers of society at large. They respond to the pathos and bitterness of living in a harsh and unjust world by turning into martyrs and reformists. They use their own pathos to identify with women as a class and become actively involved in the struggle to free women. A variation of this type is the woman who not only chooses to locate her bitterness in the symbol but becomes the symbol herself. While she works with other women she also converts herself into the issue in her own life-space and takes the stance of being a wrecker of traditions.

The third response to this encounter is the woman who becomes reflective. She takes a serious and hard look at herself and tries to own up to a great deal. She assesses the reality of her interface with the environment and instead of accusing the world of having treated her badly she holds herself responsible for having invoked the violations.

In their need to come to terms with themselves, such women give the benefit of doubt to others and take the total blame on to themselves. Going further in their understanding of the nature of the interface, they try and let go of the past and instead make a new beginning. In this moment, their reflections help them to recognise their resilience and vulnerability, the inner rhythm of their being, and the strength of their personal convictions.

Some of the women who respond in this manner postpone action for themselves and instead decide to provide a context wherein their daughters can grow up in a manner that will help them to escape the fate of womanhood. In our experience, this response is the most tragic aspect of the whole reflective confrontation with the self; tragic in the sense that these women have been unable to mobilise their own infrastructures of action for themselves.

Perhaps it is this third type of response which acts as the mirror. It serves to confront a woman with a strong sense of guilt with herself. She recognises that holding the man, society, family and traditions as being exclusively responsible for the pain, anguish and harshness of her life is only a reactive process. Her own immobility and helplessness is also responsible for all the injustice, unfairness and maltreatment she has faced.

Our discussions with many women who exhibited this response pattern showed that, ultimately, they were astutely realistic. They understood the processes of the transactions in their lives. They knew the how and the why as well as the who and the when of their humiliating experiences. However, they continued to remain frozen or very tentative while relating to the world. Many of these women, then, created settings which would encourage their daughters to take new steps. They socialised them with values of self-reliance and dignity. Though these women had not acted for themselves or explored new alternatives, they commanded respect in the social setting and were held up as role models. They had created a space which gave them value and affirmation in the eyes of society. They then hoped that their daughters would have a new future.

A Walk into the Unknown

There are some women who struggle to create a path in the shifting sand. Regardless of all the guilt, suspicion and doubts that they face, these women opt to review their lives and to create a choice for themselves. This choice is to add substantiveness to their lives. In the moment of making this choice they accept and own up to their potential of being more than just roles. Awareness of their resilience, inner rhythm and strength often spurs them to actualise these potentials.

These women seek to engage themselves in activities beyond the home. For some, the choice takes the form of beginning a new career, while others decide to promote and/or be a part of a new institution. This choice is rooted in their efforts to develop a new definition and meaning within themselves, to add to themselves and to the environment. The focus is on creating a new set of links, both for the self and the system.

The sort of engagement that women who display the first and second type of response seek is normally anchored in their disgruntlement and dissatisfaction. They have a strong need to direct their anger at the family and at society. Their stance is one of defiance, not definition; of conflict rather than negotiation. The basic theme of their response is negation of the outside, and behind this negation lurks a certain degree of self-righteousness.

The stance adopted and the choices made by women of the second stream often serve to keep the turbulence and turmoil alive. Resolution of problems and mutual understanding with the people around them is rare. Life becomes a see-saw between helplessness and defiance, victory and defeat, passivity and stress, withdrawal and conflict. The real price of this stance is actually paid by the children. Children in such families end up being torn between different adults. Their sense of belonging and psychological security is always in the balance. These children's need to survive tends to make them manipulate the people around them for their own ends and they often play one adult against the other. In their own experience they either feel indulged or brutalised. These children rarely have the occasion to confront themselves and, as such, grow up with the belief that they do not owe any commitment or loyalty to anyone.

Another response of women of the third stream is to take up careers. They bring their competence as well as intelligence to bear on the work situation and create a niche for themselves in their chosen profession. However, they do not disown their familial roles in the process. In fact, they tend to become good managers of their home, train their children to face the living process, and create harmony with relatives and neighbours in order to provide a wider network of belonging and a sort of proxy nurturance for their children. They continue to play the role of the wife and slowly encourage their husbands, who till now have played only the son's role, to seek a new integration within the family. This is often a difficult task and the women encounter many an obstacle, heartaches and occasional storms. They sometimes react and withdraw but generally most of them get a grip on the situation and hold on so that the tensions do not spread across the life-space. In the process, many of these women also create time and space where they can be with themselves, and occasionally with others, without stress. Some of our participants often talked of times of crisis and anxiety in the family which almost made them give up and retreat into negative and defiant attitudes or into passive futility. But their ability to be reflective and to be able to look at themselves without illusions provided the necessary support at such moments and they were able to persist in their efforts.

The women of the second stream who take to careers often fragment their lives into two. Both lives become arenas for struggles and fights. While they bring their talents, competence, energy and drive to succeed to the workplace, they conceive of the system as being a harsh environment and approach their male counterparts with hostility. They continue to carry the macro-symbolic identity of womanhood on their shoulders. The normal tensions created by the system, the average 'political' currents which operate in any organisation and the common masculine atmosphere which pervades most organisations, generates in such women a feeling of being discriminated against or of being denied opportunities.

Even the women who display the third type of response often live a fragmented life. These women bring their skills, competence, intelligence, their will to achieve and be successful to the work-setting. They accept their basic self-worth and often do well in the organisation. However, in their family and primary roles they take a step backwards. In action and in behaviour they give primacy to members of the family system, specifically to the husband, and often surrender to the demands of the social system. This choice reduces the stress, conflicts and tensions of interaction in the home-setting. They thus carry a larger burden but they make no complaints. The environmental process remains the same but these women have found two locations and they attempt to balance both without sacrificing either. They fulfil their potentials and find meaning in themselves.

A still smaller set of women focuses exclusively on the need to actualise their potentials. Their efforts are to force the system to respond to their design. At the manifest level, this almost appears to be a challenge. They come through as demanding, inflexible and all fired up to make or break. Their search is to create a space where there are no compulsions towards conformity or surrender. Their stated objective is to take charge of their lives and their space. In doing so, they appear to be over-stepping and acting upon the system as if to say, 'Now you know what it was like for me earlier.' The charge that they are being vindictive, autocratic, hostile and compulsive does not make sense to them. They, in fact, feel hurt by such statements.

All said and done, women of the second and third stream struggle to create a space. Their choice is to find for themselves that psychological space which has been so far been playing hide-and-seek with them. Many women start on this journey. Given the experiences they encounter along the way, some women settle down and pause and make that space their home. Others resolve to walk on and come to yet another crossroad.

These are some of the patterns we found during the course of our discussions. A review of our data suggests that in the confrontation with reality and the struggle to come to terms with it in order to create a space, many women have to face the deeply embedded assumptions of Indian society. What follows is a summary of some of these assumptions as articulated by the women we met:

Women as persons do not belong to any system except in a role. They have no personal space. They cannot make demands. Perhaps they are unwelcome intrusions or suspect visitors. They cannot be part of the system and are not to be trusted. As daughters-in-law they are received as guests, but are soon turned into *dasis* [retainers] in the family and almost become kept women in the marriage. In this role of a guest, society does not accept their desire to have any space in their own right as being a legitimate claim. Their space is always a derivative of other people's proprietory rights. Essentially, they are outsiders.

For many women, the struggle to find a legitimate space in any system or family is the most poignant aspect of their lives. Many women harbour deep resentment as a consequence. In their efforts to establish a new and meaningful engagement with the world upon reaching middle age, they often refuse the resources offered by the husband and his family. They claim that they are doing what they are out of their own choice. When they needed resources these were not forthcoming so now they do not want to accept them. The resentment and the poignancy is indeed annihilating. As such, many genuine efforts to seek meaningful new engagements with the environment tend to fail. Most of them only make the generation of economic resources their primary struggle.

Women in India have continued to struggle to establish the legitimacy of their personhood through centuries. The burden of being either an object or a role has been constantly reinforced. The tragedy of this struggle is that most women accept their commitments to the system. They give to it their best years and the best of themselves. In their struggle with reality and their attempt to cross the threshold in middle age, women also get caught up in the introjects of centuries-old tradition which sees them as being nothing other than a role. This process is very harrowing. Each encounter triggers off processes of dislocation and demands continuous reflection. The woman has to make a clear differentiation between which are reactive actions and which a response from her own location.

The experiences of the few women who have stuck to their convictions upon arriving at this new threshold are very similar. They differentiate between aggression and assertion, manipulation and acting from conviction, surrender and engagement, conformity and togetherness. They invest in people and the system for their well-being. They see themselves as being responsible for both. In their own awakening they experience other people coming alive. Most of these women sustain their struggle because of an acute sense of relatedness to the human context.

However, most of these women have no clear-cut answers to questions such as: 'Why are women denied the legitimacy of their person?' 'Why must a woman be virtuous and sacrifice her being so that her husband, children and family can become wholesome beings?' They are perhaps no longer angry and resentful, but in their new sense of dignity and integration they still hold the tragedy of being women within them. At each step they take, these women live with the fear of being alone. In each statement they make, they suffer the anxiety of being misunderstood. In each action they resort to, they face the apprehension of being stigmatised. And if they persist, they end up carrying the awesome burden of being glorified and idealised. But at no stage are they accepted as individual beings in their own right. What is the space that women struggle to create? What is the legitimacy which they need to derive? What is the definition and the design for living that they require to affirm themselves? What are the new seeds they need to plant to create a heritage they can be proud of?

7

Beyond the Horizon: Confrontation with Psychological Reality

What lies beyond the horizon? This is a question that many women ask themselves as they stand at yet another threshold. The pull of this space is experienced in the juxtaposition of the concrete and the invisible, the vision which is elusive, the touch which is withheld. The woman experiences herself as a pulsating, quivering, shapeless form to which she alone can add substance and give life. This threshold beyond the horizon is an awakening as also an invocation to create a space where she can be with the self and can also invite others.

After a long psychological journey, some women do arrive at this new threshold beyond the horizon. The woman's soul is tensile and resilient, having journeyed through the endless and arid wastes of social and psychological space. In this process, she has attempted to discover the wholesomeness of the proactive (i.e., anchored in the self) spirit of human existence. Every society and culture has some women who have crossed this threshold and created a space beyond the horizon. These women are the pioneers who add something more to themselves and make life and the process of living a little more wholesome, dignified and gracious than before. Each step on this path requires a pause to reflect deeply on the elements of the past and the present—to shut the door of the past which has been lived out and exhausted itself and to take a step into the unknown.

One of the anchors of the space beyond the horizon lies in the freedom to make a choice and to experience the present. And to experience the present, women have to free themselves from the associative universe and the overwhelming symbols of past experiences. This is a necessary step, as the present has one foot in the past and one in the future. The past contains many memories—some good, some bad; some happy, some sad; some creative, some destructive; some glowing with radiance, others with hate; some with guilt and shame, others with pride and achievement; some with the touch of wholesomeness, others with repulsion. These bitter-sweet memories have added up, drop by drop and day by day, to make life a vast panorama of experiences imbued with the magic of colours, fragrance and enchantment in the air.

In the moment of stepping into the unknown, like the tales of the cultural lore, ghosts of the past raise their heads to evoke terror and fear. Human nature is such that strangeness, newness and uncertainty create apprehensions for both men and women. Many of us hold on to certainties which are predictable and therefore comfortable, even though they have become irrelevant for the self and even others. We fantasise about having adventures and seeking out the new yet hold on to repetitive patterns; we search for uniqueness yet demand sameness and uniformity and make ourselves into predictable, known and familiar replicas of the past. For, somewhere in the continuous process of our growth, we have become frightened of both our own strangeness and the stranger in us.

The other anchor of the present lies in the space beyond the horizon—where, instead of hope there is engagement with the world, instead of dreams there is commitment, instead of aspirations there are choices, instead of ideals there are convictions, instead of bestowal and affirmation there is courage.

Time and again, the social code of conduct imposed on women and the role-taking processes defined by the cultural lore, prevent the woman from experiencing the stranger in herself which unfolds in each moment. It tames and tempers her being which is otherwise boundless and bursting with energy. Many ghosts haunt women and confront them with the nightmare of being trapped, tied at the stake, or burnt alive as a witch for making statements about her self. It evokes the terror of centuries of suffocation, strangulation and surrender. They continue to make compromises and disown their being and ultimately numb and freeze the impulse to initiate any new action.

Many a woman experiences terror at crossing the threshold to a space beyond the horizon, as this space demands that she take charge of her destiny and her life-space around her. These women struggle to take a few steps forward since their vision of their own life propels them to make a choice. They struggle to confront their own values of themselves and search for ways to encounter human existence with resilience. They rise time and again from the ashes to respond to their commitments. They reach out to experience their human spirit and the essence of life.

Indian cultural lore has taken from the spiritual heritage examples of women who have risen to destroy evil on earth. These are the Goddesses, all of them manifestations of Shakti. These Goddesses descend on earth in times of crisis, when human beings are in despair, and restore faith. Responding to this model, Indian women rise beyond their role in times of social crisis to act with the courage of their convictions only to withdraw later into socially defined roles. The cultural lore also provides role models of women who perform acts of courage, valour and bravery in times of danger and war. But here, too, once these moments have passed, they return to the roles prescribed by the social system. In short, these transient roles are designed only for moments of crisis in the system and while these models permit new responses, they are not meant to become living realities for women.

Woman after woman has abandoned the choice to make contact with the spirit of human existence within them. They mortgage themselves at various thresholds and rarely cross them to encounter the space beyond the horizon. At each new threshold they encounter the ghosts which haunt the inner space of their lives and return to being echoes and shadows. The confrontation with this threshold and the space beyond the horizon is really an encounter with the inner realities of the self, others and the system. It is a space to own up to the self and to unfold its resources. These psychological resources are designed for new role-taking and making choices for action.

At this threshold there is also space for consolidating new steps for the present. But at each such step the ghosts of the past rear their heads. The shadows of the centuries loom large and many a woman gets caught here. Struggling for their freedom, autonomy and acceptance of their self-worth, many women turn idealistic. They identify a cause. In this space some women anchor their experience in movements for liberation, the fight for equality and freedom of action, or other such worthy social causes. These issues are legitimate and are part of the space beyond the horizon. Women, then, take on the role of being spokespersons for all women. They talk of uplifting women from their secondary and subjugated status. They enter the space which belongs to womankind and where the male is experienced as a negative continuum of cumulative historical experience. Walking into this space means an encounter with the structural processes of the system. These women accept the role of contributing to a redefinition of the system. They articulate their feelings, make themselves visible for accusation, open for ridicule, and vulnerable for exploitation. In so doing, they are also invited to be part of the structures of power. Many women who accept such roles contribute to an awareness of the discriminative processes that occur between men and women, of the marginal status accorded to women in the social set-up and in work systems, the brutalisation of women in many a form, and the overall and dominant processes of dehumanisation prevalent in society. However, the mammoth social system and the invisible but ever-present structures of bondage continue to prevail.

In their role as spokespersons for all women, many women ignore a very critical dimension: they forget to explore and articulate the role of women vis-a-vis men, their counterparts. As a collectivity, every society and culture lets loose processes which are unjust, brutal, constricting and suffocating, subjugating and demanding. These processes affect women, the underprivileged, the handicapped, and even men. The reality is that such dehumanising processes operate collectively. Through the forces of evolution and growth across societies and cultures, women have experienced the rigidities of social structures and lived with the ensuing pathos. But in the articulation of this pathos and while holding on to an ideal cause, women often ignore the pathos experienced by men. Men are thus cast in the role of being the exclusive source of the victimisation and oppression of women.

Some women take a step beyond the concept of social awareness. They lay the ghosts of deprivation and denial, discrimination and comparison, feelings of being small and unworthy, and of being victims of others, of society and of circumstances. They come to grips with their own handicap of being dogmatic about people, society and situations. They identify the process by which they adopt roles based on past lacunae and deprivations. In this moment, then, women take another step to re-examine their multiple roles in the diverse systems of belonging. Women who enter this space continue their lonely and desperate struggle both at the level of the self and of the system. At the 'self' level they critically assess their role as a daughter, daughter-in-law, wife or mother, as also their role in the space beyond the family, and ask serious questions about their lives—past, present and future.

Emotive Maps

The New Daughter

At this point of time, childhood, the role of a daughter, and the associated feelings seem to belong to another place and time. Many women construct ideal images of their parents. However, revisiting that space confronts them with the realities of their parents' situation— the preoccupations, rigid boundaries and vulnerabilities with which they had lived; in short, they realise that their parents had lived with their own uncertainties and doubts. This understanding of the realities of their parents' restricted horizons, their struggles and efforts to find a meaning and an anchor in the self or the system, their socio-economic aspirations and frustrations, and the exasperations of bringing up children—all these and many more aspects of their parents' lives acquire newer meanings for women. As soon as women start to take stock of their present realities they have first to deal with the realities of the past so as to free their being, which is captive to the role of being a daughter.

Gaining freedom from the role of the daughter enables women to redefine both their roles and their relationships. The parents—now old and/or dependent, seeking comfort and security in the children— make demands, create compulsions and arouse feelings of guilt. Those women who enter the space beyond the horizon first have to transcend these processes of compulsion and guilt and demand, and respond to their parents' needs. For the first time, these women articulate their own concepts of the life-space, relationships, togetherness and the values of their role-taking. They share all this with their parents and extend the security of their love and concern for the parents without being compelled by feelings of sacrifice or of surrendering their beings. They state their choices and commitments and do not surrender to evocations of guilt and compromise. These women take the first step in the direction of creating infrastructures of relatedness while maintaining their relationships. They work for the creation of understanding rather than enter into agreements; they make statements of value rather than of role. They are willing to accept the wrath, threats and accusations of their parents. At the same time, the woman makes the effort to enable the parents to accept her, the daughter, as a mature adult and a trusted friend rather than the one with whom they can be unreasonable, illogical and irrational in the name of love and concern.

Most women attempt to redefine the parent–daughter relationship. They try to break the unilinear pattern of parents evoking guilt in the name of all they have done for their children. These women have chosen to pay the price for their new role design and definition and are unwilling to accept the price of role-taking demanded by the parents. Sooner or later, many of these women succeed in establishing this new definition—which is aimed at better understanding and is based on expressions of warmth and affection and on articulation of differences in values—in order to create harmony and understanding. There are others, however, for whom this struggle continues without a successful or meaningful resolution.

Many women, now parents themselves, have to perform the balancing act of simultaneously being daughters and mothers and managing the divergent values of the older generation on the one hand and the younger generation on the other. They have to tightly hold onto their own values, beliefs and visions so as to remain steadfast in their being.

The New Daughter-in-law

Despite being married for a decade or two, many women are not accorded the psychological acceptance and role of being a member of the husband's family. In such cases, the woman's second step is to earn the status of being a part of the family. Being a wife provided entry into the social network of the family while producing a male heir marked the beginning of being accepted into social membership. However, to earn psychological membership she also has to play the role of being a helper, the errand girl, the contributor and the adaptor.

However, all this does not create a sense of belonging or lead to membership and partnership. The woman needs to discover ways of being a co-owner of the system. This normally means that she has to accept the in-laws' and the husband's home as her own. However, this is easier said than done. Women first have to transcend centuries-old, stereotyped relationships and then try and define new modalities of relatedness. What they often discover in the process is that the mother-in-law, like her mother and herself, is equally trapped in the role-taking processes of the cultural heritage. Neither the mother nor the mother-in-law can venture beyond the internalised values of the traditional and prescribed role. They can only replay the psychodrama of social role-taking while acting out their traditional roles, and perhaps hope and wait for new responses from the daughter and the daughter-in-law. Taking this new step means that the woman, once again, has to articulate her definition of the life-space, as also her expectations of the husband, mother-in-law, father-in-law and other family members. Having articulated the new response, the woman has no other option but to persist in making statements of the self and to keep making efforts to explore newer avenues. In order to create understanding and an acceptance of differences, she must not deny the mother or the mother-in-law. In essence, what this means is that the woman has to first experience herself beyond the daughter and daughter-in-law role and thereby give herself the freedom to experience the mother and the mother-in-law shorn of their roles. This process of redefinition entails the woman accepting both herself and them as mature individuals.

Some women choose to accept the realities of the existing relationships with both their parental and in-laws' family but to respond with a new initiative. The initial phases of such a response are invariably marked by conflicts, arguments, tensions and stress all around. Often the extended family joins in to accelerate and intensify the conflict by transmitting contradictory messages to those involved. They act as the heralders and announcers of the on-rushing drama and sometimes speak against the mother-in-law, sometimes the husband but most often against the wife—the woman who is the outsider. The basic effort of the family and the community is to keep the conflict alive. Many a woman gets stuck here. It seems that, at each new step, she has to confront the ghosts of the past and lay them down in order to redefine her role. In their attempts to redefine the space beyond the role, some women lose the perspective of providing dignity and respect to existing relationships. The residues of hurt, resentment and anger, which have turned into bitterness by now, compel these women to mete out punishment to, and become vindictive and hateful towards, the presumed sources of hurt. Their pathos generates vindictiveness, their deprivations rudeness, while denials bring about hurt and they become insensitive to the pathos of others. They basically decide to vanquish all those whom they hold responsible for their past traumas.

This stance breaks up many a family. Many relationships are left with pain and anguish, and a sense of helplessness and doom prevails. Those women who cannot touch their own beings and discover the humaneness in themselves and others, unleash negative consequences both for the parental and the in-laws' family. The nuclear family—made up of husband, wife and children—often gets cut off from its primary as well as cultural moorings and ends up adrift.

Yet there are some women who transcend the process of redefinition. They survive all this and persist in their efforts. They are able to rebuild the family with emotional linkages. They sow the seeds of a new heritage, new values and a new philosophy of living. These are the women who create a family where there is space for each and everyone. They foster a tolerance of differences amongst roles and encourage committed relationships. They engender in the family the capacity to respond to individual feelings rather than to the compulsions of the roles. They establish a context where conflict, stress and hurt are as much part of a living reality as are moments of togetherness and well-being. With effort and persistence, they slowly but steadily chip away at the monolithic processes of the social code of conduct. Some women, however few in number, can thus visualise a shape, a form, a colour, a sound and a new meaning with which to create a new home.

This process of confronting in themselves their role-taking processes, of being a daughter and a daughter-in-law, dealing with the mother and mother-in-law respectively, is only one element of women's critical assessment of reality. They have yet to deal with the role-taking processes of being a wife and a mother.

The New Wife

Standing at this threshold, many women review what being a wife now means. So far, they have lived a life of fantasy and discovered the illusions and the emergent disenchantment. Some of these women have even experienced a transient interlude and discovered the hollowness and emptiness of sexual escapades and make-believe relationships. They accept that they are no longer daughters and that the lacunae experienced in the past can never be made good. Their search for comfort and protection only led them to exploit themselves and others. Their attempts to escape from the barrenness of their existence only provided them with a momentary illusion of togetherness. Their fear of themselves and of being alone only brought about indignity, humiliation and demands for surrender.

Having lived through these encounters, some women again choose to cross the threshold beyond the horizon. At this threshold, and for the first time, they encounter the male identity in themselves. The woman discovers that in the process of role-taking as a daughter and then as a wife, she had cast the husband in the role of the man—the male—who would be the replica of her father. As a wife, and anchored in the daughter role, the woman had sought protection without dependency, affection without control, love without pain, relationship without bondage—in essence, the fulfilment of all the lacunae of the past without the attendant deprivations, denials and hurts. In return for all this, she was willing to offer conformity, sacrifice, surrender and loyalty. She believed that this process would create a new world and space for her.

When confronting herself at this new threshold, the woman discovers that, in her preoccupation with carving out a life for herself, she had ignored the husband as a person. She now realises that he was equally trapped by social mores and codes of conduct and that, like her, his life was dominated by the role model of being a 'son'. She had failed to understand that her husband had his dreams, hopes and aspirations as well. He, too, had hopes of receiving all that had been denied to him. He, too, wanted a respite from playing the role of the achiever and enhancer of socio-economic status. Through his childhood and adulthood, the husband had been pushed towards careers and aspirations and had to play proxy roles to fulfil the demands of his parents. He also wanted tenderness without demand, nurturance without control, and love without tendering his pound of flesh in terms of rising in the social and economic hierarchies. He wanted to be accepted and loved for just being himself.

As such, both men and women had expected too much from their counterparts. Both the identities—male and female, husband and wife—had much to offer and a lot to receive. However, they had been caught up in trying to make good perceived lacunae, rather than offering what they had to offer and receiving what the other had to offer. Women who recognise this try and sort out what they can and wish to offer and what they want to define and create rather than just what they wish to receive.

In the process of focusing only on being a woman, they have disowned their qualities of instrumentality with the environment. They have disowned their assertiveness, their ability to act and to give shape, form and direction to people and situations. In the name of conforming to the processes of social role-taking, they have surrendered the male portion of their identity and have managed to hold anger, resentment and wrath in abeyance.

Those women who take the new step and create a space beyond the horizon, first unleash, with fury and intensity, the residues of the male identity in themselves. They tend initially to be aggressive and seek for themselves what they perceive as being the privileges accorded to men. This process has diverse expressions. Some women give themselves freedom to be impulsive. They take their freedom for granted and indulge in 'free sex' and live in defiance and with bravado. Their search for companionship leads them to social rebellion. Others, however, recognise the futility of finding meaningful relationships in such encounters. They then search for alternatives to discover fulfilment.

Some turn bitter and angry. They direct their wrath at men, women and children and turn vindictive. Nothing really satisfies them. They learn to negate, deflate, criticise and condemn. No individual, or system, or institution is good enough for them. They portray themselves as models. They accept isolation and an outsider status. However, they assume that this isolation is a consequence of their search for equality and thus hold others responsible for it. They turn self-righteous and believe that their own agony is more intense than anyone else's.

Some women, having lived through these experiences and having encountered the male identity both outside (in the shape of the husband) and within them, finally confront the issue of what it means to be a woman. This woman accepts the bio-physiological aspect of being a female just as her counterpart is a male. She discovers that she does have some choices. She finds the freedom to give shape to her destiny. She realises that she and she alone can determine the kind of woman she wants to be. In the encounter with the woman identity within herself, she discovers that she has exhausted all meanings internalised from the social system. She can no longer accept the role of being a victim or martyr. She realises that she is responsible for maintaining the sanctity of her bio-physiological being, of her psychological womanhood, of her self-worth and of her dignity. She knows that she has now to define and articulate her being as also to define the nature of her relationship with others.

Having thus freed the positive aspects of her being, the woman, instead of suffering from excruciating social guilt and inviting destruction on herself and those around her, creates space for herself. Being free, she can now reach out, without getting stuck in the social dysfunctionalities of the role of a woman. It also means facing insinuations and snide remarks from the outside world but, being anchored in the security of her inner space, the woman can tolerate this with equanimity.

When it comes to their physicality and sexuality, many women dwell on aspects of physical chastity and social stereotypes of purity. Confronted with feelings of shame and guilt, the ghosts of jealousy, possessiveness, and threat to the external male identity as also social stigma, many women tend to retreat into the social role of a pure and physically chaste wife. Therefore, the woman has to learn to differentiate between sexuality (a gross physical act) and sensuousness (the living process, the eroticism of her being). It is only in this differentiation and in the integration of her inner feelings that she can withstand social accusations and self-doubts.

These women, who lay down some of the ghosts of the past, choose to bring to the husband the dignity and grace of womanhood, rather than the subjugation and surrender of their physical femaleness. They experience a sense of freedom, discover their substantiveness, and the value of being a person. They create a space where they can invite others without shame, guilt or fear of social disapproval. They can receive without fear of contamination, and can offer without making others captive. This woman finally frees herself from the shifting sands of suffocating victimisation. She has side-stepped the captivities of the role processes, and has come out of prison to tread an unknown path. And it is here that she experiences the maturity of her being.

So far the woman has encountered many a role in herself. She has stood at many a threshold. Some women had stayed frozen and immobile while others have moved on. The role of being a daughter gave her acceptance, affirmation and a relatedness with the family. The role of being a daughter-in-law brought her either fragmentation or integration in the family. Integration brought new demands but in this she earned respect, psychological membership and a partnership in the new directions and goals of the family. She created a home, a heritage and laid the foundation for the generation to come.

The New Mother

However, the most painful encounter a woman has to live through is the role of being a mother. Here she encounters the primitive terror of losing her child. She is fiercely protective and possessive. In this role she is the progenitor, sustainer and nourisher of another human being in her body. The woman who arrives at the threshold of entering the space beyond the horizon has lived through all the social codings of a mother's role. She now has to define a new role not only for herself but also for her children.

The woman endeavours to create a space where her children can relate to her and she can relate to them with feeling rather than through role prescriptions. She is able to articulate her pathos as well as her world-view without the reactive residues of social demands and compulsions. She can state her vulnerabilities without eroding her role. She can state her strengths without being dominating and controlling and, in essence, can give her love and affection as gifts and not out of compulsion by virtue of being a mother. These women inculcate in their children a set of values to live by. They attempt to foster a sense of belonging, an acceptance of different types of people, and a feeling of relatedness with the people around. Amidst all this, the woman can accept her children's growth pangs, their occasional truancy and defiance. She joins in her children's struggle to grow up in a confusing and complex world. These women, having to some extent resolved their own beings, discover many ways by which they can bring themselves to their children.

Other women provoke their children to acquire the identity of exiles or psychological wanderers. They cannot manage the frustrations and exasperations of their other roles and can only act upon their young ones. These children become the recipients of their mother's frustrations, feelings of futility and despair.

Caught in the same cultural milieu, and sensing and experiencing the struggles, turmoil and apprehensions of the mother, the children often load her with the guilt of being a non-mother or a bad and inadequate one. Alternately, they turn the forces of annihilation on themselves. If, and only if, the mother does not get trapped in guilt, apprehension and anxiety do her children find a way of building a new relatedness with the person-mother.

The mother role is where the woman invariably gets most bogged down and where she is most unsure. Here, the biological bonding resulting from giving birth and the need to protect her psychological trust confronts the need for her to let go so that her children can be free to grow up. She encounters her need to restore and heal while providing space for her child to grow. The successful resolution of this encounter provides the woman with trusted friends. She can accept, with trust and goodwill, the fact that though she has given birth to her children they have their own identity. She can only be a witness to their unfolding and occasionally, if invited, have the privilege of giving shape and form to this process. It is tempting to join too soon and intrude or join too late and regret the missed opportunity. But the most difficult of all is to be patient yet ever ready to accept the invitation when proffered.

·These women, who have encountered many roles in the diverse systems they have inhabited, peel off layers of social processes to find in themselves and their progeny a touch of individuality. As such, they have invented the beginning of a new heritage.

The New Career Person

There is yet another world, another space and a whole set of people who exist beyond the world of family and relationships. This is the world of work—a world of tasks, responsibilities and men; of organisational structures, superiors, subordinates and colleagues; and of concrete jungles where men are predators. Here, too, women have to encounter themselves.

In this world, the woman is often naive, charming and innocent, and sometimes a victim of circumstances. She appears to need protection. Sometimes she is exploited and frowned upon. She has a job but essentially remains a daughter and a sister. Many women are captives of the prison of wage-earning and perform infrastructural service roles. They remain marginal and secondary and hope that they will be rescued. They toil and labour but they remain daughters across many roles and refuse to grow up and own their space. They are guests, living in others' space and hence are always on their best behaviour. In short, they are never themselves.

Some women are alluring, tantalising and inviting. As such, they become 'pets' and hence are sought after. Yet, they are intelligent, capable and competent but, more than that, they are charming and bring sparkle and life. In thus bringing life to work situations they actually mask their capabilities and end up with the regret of not having actualised their potentials. They marry, earn a second income and remained unfulfilled.

Then there are the doers and the performers. They like Herculean tasks and seek affirmation and confirmation in their roles. They are valued for what they do but cannot value themselves. They suffer and moan but are proud of being over-burdened. It is in this over-engagement with the routine of tasks that they obtain meaning and value of and for themselves.

There are still other women who are in search of meanings. Work, job, career and a profession are all an attempt to create a meaning for themselves. Being daughters, wives, daughters-in-law and mothers were enriching experiences but only partially fulfilling. They search for something more. Just as in the family some women contribute to the creation of a new heritage, so in the work-setting they aspire to create a new heritage. These women bring themselves to this setting which is beyond the portals of the home and away from the primary system of belonging and relationships. In this setting lie art, music, drama, painting, dance, entrepreneurship, medicine, engineering, communication and the world of finance. These women struggle to create a new space beyond the home, a space to add a meaning, define a world-view and a heritage which they can call their own.

Just as in the primary setting of the family, here too women have to confront the ghosts of the past and lay them down so as to free themselves in order to create new definitions and new meanings of themselves, others and situations. They struggle now with systems instead of roles. Earlier they had to deal with roles in the form of parents, husband, in-laws and children. Having chosen a career or a profession women have to cope with the conflicting demands of two systems—the home-setting and the work-setting. One system evokes guilt while the other waits for them to flounder. One evokes doubts and anxieties while the other makes demands. One demands surrender, the other challenges the woman.

Women who enter the interface of home and work often aspire but are confused, are committed yet waver, are determined yet fearful of the price demanded. However, in the work-setting she is on her own. She is pursued, enticed, allured. She has to make a statement, define her boundaries, make a personal choice of action, carve out a space, and command dignity for herself.

Many women begin to explore the nature of this resolution as they arrive at the threshold of the space beyond the horizon. They began by encountering their role as a daughter, wife, daughter-in-law, mother and a professional. Some women take one step at a time. Others take two and converge to a personal stance in life where they succeed in redefining the emotive maps with new meanings in all aspects of their living processes. All women who arrive at the threshold of the space beyond the horizon have accepted some freedom to give new meanings to people and situations and made some meaningful choices. Each encounter creates some space for new responses as well residues of reactivity. Both keep pace together. Redefining and redesigning one role does not mean that other roles get automatically changed. Each role has to be encountered anew in all its gruesome details and all its wilder aspects.

With each resolution and with the emergence of proactive responses, women define a world-view, a concept of life-space and of their life-role, and a level of integration of their being and becoming. At each such attempt they confront social taboos, experience punishment or are ostracised. However, each such social response generates in some women the determination to persist in generating a world-view, a life-space and newly designed roles for themselves. These new role designs mean that this woman acts from her being and creates a context without fear of becoming invisible, that she can invite others into her world without the fear of losing her space. She has to affirm herself and others without seeking restoration. She has to shape, mould, discipline and energise without controlling, possessing or usurping. She has to nurture, foster and replenish without smothering, suffocating or demanding surrender. In essence, she is enlivened and brings to life and the living processes a set of values which dignifies the human struggle to transcend pathos and create a new ethos.

It is here that women have to walk beyond the cultural lore. The cultural lore brings men and women to the finer elements of role-taking and leaves them at the edge of the precipice to take charge of their own destiny, to create a new life and shape an identity. Women then find a path to go beyond, to redefine the pathos of the past, and give birth to a new ethos. The pathos of the past holds the residues of hurt arising from role-taking, while in creating a new ethos women accept, with grace, the anguish and the pain of being human beings. The pathos of the past mortgages the present and the future and holds them at ransom, while the ethos of tomorrow tempers the soul in fire. For here there is no one to call upon, no one to blame, no one to lean upon. One has to walk perpetually into the unknown with only the self as the resource.

In creating a new ethos women accept, in essence, the role of being creators of a new heritage and not being mere inheritors. They build institutions of well-being, not monuments. They do not create a cult but replenish the system and sustain it with grace. They bring the processes of rejuvenation into play and not blind faith. Women in such a space have to go beyond the bio-social fragmentation of male–female, man–woman, and masculine–feminine role-taking and integrate, in a wholesome manner, the two elements in a single identity—a human identity. It is only by achieving this integration in themselves that women can cross the threshold into the space beyond the cultural lore.

Beyond the cultural lore lies the macro-identity of human existence which shapes the destiny of humankind. The macro-identity creates a new universe of meanings, identities and direction for humankind. It is in this uprooting from micro-roles and rerooting in the new emotive map of role definitions and in a second uprooting from the clarity of new definitions of the self and the system to rerooting in the macro-identity, that a few women find the freedom to infuse a new ethos into social institutions in order to create a new heritage.

In the next chapter we shall explore the space beyond both the cultural lore and the macro-identity. It is on the foundation provided by the latter that we can create a universe comprising a human code of conduct, relatedness and a pulsating and vibrant life.

8

Final Encounter with the Self

In the last six chapters we have recorded the transactions of Indian women in the course of their journey through bio-social and socio-psychological space as defined by the emergent realities of their era and the traditions of the cultural lore. This journey has been full of turmoil and turbulence. They have struggled on the way to find a niche in their era—a location where they can achieve a convergence of dignity, well-being and meaning, both as a role-holder and as a person in society. They have crossed many a threshold in this voyage. Along with all the joys and pleasures of playing a role and being a person, they have lived with the underlying pathos of being prisoners of the definitions and boundaries prescribed by the cultural lore. Many women find a resting place somewhere within the universe of the cultural lore. They have learnt to be content with a certain degree of dignity provided by the roles of being mothers and wives. However, a few have transversed the space of the cultural lore and arrived at a new threshold.

These women have to choose between retaining the micro-identity of role and person within the space of the cultural lore, or taking a step beyond this to integrate with the macro-identity of being human. The dilemma informing this choice is anchored in a question: Can a woman integrate and sustain in her life-space both the well-defined social and psychological forms of micro-identity and the diffused and abstract forms of macro-identity?

Some women who had arrived at this juncture shared their struggle with us. They stated that the old ghosts frequently reared their heads and threatened them. It is at this threshold that those women had to finally encounter the primary sensuality coded in the very fact of their being, biologically, women. They had to face the issue of how and where to draw boundaries and how to generate experiences of communion without being tainted with the aura of sensuality and sexuality that pushes them back into being women.

Before we go further, it would be useful to briefly examine the universe of the cultural lore and the role it plays in the lives of women. This universe is primarily a space for role-taking. It is defined and bounded by the primary assumptions which society and its culture hold about the nature of the individual, both collectively and in relatedness. The universe of the cultural lore contains, in dominant forms, a variety of prescriptions and processes for 'role-taking,' 'meaning-making' and 'choice-making'.

Individuals struggle to find meaning for themselves in the context of the era they live in. They attempt to move from the restricted bio-social role of a child to a socio-psychological role of an adult. They hope that this transition will allow them to design their role and its processes, and determine the quality of ethos and pathos which they live by. They wish to feel and act as persons apart from taking on the roles prescribed for them.

This struggle yields two streams of pathos for women. One consists of the trauma of role-taking in the contemporary social world. This universe is often anchored in the precepts and prescriptions laid down by earlier generations. But within the lifetime of individuals the phenomenology of the social world often changes so drastically that the precepts and prescriptions of the past no longer allow for playing out the role effectively. This in itself creates a stream of pathos which is largely reactive to particular people and particular situations. The other stream relates to the symbolic identity of women. The universe of this identity is heavily coded with feelings of being victimised as well as of being a prisoner of dominant males.

These two streams of pathos often surface simultaneously in many encounters, and the distinction between the two gets lost. The separately generated reactive feelings aroused by particular people and situations lose their identity in the face of the massive symbolic structure carried and kept alive by history and tradition. These two streams of pathos are linked and given coherence by the cultural lore. Besides defining the socio-psychological space for the unfolding of women's identity, the cultural lore contains prototypes of all situations and dilemmas. It offers well-defined patterns of causation, choice of action, resolutions of dilemmā and, finally, the acceptable locations from where women can act as persons and live with meaning and dignity. Yet, by its very nature, the cultural lore appears to be finite. The choices are, in fact, not open. It seems that the cultural lore actually holds together the codings of society, that it demands that individuals govern their relatedness with their life-space within the parameters of a certain mode. More than that, discovering the wholeness of one's human potential and having the freedom to act from there is not available within the mode.

All said and done, however, the cultural lore does have positive aspects. For example, it carries the conviction that a woman does not have to treat herself as a mere object made up of introjects of her social space and thus remain a mere role. It provides the woman freedom to move from the over-defined and prescribed location of a role in the social world to the status of a person and thus redefine her meanings and life-space. It also contains the message that one has to persist in the search for self-determined meanings, locations and dignity. It encourages a woman to establish her own relatedness. It also persuades her to give up the need for revenge and demands that she rises gracefully above bitterness to forgive and forget. Essentially, therefore, the positive message of the cultural lore is: Come through the struggle whole in yourself and extend this wholesomeness to people who inhabit your socio-psychological world.

The universe of the cultural lore, restricted as it is to the bio-social and psycho-social dimensions of a woman's relatedness, is a cultural device for the continuity of the ethos of living. It is also designed to sustain the consistency and stability of the meta-values and assumptions attached to being a woman in society. Consequently, the cultural lore does not deal with issues related to the macro-identities of women, which involves a search for a relatedness beyond the interpersonal world of living.

The cultural lore, as introjected and assimilated by a growing child, leaves very tenacious imprints of cognitive and emotive maps about the locations of an individual within the interpersonal world. These maps contain all the introjects. In the struggle to define their location and meaning, women have to engage in modifying the structure of the emotive maps so that the introjects are deprived of their aura of being absolute and inescapable. In this sense, the struggle of women in the cultural lore is not to overthrow the culturally postulated and promoted identity, role or personhood of women. Instead, it is a dramatic response which carries the message that the primary and secondary introjects from childhood to pre-adolescence must be reviewed, re-defined and given new meaning. Only thus will the woman be free of the absolute power of these maps and be able to move into an adult world with a certain degree of freedom.

In the normal course, a female child growing up in Indian society imbibes the cultural lore from the significant people in her life-space. She is also witness to and the recipient of their personal control, instructions and codes. These two sets of communication, however, do not necessarily match. More generally speaking, the personal behaviour of the adults around her often appears compulsive and painful. They also exhibit personal biases. As such, the direct values stated in the behaviour of significant people and the meta-values and assumptions coded in the cultural lore are loaded with a feeling of conflict.

As stated earlier, the cultural lore does not permit a departure into the macro-identity of being a woman and human. The cultural lore is a dramatisation of a confrontation where the residues of the introjects can be sorted out and individuals can re-anchor themselves. By way of the socially and culturally defined meta-values contained in the inter-personal world of the cultural lore, therefore, society unwittingly communicates the message that the roles and systems experienced in childhood can and do make illegitimate demands and exert pressure to restrict the culturally available space to an individual.

The struggle portrayed in this book relates to the life-space of women during the course of the last four decades of Indian society. We have focused on their anxieties, fears, turmoils and pathos by conscious choice. In the midst of all this, we have also shared moments of rejoicing and fullness. However, the theme of pathos has persisted and echoed and re-echoed in the being of the women we have encountered. Our review of their struggle establishes the following:

1. As compared to the scenario envisaged in the cultural lore, the scenario of the contemporary life-space of Indian women is very diverse and complex. However, the feelings aroused by the current scenario are experientially similar. This establishes an analogous association between the two.
2. Today's women not only introject the cultural lore but also introject emotive and cognitive maps from the current life-space. These two introjects clash and create a tension. In the light of introjects from the cultural lore, the introjects from the contemporary space appear to stand for selfishness, immorality, rebellion and a disowning of human values.

The new introjects, then, become associated with mixed feelings, the most dominant one being the feeling of being accused. Other feelings vary from righteousness to defiance, from commitment to disowning, from logic to compulsiveness, and from guilt and shame to indifference and anger. As such, the woman finds that she is waging a battle within herself.

The double-bind of these two sets of introjects persists with many women. Those who gather enough strength and conviction to act on the basis of the current introjects often find that their male counterparts do not appreciate their behaviour. Actions based on the new introjects seem to invoke threats of punishment, accusations and condemnation. Consequently, women end up feeling used and cheated. Although they are outwardly angry with men, their anger is really directed at their own helplessness and inability to achieve dignity for themselves.

Thus the scenario of contemporary life, characterised both by beckoners and inhibitors, has left Indian women in a double-bind where feelings of doubt and isolation and feelings of conviction and assertion alternate as if on a see-saw. The struggle of contemporary women to move from a bio-social role to psycho-social personhood does not seem to be as smooth as the lives of heroines in the cultural lore. In most cases, the outcome remains dubious and the majority of women remain unresolved and uncertain.

In traditional Indian society, a woman could always turn to spiritualism and mysticism and in doing so she could minimise the obligations of prescriptive roles or even completely abandon them. While she could be censured for this, she at least had the freedom to make such a choice. However, the life-space of modern women is heavily rooted in the ethos of secularism and scientism. The traditional option does not seem as viable. In some instances, women have actually felt guilty or embarrassed to express such feelings. Only a few women of today have turned to the spiritual option. However, in most such cases they lose the battle by becoming disciples of, and hence dependent on, a male guru. In short, they end up where they started from.

The second component of the ethos of contemporary life is the search for equality in terms of status, role, personhood and of being and becoming. At this new threshold in her encounter with the macro-human identity, the modern woman often gets caught up with issues concerning the ethos of equality. Consequently, most of these women find themselves entrenched in the new personhood they have carved out for themselves. They consider it to be a precious gift which they have given to themselves. Their need to preserve, express and enjoy it is, therefore, high. Risking it for the sake of an illusive macro-identity seems to be a dubious choice to make. The fact that this new person-hood is not generally acceptable in their own living space makes them even more determined to hold on to it. However, the very freedom that they struggled for and thought they had achieved is, in reality, a prison. Perhaps their own need to be consistent as well as to find security in their own person also serves to make them dig their heels in. This process prevents any movement towards the threshold where the journey towards the macro-identity can begin. These women tend to take on a defensive stance as well to make a defiant statement of their personhood. Like many thresholds which women have crossed, the threshold of the final encounter is also a twilight zone, where opposites and contradictions intermingle, dance in harmony or with discordance, create excitement and exhilaration as well as apprehensions and fears. The temptation to turn to the old familiar world is quite high.

Those who persist in their journey across this threshold find themselves in a bind. They discover that even the concept of a woman's macro-identity is anchored in another level of the cultural lore. For, at this stage, they are conceived as Shakti. The cultural lore has woven a universe of mystery around this concept. Shakti is a counterpoint to the male. She is postulated as the creator, the destroyer, the nourisher and the sustainer, and the withholder or giver of abundance and plenty. Alternatively, she is a mystery, an enigma and the holder of the secret knowledge of creation and so man has to propitiate her through devotion and homage.

In the experience of many women, the identity of Shakti is analogous to the social identity of *bhogya* wherein she is postulated as a slave who is to be possessed or as a tantaliser who is to be captured and violated. In the deepest experiential sense, women discover that the two counter *locii* still leave them open to manipulation by men. This discovery reinvokes feelings of futility. It seems that the cultural lore has completely imprisoned the spirit of women. It does not even allow them to respond to their existence.

At this point, it is necessary to explore the universe of the macro-identity. It is indeed a new kind of space. In the universe of the macro-identity, the primary fragmentation of men and women ceases. It is a space of being human. It is also a universe where human beings can experiment with their own potentials and qualities in order to seek and establish their relatedness with the cosmos. In the tradition of most societies in the world, this space has come to be identified with humankind's search for spiritual realisation. In the past, both men and women have come up with new meanings for their living. They have created new definitions and assumptions about the nature of human beings collectively, in their relationship to one another individually and to the cosmos as a whole. Their experiences, discoveries and articulations have frequently become the inspirations for a new religion or a new philosophy.

In transmitting their own philosophy for living, they and their followers have redefined humankind's life-space. Many of the old role definitions have been modified. Some new meanings and choices, so far tabooed, have been opened for action. New additions have been made to the cultural lore. In the Indian context, these attempts have even found a place in the overall cultural fabric. Ideational freedom and changes have often been achieved by means of these attempts. However, the role-space has often remained constricted. Even the cultural lore has very often been assimilated into these new ideas. Thus, the contribution of the sages, which could have triggered off an overall dynamic action for change, has often been contained within a limited frame.

Men and women of today who reach this threshold often experience a major problem. The ethos of secularism and scientific idealism does not allow them to recast their search for relatedness with the cosmos into a spiritual frame. While their focus is grounded in the unfolding of their human potential and qualities alone, they do not have any conception of a space to walk towards. Many women, in fact, have been tempted to stop at this threshold and become the spokespersons of the woman's struggle. Consequently, women arriving at this threshold often experience a great deal of loneliness. Interestingly, their arrival at this threshold is also in loneliness. During their struggle they meet others who are located at the same point. These meetings create moments of intimacy and empathy, provide a respite, replenish the individual, and reinforce the woman's commitment to continue the struggle. These meetings, however, are only transient.

The people met in such moments are fondly remembered; but very rarely, if ever, have any enduring relationships evolved as a result. Surprisingly, for most women these encounters rarely take place in their own locale or social settings. Sometimes these encounters are with people who are not of the same cultural or ethnic background. Perhaps a cross-cultural encounter is essential to release a fresh momentum in the direction of the human identity—i.e., beyond the universe of the cultural lore.

Why do many women freeze at this threshold? Our speculation is that they lack adequate language and metaphor to articulate their feelings and to mould their behaviour. They are unable to present themselves in a way in which they can distinguish themselves from the continuity of feelings and behaviour of the people around them. As a result, they get swamped with old ghosts, lest they be misunderstood. Similarly, they do not appear to receive any support in their experimentation with the self. This need to obtain support also raises a ghost from the past—that of being exploited. The tension thus builds up and the women who wish to walk alone often decide that the price is too high. Hence, in loneliness and with tension, sometimes with anger, these women tend to stay put.

Women have another choice at this threshold—the choice of becoming self-born. This process involves a proactive stance. The woman has to re-evaluate the introjects from the cultural lore and the living models of significant people in her life. This review also assists her to recognise and decode the symbolic associates of the introjects. On the whole, this process culminates in the woman achieving a clarity about the boundaries of that which is hers and that which is part of the introjects. This, in turn, has the effect of dissolving the anger and bitterness and locates the woman in the purity and potency of the existential self.

For some women, this effort to be self-born opens the door to new aspirations, visions and ambitions. The resultant sense of freedom and ease with which to pursue and explore the new direction create a resurgence of spirit. Somewhere along the way, however, they discover that they have lost their sense of balance and acumen when they encounter new symbols of the old introjects in their life-space. This invokes their wrath as well as disdain. They hide their fear of becoming contaminated by the introjects. Essentially, the hold that the old introjects have on the psyche of these women has not been completely shaken off. Women have talked at length about their recurrent encounters with old introjects and the storms this has generated in their lives. Thus does the cycle of discovery and rediscovery continue.

The encounter with the macro-identity of human beings is a serious one both for women and men. It is anchored in the very biological fragmentation of human beings into two distinct body forms. Each of these body forms may be adequate unto itself for functional transactions with the social world around it. However, deep somewhere in this fragmentation lie residual feelings of being incomplete in oneself. The metaphor of human existence seems to be dominated by the search for union vis-a-vis social transactions. A woman's search for that pure form of relatedness where the two halves can be one seems to be the eternal dream, the essential vision, and is the theme of myths, poetry and cultural lores the world over. This search for union and assimilation into one existence has been institutionalised by society in the sacrosanct bond of marriage. Marriage, then, is the legitimate space where this union and merger is acceptable. All other social spaces and identities are out of bounds. The marriage vow in all cultures carries shades of the same commitment: 'For better or for worse, till death do us part.'

Somewhere during the course of the agrarian era, women were allocated the role of being carriers of virtue, idealism, ethics and of perpetuating culture. But, simultaneously, they were attributed with the disposition of being unstable, temperamental, emotionally immature and sensuous. As such, they were suspected of actively seeking to betray the role of being the upholders of virtues. Hence, they became objects which required control and protection. Indian literature is rife with women who are in active search for a union outside marriage. *Katha Sarit Sagar* and *Kissa Tota Maina* describe various types of *abhisarikas*. Thus, the recognition of the very fundamental search to achieve a wholeness of the incomplete being through union and merger, ended up being heavily loaded for women in terms of sexual morals and virtues. This search became taboo and brought on accusations when attempted. If mythological stories and the cultural lore are to be believed, women were punished not only for pursuing this search but even for thinking or fantasising about it. The attribute of being chaste in all aspects of *manasa, vacha* and *karmana* ('in mind, words and action') became a burden.

Yet the search for the union and the merger and for ways to transcend the bio-social boundaries of their own self, is fundamental to both men and women, perhaps more so for women. Essentially, it is a tandem relationship of two body types trying to experience their essential oneness of spirit. The social order, however, seems to transfer the burden of maintaining the purity of this relationship entirely on to the shoulders of women.

According to folklore, it is the woman who contaminates and destroys a union and she is forced to rehabilitate herself over and over again. This idea is illustrated in the story of Shakti, the consort of Shiva, as Parvati or Sati and in her various manifestations as Kali and Devi. The mythological stories associated with Shakti are interesting. Sati, the original form born of Daksha, is conceived first as an ideal daughter. However, her husband Shiva is not acceptable to her father. As a result, she is exiled from her father's home. Daksha once performed a major *yagna* but did not invite Shiva as one of the gods. Sati, claiming her right of being a daughter, travels to her father's home and witnesses not only the lack of welcome for her but also insults being heaped on her husband. In her anguish, she jumps into the sacrificial fire and ends her life. What follows is an aftermath of *thandava*. Sati is born again as Parvati to Himavan (the mountain). She has to undergo severe penance to seek union with Shiva once again.

In another incident, Parvati is tempted to test the authenticity of Rama's status of being an *avatar* of Vishnu. She transforms herself into the image of Sita who has been kidnapped by Ravana. While searching for Sita, Rama encounters Parvati in the guise of Sita. He, however, recognises her as Parvati and pays her homage. Parvati returns to Shiva but he turns her out for this act and she is once again separated from Shiva. This story is repeated, in one form or another, from era to era.

How important the issue of the purity of the two body types is, is illustrated in these stories concerning Shakti, the macro-identity of women. In Parvati's story, physical union is denied. Ganesh is a virgin concept. He was created from the perspiration and dust of Parvati's own body. Karthikeya, Shiva's other son, is born of Shiva's seed independently and then handed over to Parvati to be brought up. Most of her other forms—Kali, Durga, Chandi, etc.—are similarly isolated women who invoked their magic and potency to destroy evil men and to bless the good.

On the whole, the concept of the macro-human identity postulated in the form of Shakti depicts women as continuing ceaselessly to struggle for location, dignity, belonging and togetherness. It seems that the universe of bio-social roles, personhood and the macro-human identity of women in social transactions reflects the same pattern—that of an isolated person who can be of use to the world but can never find her own fulfilment.

Fragmented in two distinct body types, women and men seek unity and communion with each other. Together and separately they go through two struggles—one, to unite and create an integrated existence and thus discover their wholesomeness in relatedness; and the other to unfold their spiritual being and enter a stream parallel with the cosmos. The very fact of the fragmentation creates the space for their transactions and their struggles. This is the space which society and culture possess and define. The codes and values of society are major determinants of their being, becoming and belonging together.

This encounter with her counterpart frees the woman from her moorings in the social role. It propels her psychological being to strive for communion. Simultaneously, it awakens her existential sensuousness and eroticism in which are anchored both her social role and her psychological being. This communion acquires the intensity of emotions, where the fulfilment of all the lacunae of the past unfolds the psycho-drama of surging hopes and sinking disillusionments. The whole process acquires the semblance of a sensual escapade. It also acquires strong modalities of early adolescence in behaviour and feeling.

The woman had sought from her counterpart to be held in togetherness; a space to weep and let the accumulated pathos of the centuries exhaust itself through expression and understanding. However, the reality of the experience seems to have once again mortgaged her to a sense of futility and isolation. It has been an endless search across dreary wastelands and marshy swamps, this search for a space, an encounter, a context, a person—an identity—to touch, to enliven, to behold and to walk with on the path of the unknown. In this search, the woman got lost in the labyrinth created by the allure of a beautiful relationship. At various points in this labyrinth, the woman continues to recognise the repeated harrowing and ravaging experiences as well as fulfilment of her hopes and dreams with her counterpart. Similarly, at each of these pauses, a part of each woman urges: 'Let go—begin with yourself. If need be, incur the wrath, face all the accusations, pay any price, but state your convictions and live by them.' Another part heaps remorse and anger upon her for allowing herself to be cast in a mould and being forced to silence her soul. The eternal dialectic—let go and act; be and live and hold on; and hold still and hide and disown the self—continues remorselessly. In the analogy of the psycho-drama of the identity at the magic threshold, it seems that these are the yes and no parts of the woman. The judge—the third partner, the deciding partner—in her being seems to have got lost somewhere.

The monologue persists and the judge remains silent as each new step of the identity threatens the role with loss of affection and invokes the fear of being dislodged from the make-believe haven and sundered from empty interpersonal relations. The foundation of the role identity is formed by the need to hold on to the available tenderness, the touch and the soothing voice both within and without. To give up all this means experiencing one's being in its raw and naked state. The fear of exposing this being reminds the woman of the moment of birth when the phenomenological world first touched her being and became a compulsion. It is the moment of coming alive when the search began and got confused and converted into a search for affection and transient softness, tenderness and care. The question the woman confronts at this stage is whether she can trust her resources enough and differentiate her search for human regard from the search for love. Can she really distinguish between human dignity and transactional social dignity?

The dominant feeling garnered from the long history of woman's relatedness with man has left an ever-burning scar in which the threats accompanying her search in life have become permanently anchored. History is full of pathos and her experience of the threats of deprivation are forever alive. This in itself has become a major block which women have to break through by themselves at the new threshold leading towards a human identity. Their cumulative social and cultural identification with womanhood at this threshold comes alive and becomes active. Besides pathos, this identification also contains seething anger and impotent rage. This anger and rage is often experienced as existential. It may be so. However, women often relate this anger and rage to some specific event.

Some experiences with the counterpart have generated a rage of such intensity that expressing it can only demand destruction. In mythology, the *asura* has to be trampled underfoot, his blood has to be drunk and his seed—i.e., the ability to rise again and again—has to be destroyed forever. For some women, the erstwhile counterpart becomes the symbol of *asura* and destruction is let loose. For some women, however this destructive anger is directed towards the self. Normally, it is a mixed pattern: some of the destruction is towards the self and some of it towards the counterpart or other symbols of the counterpart.

This blending of the existential search and sensuous eroticism with the counterpart becomes another setting to experience a new pathos. It revives the intense pathos of woman's identity through history. The intensity of this pathos is like a final slashing, which evokes in her the search for her existential spirit and spiritualism. The status of women has very often been one of 'mother–whore' or courtesan, as often described in the cultural lore. But her own experience of herself is also full of dual images—she is simultaneously the ideal and the cursed; the deity and the demon; the innocent and the temptress; the destroyer and the preserver She knows that she loves, gives herself with abundance, withstands the evaluations and accusations of the social system and yet retains her personal sense of dignity.

This book is primarily the saga of women. We have, to a large extent, attempted to articulate the vast array and vicissitudes of the experiences and feelings of women which lie.behind their continuous efforts to adapt and conform to the socially desirable performance of their prescribed role. They bring to this role their ability to give birth and their never failing desire to bring to this world the grace that is the quality of the human spirit. But the journey is also punctuated with fear, despair and shame. They experience strength and despair, futility and courage, in movement and in action. Their very existence is tied to their counterpart, the man. Their lot is to be pursued either with respect and homage or in possession and control. Even in their moments of success, fulfilment and glory, they cannot forget that they are dispensable and can be discarded without notice. The threat of violation and of being ejected from the status of being human and women as individuals are caught in a web. One may call this the web of destiny, futility or meaninglessness; but the web is real. Within this web there are only a few places to pause and only limited paths to choose from. And each route leads to another pause. Each of these pauses are also thresholds—thresholds for the renewed struggle to move away from the status of a bio-social role to that of a human identity. Each of these pauses or thresholds are the beginnings of a resumed search, the endless search to find a place, a space, a context, a companion. And then, as counterparts, to empower each other to experience dignity and well-being on the one hand, and to reach beyond the horizons into the glory of the world to be on the other.

While women are perpetually trapped in the struggle and monologue that we have described, they do often discover that they are held in regard by quite a few men. Also, some men do hold them in love. But they rarely experience being held in regard and with love simultaneously by one person. This is the result, partially, of residues from earlier encounters with the counterpart. At that encounter she has felt her well-being. A flood of joy and tears has washed away aeons of pain and anguish. The tragedy which made her lose her ambience with her counterpart had brought her back to repeated monologues with herself. The tragedy also shakes the woman and awakens her soul into reality. So far it has been lulled into sleep by fantasies and dreams. The awakening propels her to define her values and convictions to live by. She makes the commitment to take her destiny in her own hands. However, the final issue of exploring her existential eroticism and sensuality at the level of the macro-identity remains. The discovery of the ever-rejuvenating, ever-green and replenished powers of the macro-identity have to be experienced through this exploration. It is here that the woman can discover the magic in the music of the cosmos which beckons to integrate her being and becoming and to create the new ethos and heritage for humankind.

The woman, having lived through the encounter with the counterpart, explores her bio-existential reality with herself. She has awakened and enlivened her existential being. She has experienced the sensuousness of her life and the eroticism of her being. She has found her anchor within and discovered the sanctity of her body. And she has struggled to flow towards the macro-existential being of hers anchored in the spiritual identity.

The woman's identity anchored in the bio-existential reality walks a razor's edge. If she succeeds at crossing the threshold she remains once again anchored in the bio-existential modality. If she fails then she is bereft of her own feelings and the sources of her replenishment. The spring of life of her being goes dry. She lives through the bio-social psycho-drama of barrenness, frigidity and being doomed. Her search for the existential spiritual encounter appears to be a mirage. She struggles to rise from despair to touch the existential spiritual being of her own identity. Herein lies the final threshold to the final encounter with her soul which will enable her to rise above the ashes and to walk across. In taking this step she sheds the pathos of centuries and releases her being from captivity. She awakens the soul from the slumber of millenias. Her search has been for the unknown, to create a location and to enliven the process of living. There are no regrets but an invitation and an awakening to touch the spirit of human existence.

Such an exploration alone can exhaust the psycho-drama of women's history in pathos. It is only then that she can arrive at the point where from within her awakened soul she can face the simultaneity and dualities of her life-space: the pulsating throb of life and the numbness, the nectar and the poison. Her soul awakens to be tempered through these and to emerge purified. This cleansing and tempering gives rise to an identity which like a phoenix is ever ready to create a life-space and enrich the spirit. In this tempering, the woman awakens her power to create a space as vast as the ocean both gentle and furious; space as boundless as the sky both gloriously bright and gloomy; space as illusive as the wind which whispers and storms; space as intense as the fire which softly warms and cheers and burns; and, finally, a space as resourceful as the earth with both limitless powers to replenish and emptiness. It is to discover these spaces that she invites herself to step across the threshold.

How does such a woman experience herself, her being, her becoming, her space and her identity? She accepts her definition of herself as being multifaceted. She experiences and owns her qualities of magic, of mystery and is fearful of her powers. She has the touch to soothe the rawness of herself. She owns her magic of enlivening life as well as her destructiveness and she can experience the ever-changing flux of push and pull and yet hold steadfast in her being. By her energy she invokes pulsating life and melts the frozen spirit, lives through excruciating pain to enliven the numbness and breathes life into her being and that of others and into the system.

She has no residues of shame, guilt, anger, resentment, agony, anguish, scars, wounds, bitterness and hate. She has created her space, and is self-born. The struggle of her identity is to now create a new ethos and a new heritage imbued with the spirit of human existence and beckoning to journey on the path of life. She is forever ready to die many a death only to come alive again and again.

A Glossary of Festivals, Characters, Terms and Concepts

abhisarika is a Sanskrit word denoting a woman who steps out of her role boundaries to seek union with a relevant male in order to fulfil her own identity. Sanskrit literature describes various kinds of *abhisarikas*. Popular belief associates *abhisarikas* with women who seek fulfilment of their sensual and sexual needs outside marriage.

Ahalya is a figure mentioned in the epic *Ramayana*. She was the wife of sage Gautama. Indra, the king of gods, who was besotted by her beauty, disguised himself as the sage and approached her. When Gautama, who was away for his morning rituals, returned to the hermitage and found them together, he cursed them and Ahalya was turned into a stone. For more than a millenium Ahalya remained thus. When Rama (q.v.), the seventh incarnation of Vishnu, was passing through the forest, he came across the petrified Ahalya and touched her with his feet. This released her from the curse and she resumed her own form. She is one of the *panchkanvas* (five virgins).

Ahilyabai (1725–1795) was the widow of Khande Rao, the son of Malhar Rao Holkar of Indore. After Malhar Rao's death in 1766, she became the regent of the Holkar kingdom on behalf of her son Male Rao. After the latter's death she became the ruler. She exercised tremendous power and was held in high esteem by other chieftains and rulers. She was a woman of unusual genius and is remembered for her benevolence. Many temples, roads and other public utilities were constructed during her reign.

Amrapali was a renowned courtesan in the kingdom of Vaishali during the Buddhist period in India. She was highly educated and accomplished and has contributed poems to the *Therigatha* collection. She played a significant role in the struggle of Vaishali against Bindusar, the father of Ashoka the Great. She later renounced the world and joined the Buddhist order.

Anandmai Ma is a twentieth century saint. She was born in 1896 in Tripura district and attained self-initiation in 1922 in Bajitpur (both places are now in Bangladesh). Her husband Ramani Mohan Chakravarty was a staunch devotee and had been initiated by her. She devoted her life to the worship of the Lord and had many followers.

Anasuya was a virtuous woman who is referred to in the *Ramayana* and in the *Bhavisya Purana*. She was the wife of sage Atri whose ashram was situated on the banks of the Ganges in Prayag or modern Allahabad. When the three gods—Brahma, Vishnu and Rudra—tried to seduce her, she cursed them. Rama (q.v.) and Sita (q.v.) on their way to their fourteen-year exile visited the ashram where Anasuya inducted Sita into the ethos of being a good wife.

ardhangini is a Sanskrit term connoting one of the role aspects of a woman as wife. The woman is supposed to represent one half of the personality and body of man.

Arundhati was a chaste and virtuous woman from the Vedic period of India, known for her powerful asceticism and devotion to her husband Vashistha. According to popular belief, she was united with her husband after she died and took her place alongside her husband in the constellation of Saptarishi (Ursa Major). She is the personified form of the Morning Star.

Arya Samaj is an organisation founded by Swami Dayanand Saraswati (q.v.) in the early nineteenth century. It was the harbinger of the revivalist movement in modern India and a forum to unite Hindus for the sake of reformation. It was a response to the challenge of Christianity and did much work in the field of education by establishing Dayanand Anglo-Vedic colleges and *gurukuls* throughout India. The Arya Samaj fought against the many ills of Indian society like the caste system, untouchability and child marriage.

avatar is a Sanskrit word which connotes one who descends; hence it implies the incarnation of one of the gods in mortal form. In practice, the word is used primarily for incarnations of Vishnu.

badi bahu is a Hindi phrase denoting the eldest daughter-in-law in a family.

bahu is a Hindi word derived from the Sanskrit term *'vadhu'*. In the literal sense it means bride and is sometimes used to connote wife.

Balram, the seventh son of Vasudeva and Devaki, was the elder brother of Krishna (q.v.). He was a great warrior. It is said that he broke away from the cattle culture of the Yadavas and promoted the development of agriculture. He was also known as Samkarsana, that is, one who draws or ploughs. His chief tool in war and work was the plough.

bhabhi is a Hindi word denoting one kind of relationship between a man and a woman. The woman in this case is the wife of the elder brother, or cousin, of the man. The younger brother or cousin of the woman's husband is called *devar*. The *devar-bhabhi* relationship is often dramatised in Indian folk literature and myths. The relationship between Sita (q.v.) and her brother-in-law Lakshmana is the most idealised one.

Bharvada is the name of a community found in Saurashtra which is a part of Gujarat on the west coast of India. Bharvadas are known for their lifestyle, music, dance and attire which are believed to be similar to that of the Yadavas—the clan to which Lord Krishna belonged.

bhikshuni is a woman who renounces her home and married life to devote herself to religion under the guidance of a spiritual teacher. Both Jainism and Buddhism initiate women into religious life. The process is analogous to becoming a nun in Christianity.

bhogya is a Sanskrit word indicating one that is enjoyed for pleasure. In a limited sense it implies a woman or women as a class and, according to this interpretation, women are both the source as well as the object of enjoyment and fulfilment.

bio-social role modality indicates the characterisation of behaviour, prescriptive or emergent, which is related to the appropriateness of the age and social status of the individual.

cathexis is a concept used in psychoanalysis. It means the conscious or unconscious engagement of an individual's psychic energy with an object of transaction, as also a strong attachment to certain objects of transaction.

chachi is a Hindi word denoting the relationship between a woman and her kin who are the offspring of her husband's elder brother. The offspring could be either male or female.

Chandi is a form of Shakti (q.v.).

Chattopadhyay, Sarat Chandra, was a famous Bengali novelist of the early twentieth century. His novels were widely read in India during the thirties and the forties. He is well known for his sensitive portrayal of Indian women and for his depiction of the ambivalence characterising Indian society at that time.

Chitrangatha is a character from the epic *Mahabharata*. She was the princess of Manipur and was well versed in the art of warfare. Arjuna fell in love with her and married her.

chuddail is a Hindi word denoting a form from the world of evil spirits. This particular manifestation is believed to disturb people, inflict pain, threaten and even devour human beings. The word is also used as an attribute and abuse for a woman whose temperament and behaviour evoke similar feelings in people.

Damayanti was a princess who married King Nala after hearing about his fame and virtues. Nala lost his kingdom in a game of chance called *chaturang* and was exiled from his kingdom. Damayanti followed her husband into the forest where Nala abandoned her while she was asleep. She wandered about in the forest looking for him and was finally taken home by her parents. A search for Nala was launched and they found that he was engaged by King Rituparna as his charioteer. They were finally united and Nala was able to win back his kingdom through the game of dice.

Dashratha literally means possessing ten chariots. He was the father of Rama (q.v.) and the king of Kosala and his capital was at Ayodhya. He had three queens, of whom Kekaiyi (q.v.) was his favourite. For a long time he did not have an heir but after intense worship four sons were born to his queens. When he decided to nominate Rama as the heir apparent to his kingdom, Kekaiyi intervened as she wanted her own son, Bharat, to be crowned king. Dashratha was bound by a promise to fulfil this desire of his queen. After Rama and Sita (q.v.) were exiled, he died of a broken heart.

dayan is a Hindi term which is synonymous to the term *chuddail* (q.v.). A *dayan* is supposed to have bigger, protruding teeth and a more hideous face as compared to a *chuddail*.

devdasi is a word found in both Sanskrit and Hindi. It is used to refer to women who are dedicated by their family to a temple to serve God through music, dance and other services. In Shaivite temples, *devdasis* became an institution. This practice eventually led to the creation of a class of women who were linked to the temple and whose main function was to serve God. In later years, however, the practice deteriorated and was equated with prostitution. These women made themselves available to visiting pilgrims and others in the vicinity of the temple.

Devi literally means goddess. Durga, Parvati, Uma, Gauri, etc., are manifestations of Devi. In a broad sense, the term is used to connote a woman. The word may also be part of a woman's name, for instance, Kamala Devi.

devrani is a Hindi word. Among two brothers, the wife of the younger is referred to as *devrani* by the wife of the older. For instance, Kunti (q.v.) was the *devrani* of Gandhari (q.v.) as their husbands, Pandu and Dhritarashtra (q.v.), were brothers.

Dhritarashtra is a character mentioned in the epic *Mahabharata*. He was the eldest grandson of King Shantanu of Hastinapur. As he was born blind, he could not occupy the throne of Hastinapur and had to abdicate in favour of his younger brother Pandu. Later, this became the source of contention between the Kauravas and the Pandavas and led to the battle of Kurukshetra.

Draupadi is a central figure in the *Mahabharata*. She was the chief queen of the five Pandava brothers and daughter of King Drupada of Pancala. She was the goddess Lakshmi while the Pandavas were Indra in their previous birth. Following the curse of Lord Sankara, she was born as Draupadi and the Pandavas as the five incarnations of Indra. Draupadi is depicted as a pious, dutiful, learned, courageous and truthful woman in the epic, who shared the joys and tribulations of her husbands. She is regarded as one of the *panchkanyas* (five virgins).

Durga, or difficult of access, is an epithet of Shakti (q.v.) in her fierce aspect. She rides a lion and carries weapons in all her hands. She is worshipped by some people in that form. She killed the demon Mahisasur and in this aspect is known as Mahisasurmardini.

Durgavati was the queen of Gondwana and the princess of Chandebla. After the death of her husband she became regent for her minor son, Vir Narayana. She fought many wars and in 1564 she successfully spurned the attack by Asaf Khan, subedar of the Mughal Emperor Akbar. However, Akbar sent his forces once again to attack her kingdom. Her son Vir Narayana was wounded and her kingdom was annexed by the Mughal emperor. Durgavati chose to kill herself rather than fall into the enemy's hands.

Gandhari was the wife of Dhritarashtra (q.v.) and the mother of the Kauravas. Her love and devotion for her blind husband was so intense that from the day she married him, she blindfolded herself and refused to see the beauty of the world because she could not share it with her husband. Gandhari and Dhritarashtra renounced the world after the battle of Kurukshetra in which all their hundred sons were killed.

Ganesh is the lord of hosts. This elephant-headed son of Shiva is variously known as Gajanana, Ganadhipa, Ekadanta, Lambodara, Vighnesa. He is one of the central deities of the post-Vedic Hindu system. According to ancient texts, he was created by Parvati (q.v.) alone. Before Hindus undertake a journey or a project or any auspicious ceremony, Ganesh is remembered and honoured so that the venture is successful.

Gargi was one of famous women sages of the Vedic period. She was a reputed scholar and philosopher and composed some of the sacred hymns found in the Vedas. She challenged Yajnavalkya's claim to superior knowledge in the philosophical contest held at the court of Janaka. She proved to be an intellectual match for Yajnavalkya who threatened her when she questioned him about the ultimate truth.

griha lakshmi is a term found in both Sanskrit and Hindi. It literally means the goddess of prosperity of the home. This word connotes that aspect of the role of a housewife which ensures the prosperity and well-being of the family.

gurukul is a Hindi term, the Sanskrit equivalent being *gurukula*. It means the place where the teacher resides. In practice, the word denotes an institution of education organised around the philosophy and ethics of a particular teacher. According to ancient Hindu tradition, *gurukuls* were situated away from the cities. A child at the age of five or six years would leave his home and join the *gurukul* to learn all that was required for effective functioning in society.

havan is a Sanskrit term indicating the ritual performance of sacrifices to the holy fire or *agni*. It is the central aspect of *yagna* (q.v.) and household worship.

Hidamba is referred to in the *Mahabharata*. She was the sister of the demon chief, Hidimb, and lived with him in the forest. When the Pandavas fled from Varnavata, they sought refuge in the forest where Hidamba lived with her brother. Hidamba saw Bhima and fell in love with him. Fully aware that she could not win his love as long as she was in her hideous demon form, Hidamba transformed herself into a beautiful maiden in an attempt to entice him. Bhima married her and she gave birth to a son named Ghatotkacha.

identity is a concept frequently used in the social sciences. Erikson used the term to describe the pattern of the human ego at different stages of life. Erikson also talks of role identity. The other types of identity are ethnic identity and professional identity. In this book, the term is specifically used to denote that structure of the individual which determines the processes of meaning-making and choice-making in life-space. It is also referred to as socio-psychological identity and bio-psychological identity. In the former, societal determinants play a significant role while in the latter biological factors are dominant. In psychological identity, the personal value structure plays an important role.

infrastructure, as used in this book, relates to the organisation of contextual elements within which a structure of action, decision or any human aspiration is located. It also refers to the organisation of institutional variables as opposed to task variables.

instrumental role and **instrumentality** are terms frequently used in the social sciences. These terms indicate the quality of action which is directed to achieve goals. In contrast to instrumentality and instrumental role, the concept of expressive role has been used to denote action which is related to the expression of feelings and values. Often, instrumentality is attributed to the masculine identity and expressiveness to the female identity.

Jain, Jainendra Kumar (1905–1988), was a very prominent Hindi novelist and philosopher. In his novels and short stories he highlighted women's personality and individuality and dwelt at length on the man-woman relationship. Often controversial, his forte was his ability to delineate the emotions of his women characters. He is also known for his sensitive depiction of the social and political problems facing Indian society. Jainendra Kumar wrote ten novels and ten collections of short stories, including *Tyagpatra*, *Parakh* and *Muktibodh*.

jethani is a Hindi word that denotes the relationship between two women who are married to two brothers in a family. The wife of the elder brother is the *jethani* of the younger brother's wife who is called the *devrani* (q.v.). The *jethani-devrani* relationship, like the *bhabhi-devar* relationship, is often dramatised in Indian folklore.

kaki is a Hindi word synonymous with the word *chachi* (q.v.). In some parts of North India these two words are used alternately. In some communities and ethnic groups the term *kaki* is more commonly used.

Kali, or the black goddess, is born of anger and drinks blood. She wears a garland of human skulls and carries a skull in her hand which is used for drinking blood.

Kalidas was a renowned Sanskrit epic poet and dramatist from Ujjayani, the capital of the Malavas. He wrote under the patronage of Vikramaditya, who founded the era of the Malavas in the middle of the first century before Christ. His work reflects the beauty of human life, the splendour of art and the glory of the senses. It also mirrors his age—one of the greatest periods in Indian civilisation. *Kumarasambhava*, *Abhijnana-sakuntalam* and *Meghdoot* are among his works.

Kannagi is the heroine of the Tamil epic *Silapathikaram* written by Illango Addigal. Kannagi, whose husband is beheaded on a false charge, confronts the court and proves that the life of an innocent man has been taken in the name of justice. In her anger she is supposed to have burnt the city of Madurai.

Karthikeya is the six-headed son of Shiva who was born from the seed of Shiva in the hands of Agni (God of Fire). He had six heads so that he could respond simultaneously to six women who claimed to be his mother. Shiva intervened and told Parvati to bring him up.

karva chauth is the fourth day of the fortnight of the dark moon in the month of Kartika of the Hindu calendar which corresponds to October-November in the Gregorian calendar. On this day, married women fast and perform rituals and offer prayers for the long life and well-being of their husbands.

katha means a tale in Sanskrit. *Kathas* is the plural. Not every story is a *katha*. The term *katha* originated from the oral tradition of reciting tales from the *Puranas* about gods and goddesses and their interaction with the lives of men. A different term is used to denote the modern written form of stories.

Kekaiyi was the favourite queen of King Dashratha (q.v.) of Kosala and the mother of Bharat. She plays a pivotal role in the epic *Ramayana*. She compels King Dashratha to coronate her own son Bharat and exile

Rama (q.v.), Dashratha's eldest son, to a forest for fourteen years.

Keshav, Maharishi Karve Dhondo (1858–1962), was a social reformer. He established the Widow Marriage Association and laid the foundation of the first women's university, the SNDT University, in 1916. He is well known for his work in the fields of education and social welfare.

Krishna, the eighth incarnation of Vishnu, plays a central role in the epic *Mahabharata* and in the *Bhagvata Purana*. He was the eighth son of Vasudeva and Devaki and the younger brother of Balram (q.v.). When Arjuna refused to fight in the battle of Kurukshetra againt the Kauravas, Krishna preached to him about one's *dharma* or duty. He said that each man may choose his own path to God according to his nature. A Kshatriya, he said, must fight for righteousness and he must do so without being attached to reward or success. Krishna emphasised right action which was free from all desire.

kshatra is a Sanskrit word with several connotations. It essentially means an umbrella. However, in its usage it has become a symbol of patronage extended to dependents and subordinates.

Kunti was the chief queen of Pandu, the grandson of Shantanu. She was the sister of Vasudeva and the aunt of Krishna (q.v.). Her character is described in all its facets in the epic *Mahabharata*. As a maiden she so pleased the sage Durvasas with her services, that he granted her the power to invoke any deity she liked. The consequence was the birth of Karna from the Sun God. However, being a maiden, she was forced to abandon her son. She was a dutiful and loving wife. She accompanied her sons to the forest after they lost their kingdom but she exhorted them to fight against the Kurus and reclaim their kingdom.

Lakshmibai, Rani of Jhansi, was the queen of Jhansi whose kingdom was illegally annexed by the British after the death of her husband. She was one of the Indian rulers who fought in the first war of independence in 1857. She died on the battlefield and is remembered for her valour.

Leelavati is the name of a mathematical treatise on algebra written by Bhaskaracharya somewhere between the second and fourth century A.D. It is believed that Leelavati was also the name of his widowed daughter. He inducted her in the knowledge of algebra and named his treatise after her.

Lopa Mudra was a learned woman and a contemporary of Parshuram, an incarnation of Vishnu. Some of the Vedic hymns have been composed by her.

mama is a Hindi term denoting the maternal uncle or the mother's brother.

mami is the Hindi nomenclature for the wife of a *mama* (q.v.).

Mandodari was the chief queen of the demon King Ravana of Lanka. She is portrayed as a noble and majestic figure in the *Ramayana*. Though she was proud of her husband's prowess, she was not blind to his faults. She tried to persuade Ravana to make his peace with Rama (q.v.) and thus avoid a confrontation with him.

Manjari is a fictional character in the historical novels of the Gujarati novelist, K.M. Munshi. She is the wife of a soldier who rose to become one of the most important commanders of the Solanki kings of Gujarat in the eleventh century. She is portrayed as the strength behind her husband.

Manu Smriti falls in the category of sacred literature and is regarded as one of the most authoritative and respected law books in India. The largest number of commentaries are written on this text. Authored by Manu, the text records the primary codification of social structure as well as the matrix of role relationships in Indian society. According to Hindu mythology, Manu is the progenitor of the human race and human beings are called *manava* after him. He is believed to be the sole survivor after the great destruction of the universe.

map: emotive and cognitive. The word map is used here in the tradition of the social sciences where an individual acquires an image or a general mapping of his field of transaction in society or in life. The emotive map is that part of the experienced understanding of the world which is determined by the flux of emotions in transactions. The foundations of emotive maps are primarily laid during childhood, when a critical appraisal of the boundaries between the self and the outside reality is not well developed. Emotive maps play an influencing role in associations and symbolic transferences (q.v.) and in such expressions as poetry and painting. The cognitive map represents that experienced understanding which emerges after the critical faculty for drawing boundaries between the self and the outside reality has been activated. It relates more to the contraction of reality, both inner and outer. It also plays a dominant role in logical thought, and is related more to 'concept' than to 'symbol'.

Meera was a sixteenth century queen and saint who was married against her will. She was a staunch devotee of Lord Krishna and spent most of her time in the worship of the Lord. Her in-laws resented this. She finally gave up her life by accepting the poison sent by her father-in-law.

mermaid is a mythological character, the upper half of whose body is that of a woman and the lower half that of a fish. The mermaid is often found in stories about sea adventures. Hans Christian Andersen wrote a fairy tale about a mermaid. To commemorate this, a sculpture of a mermaid was installed in Copenhagen, Denmark.

Munshi, Kanaiyalal Manaklal (1887–1971), was born in Broach in Gujarat. At Baroda College he came under the influence of Aurobindo Ghosh and joined a revolutionary group. He later joined the Congress and participated in the Salt Satyagraha in 1930. He was a lawyer by profession and handled many cases connected with the Quit India Movement. He had an illustrious career and made significant contributions in the field of eduation. Apart from the Bharatiya Vidya Bhavan (1938), many other institutions owe their existence to him. Munshi firmly believed that traditional values could subsist side by side with a liberal/progréssive outlook. He is also known for his novels in Gujarati. His works include *City of Paradise & Other Kulapati Letters, Glory that was Gujaradesa*, and *Bhagavad Gita and Modern Life*.

Padmini was the queen of the Maharaja of Chittor, a kingdom in Rajasthan, and was known for her beauty. History tells us that Alauddin Khilji attacked Chittor in an attempt to possess her. Rather than fall into the enemy's hands, Padmini thought it fit to end her life and save the virtue of the Rajput clan. Hence she led the first recorded self-immolation of Rajput women.

Parvati is the daughter of Himalaya and the consort of Lord Shiva. It is said in the *Brhaddharma Purana* that Shiva is man and Parvati is woman; together they are the cause of creation. All men have Shiva as their soul and all women are Parvati. Shiva has the form of the male sign (*linga*) and Parvati has the form of the female sign (*yoni*); the universe, moving and still, has the sign of Shiva and Parvati. In other words, they represent the enactment of the psycho-drama between man and woman in Hindu mythology. They are repeatedly united and separated and Parvati has to do severe *tapas* to be united again with Shiva.

pativrata is a term both in Sanskrit and Hindi. It denotes women who are virtuous and chaste in thought, feeling and body, and are totally obedient to their husbands.

pravachan is a Sanskrit word which has the same implications as the word sermon in English.

prisoner's dilemma refers to a particular kind of experimental situation involving two parties. These experimental situations are created to study many kinds of behaviours—frustration and aggression, trust and suspicion, cooperation and conflict—in social science laboratories. Luce and Raiffa (1957) have described the 'dilemma' in the following words:

> Two suspects are taken into custody and separated. The district attorney is certain they are guilty of a specific crime, but he does not have enough evidence to convict them at a trial. He points out to each prisoner that each has two alternatives: to confess to the crime the police are sure they have done or not to confess. If they both do not confess then the district attorney states that he will book them on some trumped up charge . . .; if they both confess, they will be prosecuted, but he will recommend less than the most severe sentence; but if one confesses and the other does not, then the confessor will receive lenient treatment for turning state's evidence, whereas the latter will get the 'book' slapped at him.

Other investigators who have used the prisoner's dilemma game—with certain variations—to study human behaviour include Morton Deutsch

(1958) and his associates: Deutsch and Kauss (1962); Ravich, Deutsch and Brown (1965); Hornstein and Deutsch (1967); and Rapport (1963) and his associates and students.

priya is a Sanskrit term connoting a beloved. The term is normally used for any woman who is dearly loved though the man may not be married to her.

proactive means initiating an action anchored in the self rather than one which is determined in the context of the external environment.

psycho-social personhood implies the characterisation of behaviour wherein an individual transcends the limitations of bio-social role modality and establishes an individual status as a person. This status is independent of the prescriptive or emergent social role.

Rama, the eldest son of King Dashratha (q.v.) of Kosala and a descendant of Raghu, is regarded as an incarnation of Vishnu. He is a central figure in the epic *Ramayana*. Bound by duty to fulfil his father's promise to Kekaiyi (q.v.), Rama spent fourteen years in exile. He believed that Kekaiyi was not to be blamed for his exile as she was a passive instrument in the hands of fate. The epic *Ramayana* tells us that when Ravana had become very powerful and was committing atrocities against the Devas, they requested Vishnu to take birth in a human body and put an end to Ravana and his atrocities. Thus Vishnu was born as Rama.

Rambha is a celestial nymph who was sent by Indra to entice the sage Vishwamitra and divert him from his meditation. Recognising the fact that Rambha had been sent by the Devas to tempt him, Vishwamitra cursed her to turn into a stone for ten thousand years.

residual feelings are feelings which an individual is left with at the end of any transaction. In general, residual feelings are reactive.

Roy, Raja Rammohun (1772–1833), was born in an orthodox Brahman family at Radhanagar in Bengal. His early education included the study of Persian and Arabic. He later studied Sanskrit at Benares and devoted himself to the study of ancient Hindu texts and scriptures. Between 1803 and 1814 he was in the employ of the East India Company and this association was instrumental in his study of modern Western thought. He was distressed by the religious and social degeneration of Bengal and worked hard for the emancipation of women and the abolition of *sati-pratha*. As a result of his efforts, the British Parliament passed an act abolishing this practice. He paved the way for the synthesis between Eastern and Western social values.

rucha/richa can be pronounced either way. *Rucha* is a revelation which is supposed to appear to a rishi engaged in *tapas* for enlightenment. *Richa* denotes a Vedic stanza signifying such revelations.

sadhak is a term found in both Sanskrit and Hindi. It denotes an individual who dedicates his efforts to achieve supreme expertise in the use of spiritual knowledge and skills.

sahadharamini is a term found in Sanskrit and Hindi. Like the term *griha* *lakshmi* (q.v.) it connotes another aspect of the role of a housewife. As a *sahadharmini* the wife is seen as the co-holder of the religious and ethical duties of the family tradition along with her husband. None of the Vedic rituals can be performed by a man alone. It is through the cooperation of his wife that a man can perform these rituals. Hence the term '*saha*' means cooperation.

saheli is a Hindi word denoting the relationship between two women who are friends. These women are not related through kinship or blood ties.

sampradaya is a Hindi and Sanskrit term. In Sanskrit it implies the handing down of knowledge from one generation to another. In Hindi the term connotes a sect which may be related to religion.

samskaras is the plural of the Sanskrit and Hindi term *samskara*. The word connotes the social and psychological heritage of ideals and ethical practices internalised through early socialisation. It also denotes a group of Hindu rituals which an individual observes during the passage from birth to death. In Sanskrit, the term refers to the action of the individual in thought, word and deed, stored in the form of merit and demerit, which is manifested in a new body, specially when reinforced by the desire for future life.

sandhya is a word found in Sanskrit and Hindi which symbolises the mode of individualised meditative prayer which a follower of Vedic religion recites at dawn, noon and dusk. The term also implies the dusk or evening period of the day.

Saraswati, Swami Dayanand, was born in Tankara in Morvi state of Gujarat. He was the chief architect of socio-religious reform movements in India in the early nineteenth century. He tried to liberate Hindu society from the bondage of untouchability, superstition, orthodoxy and idolatory. In a society wherein a myriad of gods were worshipped, Dayanand propounded the concept of monotheism. He founded the Arya Samaj (q.v.) as a forum to unite Hindus for the sake of reformation. All his writings, speeches and activities are proof of the fact that he was eager for social and religious reform. He outlined a comprehensive system of education based on moral and religious values. To realise these ideals, his followers established Dayanand Anglo-Vedic colleges and *gurukuls* throughout the country.

Sati is one of the incarnations of the Mother Goddess. She was known as Parvati in a later birth. She was the consort of Shiva and the daughter of Daksa. Sati gave up her life because she was unable to bear the calumny of her husband by her father. Sati means a chaste woman, hence it may be used to denote any chaste and virtuous woman.

sati-pratha is a word in Hindi and Sanskrit. In Sanskrit the term 'sati' refers to a chaste woman. In Hindi the word *sati-pratha* refers to the convention of women burning themselves on the funeral pyre of their husbands. Since the practice of women immolating themselves is a later development and was not found in Vedic India, the Sanskrit term does not connote this meaning.

Satyavati was a young and beautiful fisher girl who plays an important role in the *Mahabharata*. Being a fisher girl she used to smell of fish. Sage Parashar was besotted by her beauty and promised her that instead of smelling of fish she would exude the fragrance of a lotus if she joined him in sexual pleasure. She accepted his offer and this union led to the birth of Vedavyasa. Subsequently, King Shantanu of Hastinapur saw her and fell in love with her. He wished to marry her. But Satyavati's father rejected the offer and Shantanu was heartbroken. Shantanu, however, persisted and Satyavati's father relented and agreed to give Shantanu his daughter in marriage on the condition that his daughter would be the chief queen and her progeny would inherit the Kuru kingdom. He also added that the eldest son of Shantanu and his first queen should promise to give up his claim to the throne. Prince Devavrata renounced his claim to the throne and promised not to marry so that his father could marry Satyavati.

Savitri was a princess who was asked by her father to find a suitable husband. She chose Satyavan, a prince living in exile with his blind parents, even though she knew that Satyavan would die within a year of marriage. On the fatal day that Satyavan was destined to die, he felt a sharp pain in his head and collapsed. Savitri then encountered Yama, the God of Death, and requested him to grant her her husband's life. Yama was pleased by her devotion and asked her to name any boon other than the life of her husband. She asked to be blessed with a hundred sons and Yama granted her this wish. But for a chaste woman this was not possible without a husband. By her single-minded devotion and tenacity she thus brought her dead husband back to life and attained immortal fame and glory. Savitri personifies triumph over death for the sake of the husband.

secondary socialisation is the internalisation of institutional or institution-based 'sub-worlds'. It is the acquisition of role-specific knowledge, the roles being directly or indirectly rooted in the division of labour. These 'sub-worlds,' internalised in secondary socialisation, are partial realities in contrast to the base-world acquired in primary socialisation. It is a process through which an organisation inducts new entrants into the ways and norms of role play and life-style. Education provides secondary socialisation as against primary socialisation which is achieved in the family.

shakti literally means power. In Hindu mythology *shakti* refers to the active and creative power of a deity which is personified as his wife.

Shakti is believed to be the source of life, and can be compared to the Mother Goddess in the universal myth. Durga (q.v.), Kali (q.v.) and Chandi (q.v.) are different manifestations of Shakti.

Shakuntala is the central figure in *Abhijnansakuntalam*, the famous play of Kalidas (q.v.). She was the daughter of sage Vishwamitra and the celestial nymph Menaka. Menaka was instructed by Indra, the king of gods, to tempt the great sage. After Menaka conceived and gave birth to a girl she went to her abode in heaven. Vishwamitra abandoned the child who was brought up by Kanva, an ascetic in his ashram. One day Dushyant, the king of Hastinapur, came to the ashram and saw Shakuntala. They fell in love and got married according to the gandharva form of marriage. Subsequently Dushyant left for his kingdom, promising to return soon. When sage Durvasas came to the ashram, Shakuntala was lost in her dreams and did not greet him, whereupon the sage cursed her that whoever she was thinking of would not recognise her. When Shakuntala's friends pleaded, the sage relented and added that the person would recognise her only when she produced a memento. When Shakuntala went to Hastinapur, Dushyant did not recognise her and she could not show him the ring he had given her as she had lost it. However, the ring was found and Dushyant recalled everything. Shakuntala gave birth to a son named Bharata. India came to be known as Bharat after him.

Sita is believed to have been born out of a furrow in a field ploughed by Janaka, the king of Videha. Mithila being the capital of Videha, therefore Sita is also known as Maithili. The wife of Rama (q.v.), the seventh incarnation of Vishnu, her life was beset with a series of misfortunes and sufferings. She was abducted by the demon King Ravana which led to a battle between Rama and Ravana. Her purity, steadfast devotion and loyalty to Rama are held up as ideals for a Hindu wife.

structure of life-space. Each individual has a certain life-space which includes his aspirations as well as the various objects and choices available to him. This space has a certain structure which is partially defined by society and partially by the ethos of culture.

Sukhobai, Sant, was among the early saint poets of India. It is believed that she established the tradition which saint poets like Guru Nanak, Kabir and Ravidas emulated. She lived in the ninth century.

Sulochana is also referred to as Sati Sulochana. She embodies the ideal of a virtuous and devoted wife who is the source of inspiration and strength for her husband. She was the wife of Meghanath, the eldest son of Mandodari (q.v.) and Ravana. When her husband was killed in the battle against Rama (q.v.), she faced the armies of Rama to claim the body of her husband so that she could perform *sati*.

Surdas was a saint poet of the sixteenth century who was a devotee of Lord Krishna. His works are dedicated to the Lord. He was a contemporary of Tulsidas and is the author of *Sur Sagar*.

Surpanakha is a character mentioned in the *Ramayana*. She was the sister of the demon King Ravana and the sister-in-law of Mandodari (q.v.). The area around Panchvati was under the rule of her brothers, Khara and Dooshana. Rama and Sita (q.v.) stayed at Panchvati during their fourteen-year exile. After seeing Rama, Surpanakha wanted him to leave Sita and live with her. When Rama refused, she turned to Lakshmana, the younger brother of Rama, who cut off her nose at her proposition. Angered by this insult, she complained to Ravana. This led to the abduction of Sita and the battle between Rama and Ravana.

symbolic transference is a concept used in psychoanalysis. The attitudes and feelings that a person has experienced in childhood or at different stages of life are used either in their totality or in part to perceive or interact with a new figure in present transactions.

Tantalus is a character from Greek mythology. He was a son of Zeus and was punished for revealing the secrets of the gods. He was condemned to remain in Tartarus and was made to stand in water that ebbed every time he tried to drink, and surrounded by overhanging grapes that drew back every time he reached for them.

Tara is a character mentioned in the *Ramayana*. She was the wife of the vanar King Sugreev of Kishkindha. Sugreev was the younger brother of Vali. Vali declared war on Sugreev, drove him out of his kingdom and married Tara. Sugreev, living in exile, sought Rama's (q.v.) help to defeat Vali and recover his kingdom. After Rama killed Vali, Sugreev and Tara were reunited.

thandava refers to a form of dance which Shiva performed in anger with the corpse of Sati (q.v.) on his shoulder. This dance led to the massive destruction of the world. Shiva was eventually appeased and he gave up the body of Sati.

Tripurasundari denotes the status of a woman initiate in the Shaivite Tantric system. The woman is often chosen before she reaches puberty. She is regarded as the medium identity of Shakti. The *sadhak* (q.v.) practices Tantra to achieve supernatural powers. These Tantric practices are centred around Tripurasundari. This term also refers to one of the manifold manifestations of Shakti (q.v.).

The Mother is a title. In the context it refers to a spiritual companion of Sri Aurobindo. She was born in Paris in 1878 and came to Pondicherry in 1914 and instantly recognised the Master. The task of implementing Sri Aurobindo's vision devolved upon the Mother. She worked towards the creation of a new world, a new humanity, embodying the new consciousness. The Aurobindo Ashram was built by the Mother. The Auroville project is also an attempt to establish harmony between body and soul, spirit and matter, in the collective life of humanity.

Trishanku was the famous king of the Solar dynasty who was so much in love with the beauty of his own body that he could not bear the thought of parting with it at death and desired to go to heaven in that body. He requested his preceptor Vashistha to help him fulfil this desire. Vashistha advised him to give up attempting the impossible. Dissatisfied with the sage's response, he then approached the sage's sons and they ridiculed him. Trishanku told them that since they and their father were incapable of helping him, he would find others who were more capable. Vashistha's sons then cursed him and turned him into a Chandala (a low caste community which lives on cremation grounds). Trishanku approached Vishwamitra and narrated his tale of sorrow. Vishwamitra promised to send Trishanku to heaven. A great *yagna* was organised and all the great sages were invited. When Trishanku reached heaven he was refused entry and Indra pushed him down. As Trishanku fell he shouted out to Vishwamitra for help. Vishwamitra told him to stop in mid-air and began to create another universe for him to rule. However, the Devas intervened and entreated Vishwamitra to aesist. Thus Trishanku hangs in mid-air. According to one story, he became a part of the constellation called the Southern Cross. He symbolises a person who, without personal effort and ability, desires rewards which are beyond human endeavour.

Tulsidas was a saint poet and a follower of Ramananda. He has immortalised himself by his Hindi translation of the *Ramayana*. He also wrote the *Ram Charit Manas*. He was a contemporary of Rahim during the reign of the Mughal Emperor Akbar. His *Barvai Ramayana* is a tribute to Rahim.

Yagna is a sacrifice, a religious ceremony accompanied by oblations, obeisances and hymns. At the *yagna*, before one or more fires are ceremoniously kindled, favourite articles of food are offered amidst the chanting of verses. The *yagna* was originally intended to secure the goodwill of the gods for happiness and a heavenly life after death.

Suggested Readings

Aggarwal, R.C., 'Women's Lib. in India,' *Social Welfare*, Vol. 20, No. 10, January 1974, pp. 11–12, 28.

Altekar, A.S., *Position of Women in Hindu Civilization: From Pre-historic Times to the Present Day*, Delhi: Motilal Banarsidass, 1962.

Amin, U., 'The Acceptance of Equality,' *Seminar*, No. 52, December 1963, pp. 32–34.

Anant, S., et al., *Women at Work in India: A Bibliography*, New Delhi: Sage Publications 1986.

Bader, C., *Women in Ancient India: Moral and Literary Studies*, Varanası: The Chowkhamba Sanskrit Series Office, 1964.

Baig, T.A. (ed.), *Women of India*, Delhi: Publications Division, 1958.

Banerjee, N., *Women Workers in the Unorganized Sector: The Calcutta Experience*, Hyderabad: Sangam Books, 1985.

Bhoite, A., *Women Employees and Rural Development (Problems of Employed Women in Rural Areas)*, Delhi: Gian Publishing House, 1987.

Billington, M.E., *Women in India*, London: Chapman & Hall, 1895.

Chattopadhyay, K., *The Awakening of Indian Women*, Madras: Everyman's Press, 1939.

——————, 'The Struggle for Freedom' in T.A. Baig (ed.), *Women of India*, Delhi: Publications Division, 1958, pp. 14–31.

Chauhan, Indira, *Purdah to Profession: A Case Study of Working Women in M.P.*, Delhi: B.R. Publications Corp, 1986.

Chettur, U., 'Woman Invades Man's World,' *Yojana*, Vol. 11, No. 1, 26 January 1967, pp. 32–36.

Cormack, M.L., *She Who Rides a Peacock*, Bombay: Asia Publishing House, 1961.

Cousins, M.E., *Indian Womanhood Today*, Allahabad: Kitabistan, 1947.

Das, R.M., *Women in Manu and His Seven Commentators*, Varanasi: Kanchana Publication, 1962.

Dasgupta, K. (ed.), *Women on the Indian Scene: An Annotated Bibliography*, New Delhi: Abhinav Publications, 1976.

Dasgupta, S.B., 'Evolution of Mother Worship in India' in Madhavananda Swami and R.C. Majumdar (eds.), *Great Women of India*, Mayavati: Advaita Ashram, 1953, pp. 49–86.

Datta, N.K., 'Widows in Ancient India,' *Indian Historical Quarterly*, Vol. 14, No. 4, December 1938, pp. 661–79.

Desai, A.R., 'India's Path of Development and Women,' Paper presented at National Conference on Women's Studies, 20–24 April 1981, Bombay.

Desai, N., *Women in Modern India*, Bombay: Vora Publishing House, 1957.

Deshmukh, D., 'New Dimensions of Women's Life in India,' *Social Welfare*, Vol. 3, No. 9, December 1956, pp. 3–6, 29, 31, 48.

Deshpande, D.Y., *Women, Family and Socialism*, Bombay: Hind Kitabs, 1948.

Fuller, M.B., *The Wrongs of Indian Womanhood*, New Delhi: Inter-India Publications, 1984.

Gallichan, W.M., 'The Cult of Woman and Love' in *Women under Polygamy*, London: Holder and Hardingham, 1914, pp. 71–85.

Gokhale, B.G., *Ancient India: History and Culture*, Bombay: Asia Publishing House, 1952.

Gupta, B.A., *Position of Women among Hindus, Moslems, Buddhists and Jains*, Calcutta: Superintendent of Government Printing, 1901.

Gupta, G.R., and **H.C. Ganguli**, 'Marriage–Work Interaction: A Study on Indian Women,' *Indian Journal of Clinical Psychology*, Vol. 9, No. 2, September 1982.

Haksar, Nandita, *Demystification of Laws for Women*, New Delhi: Lancer Press, 1986.

Hate, C.A., *Changing Status of Women in Post-Independence India*, Bombay: Allied, 1969.

Hemalatha, P., and **M. Suryanarayana**, 'Married Working Women: A Study on their Role Interactions,' *Indian Journal of Social Work*, Vol. 44, No. 2, July 1983.

Hirway, Indira, *Denial of Benefits to Women Workers: A Study of the Factory Sector in Gujarat*, New Delhi: Oxford & IBH, 1986.

Horner, I.B., *Women in Early Buddhist Literature*, Kandy: Buddhist Publication Society, 1961.

Iyer, K.V., 'Place of Women in Indian Society' in National Council of Women in India (ed.), *Long-term Educational and Training Programmes for Advancement of Women in Asia*, Bombay: NCWI, 1967, pp. 132–38.

Jain, D. (ed.), *Indian Women*, New Delhi: Publications Division, 1975.

Jayal, S., *Status of Women in Epics*, Delhi: Motilal Banarsidass, 1966.

Jhabvala, R., *Working Women: Myth and Reality (Experiences of a Group of Muslim Women Workers)*, Ahmedabad: SEWA (mimeo), 1979.

Jose, A.V., *Employment and Wages of Women Workers in Asian Countries: An Assessment*, New Delhi: International Labour Office, 1987.

Kapur, P., *Marriage and the Working Woman in India*, Delhi: Vikas Publishing House, 1970.

——————, *The Changing Status of the Working Woman in India*, Delhi: Vikas Publishing House, 1974.

Karlekar, M., *Poverty and Women's Work: A Study of Sweeper Women in Delhi*, Delhi: Vikas Publishing House, 1982.

Luthra, P.N., 'Women in the Age of Science and Technology,' *Social Welfare*, Vol. 22, No. 1, April 1975, pp. 4–5.

Madhavananda Swami and R.C. Majumdar (eds.), *Great Women of India*, Mayavati: Advaita Ashram, 1953.

Manmohan Kaur, *Role of Women in the Freedom Movement, 1857–1947*, New Delhi: Sterling Publishers, 1968.

——————, *Great Women of India*, New Delhi: Sterling Publishers, 1969.

Mies, Maria, *Indian Women in Subsistence and Agricultural Labour*, Geneva: International Labour Office, 1986. (Indian reprint: New Delhi: Vistaar, 1987).

Mukerji, D.P., 'The Status of Indian Women,' *International Social Science Bulletin*, Vol. 3, No. 4, Winter 1951, pp. 793–801.

National Commission on Self Employed Women and Women in the Informal Sector Report, New Delhi, 1988.

Nivedita, Sister, *The Web of Indian Life*, Almora: Advaita Ashram, 1950.

Parikh, I.J., 'Women in Work and Life' in *Towards Continuing Education*, New Delhi: PECCE, 1981, pp. 124–26.

——————, *Women in Management*, Ahmedabad: Indian Institute of Management, 1982.

——————, *Models of Role Identity in Indian Women: Barriers to Growth*, Working Paper No. 409, Ahmedabad: Indian Institute of Management, February 1982.

——————, 'Management Training: Issue of Mixed Groups or Single Sex Groups,' Workshop on Women, Training and Management organised by Ecole des Hautes Etudes Commerciale, Montreal, Canada, 17–21 August 1987.

——————, 'Management Training in Third World Countries,' Workshop on African Women, Development Planning and Management organised by UNDP/EDI/ILO, Douala, Cameroon, West Africa, 30 November–4 December 1987.

Parikh, Indira J., and P.K. Garg, *The Maid for All Seasons. Women Managers: A Struggle against Stereotypes*, Ahmedabad: Indian Institute of Management, 1982.

——————, *Report on Training for Trainers: A Programme for Women Managers*, Ahmedabad: Indian Institute of Management, 1986.

Parikh, I.J., and Rakesh Kumar, *Research on Women in Management: A Developmental Perspective*, Working Paper No. 663, Ahmedabad: Indian Institute of Management, March 1987.

Pereira, B.F., 'Organizational and Personal Correlates of Attitudes Toward Women as Managers,' *Indian Journal of Social Work*, Vol. 39, No. 3, October 1978.

Pool, J.J., *Famous Women of India*, Calcutta: Susil Gupta, 1954.

Prabhu, P.N., *Hindu Social Organisation: A Study in Socio-psychological and Ideological Foundations*, Bombay: Popular Prakashan, 1971.

Prasad, S.S., *Tribal Women Labourers: Aspects of Economic and Physical Exploitation*, Delhi: Gian Publishing House, 1988.

Puri, B., 'Can We Identify the Mother Goddess Cult at Mohenjodaro?,' *Quarterly Journal of th. Mythological Society*, Vol. 34, No. 263, Oct.–Jan. 1943/1944, pp. 159–64.

Raj, M. Krishna, *Women Studies in India: Some Perspectives*, Bombay: Popular Prakashan, 1986.

Ramanamma, A., *Women in Indian Industry*, Delhi: Mittal Publications, 1987.

Rani, K., 'Job Motivations for Working Women,' *Journal of Social and Economic Studies*, Vol. 3, No. 1, March 1975.

——————, 'Performance of Job Role by Working Women,' *Indian Journal of Social Work*, Vol. 37, No. 3, October 1976.

Rao, S., 'Educated Woman as an Economic Partner: A Comparison with the West' in N.B. Sen (ed.), *Development of Women's Education in New India*, New Delhi: New Book Society, 1969, pp. 130–39.

Reddy, C.R., *Changing Status of Educated Working Women: A Case Study*, Delhi: B.R. Publications Corp, 1986.

Science and Technology for Women: A Compendium of Technologies, New Delhi: Department of Science & Technology, 1982.

Sengupta, A.K., 'Indian Woman—Her Position and Problems in Modern Times, *Journal of Family Welfare*, Vol. 10, No. 4, June 1964, pp. 51–59.

Sengupta, P., *The Story of Women of India*, New Delhi: Indian Book Company, 1974.

——————, *Women in India*, Delhi: Information Service of India, 1947.

Sengupta, S., 'Socio-cultural Organizations of the People of India with Special Reference to Women,' *Folklore*, Vol. 10, No. 8, August 1969, pp. 282–304.

Seth, M., and **M. Bhatnagar**, 'Personality Factors in Relation to the Adjustment of Children of Working and Non-working Mothers,' *Child Psychiatry Quarterly*, Vol. 13, No. 2, April–June 1979.

Shastri, S.R. *Women in the Vedic Age*, Bombay: Bharatiya Vidya Bhavan, 1960.

Shridevi, S., *A Century of Indian Womanhood*, Mysore: Rao and Raghavan, 1965.

Singh, A.M., and **A.K. Viitanen**, *Invisible Hands: Women in Home-based Production*, New Delhi: Sage Publications, 1987.

Singh, D.K., 'Women Executives in India,' *Management International Review*, Vol. 20, No. 2, 1980.

Socio-economic Conditions of Women Workers in Textile, Khandsari and Sugar Products Industries, Delhi: Indian Labour Bureau, Controller of Publications, 1985.

Sreenivasan, M.A., 'Panchakanya—An Age-old Benediction' in D. Jain (ed.), *Indian Women*, New Delhi: Publications Division, 1975, pp. 53–58.

Status of Women in Gujarat, Gandhinagar: Gujarat Directorate of Economics & Statistics, 1987.

Surti, Kirtida, *Some Psychological Correlates of Role Stress and Coping Styles in Working Women*, Ahmedabad: Gujarat University (thesis), 1982.

Survey on Socio-economic Conditions: Women Home Workers in Ahmedabad, Nadiad: Shranjivi Mahila Sewa Trust, 1987.

Thapar, R., 'Through the Ages,' *Seminar*, No. 52, December 1963, pp. 15–19.

——————, 'Looking Back in History' in D. Jain (ed.), *Indian Women*, New Delhi: Publications Division, 1975, pp. 3–15.

Thomas, P., *Indian Women through the Ages: An Historical Survey of the Position of Women and the Institutions of Marriage and Family in India from Remote Antiquity to the Present Day*, Bombay: Asia Publishing House, 1964.

Uploankar, A.T., 'Social Background and Occupational Aspirations of College Students,' *Indian Journal of Social Work*, Vol. 43, No. 2, July 1982.

Varadappan, S., 'Indian Women: A Product of Tradition and an Aspirant of New Vistas,' *Social Welfare*, Vol. 21, No. 7, October 1974, pp. 1–4, 27.

Venkatarayappa, K.N., *Feminine Roles*, Bombay: Popular Prakashan, 1966.

Vohra, Roopa, and **A.K. Sen**, *Status, Education and Problems of Indian Women*, Delhi: Akshat Publications, 1986.

Wasi, M., 'Professional Women in India: Dangerous Corners,' *Monthly Public Opinion Survey*, Vol. 18, No. 1, October 1972, pp. 17–20.